STAND FIRM
YE BOYS FROM MAINE

STAND FIRM
YE BOYS FROM MAINE

The 20th Maine and the Gettysburg Campaign

FIFTEENTH ANNIVERSARY EDITION

Thomas A. Desjardin

OXFORD
UNIVERSITY PRESS

OXFORD
UNIVERSITY PRESS

Oxford University Press, Inc., publishes works that further
Oxford University's objective of excellence
in research, scholarship, and education.

Oxford New York
Auckland Cape Town Dar es Salaam Hong Kong Karachi
Kuala Lumpur Madrid Melbourne Mexico City Nairobi
New Delhi Shanghai Taipei Toronto

With offices in
Argentina Austria Brazil Chile Czech Republic France Greece
Guatemala Hungary Italy Japan Poland Portugal Singapore
South Korea Switzerland Thailand Turkey Ukraine Vietnam

First issued as an Oxford University Press paperback, 2001

Oxford University Press, Inc.
198 Madison Avenue, New York, NY 10016

ww.oup.com

Oxford is a registered trademark of Oxford University Press

Library of Congress Cataloging-in-Publication Data
Desjardin, Thomas A., 1964–
Stand firm ye boys from Maine : the 20th Maine and the Gettysburg
Campaign / Thomas A. Desjardin.—Fifteenth anniversary ed.
p. cm.
Includes bibliographical references and index.
ISBN 978-0-19-538231-0
1. Gettysburg Campaign, 1863. 2 United States. Army. Maine Infantry
Regiment, 20th (1862–1865)—History. 3. Maine—History—Civil War, 1861–1865—
Regimental histories. 4. United States—History—Civil War, 1861–1865—Regimental
histories. I. Title.
E475.51.D44 2009
973.7'349—dc22——2009031635

Printed in the United States of America
on acid-free paper

This volume is dedicated to the forty-eight men of the 20th Maine Volunteer Infantry Regiment who gave their lives as a result of the Gettysburg Campaign.

Aaron Adams • Charles Beadle • Charles Billings • George Buck
Willard Buxton • Stephen Chase • Seth Clark • Alvin Cutler
Frank Curtis • Moses Davis • William Davis • Melville Day • Isaac Estes
Lewis Flanders • Elliott Fogg • Elfin Foss • John Foss • Benjamin Grant
Charles Hall • William Hodgdon • Goodwin Ireland • William Jordan
Warren Kendall • James Knight • Iredell Lamson • Isaac Lathrop
George Leach • John Lenfest • Alexander Lester • Arad Linscott
Andrew Mabury • James Merrill • William Merrill • George Noyes
Willard Pinkham • Stephen Prescott • John Reed, Jr. • Gardiner Schwartz
Joseph Simpson • Alva Small • Charles Steel • Oliver Stevens
Thomas Townsend • Paschal Tripp • Orrin Walker
Sanford Wentworth • John West • Oscar Wyer

CONTENTS

MAPS

ABBREVIATIONS

ADH   Alabama Department of Archives and History, Montgomery, Alabama

AMS   Private Collection of Abbott and Marjorie Spear, Warren, Maine

BCL   Hawthorne-Longfellow Library Special Collections, Bowdoin College, Brunswick, Maine

GNC   Gettysburg National Cemetery, Gettysburg, Pennsylvania

GNP   Gettysburg National Military Park, Gettysburg, Pennsylvania

LC   Library of Congress, Washington D.C.

LCN   *Lincoln County News*, published in Waldoboro, Maine

MSA   Maine State Archives, Augusta, Maine

MHI   U.S. Army Military History Institute, Carlisle, Pennsylvania

MHS   Maine Historical Society, Portland, Maine

NA   National Archives, Washington, D.C.

NHS   New Hampshire Historical Society, Concord, New Hampshire

NOR   Norlands Living History Center, Livermore, Maine

NYS   New York Historical Society, New York, New York

PHS   Pejepscot Historical Society, Brunswick, Maine

SVM   The Shore Village Museum, Rockland, Maine

UMi   William Clements Library, University of Michigan, Ann Arbor, Michigan

UMO   Fogler Library Special Collections, University of Maine, Orono, Maine

UOA   Sterne Library Special Collections, University of Alabama, Tuscaloosa, Alabama

PHOTO CREDITS

Preface

> Boots, Pejepscot HS; Sword, Bangor HS; Revolver, Maine State Museum; Flag, Maine State Museum; Memorials, Author's collection.

Chapter One

> Sam Keene, Maine State Archives (MSA); Holman Melcher (1864), MSA; Adelbert Ames, MSA; Sgt. Albert Fernald, MSA; Joshua Chamberlain (1860 Yearbook photo), Bowdoin College; Joshua Chamberlain (1862), Pejepscot HS; Ellis Spear, MSA; Walter Morrill, MSA; John Chamberlain (1858), Pejepscot HS; Tom Chamberlain, MSA; William Livermore, GNMP, Charles Hamlin.

Chapter Two

> Atherton Clark, MSA; Musicians of the 20th Maine, Pejepscot HS; William Oates, from Oates, *The War...*; Michael Bulger, Alabama Dept. of Archives and History; Elisha Coan, Bowdoin College; Henry Sidelinger, MSA; Joe Land, MSA; Officers of the 20th Maine, Abbott and Marjorie Spear; Waud sketch, Library of Congress.

Chapter Four

> Looted dead, National Archives, courtesy William A. Frassanito; Trostle house, Library of Congress, courtesy William A. Frassanito; Trostle barn, Library of Congress, courtesy William A. Frassanito; Isabella Fogg, Ruth Kintzer.

Chapter Five

> Lavinia Lenfest, Pejepscot HS; The Battle Flag, Abbott and Marjorie Spear; Choosing a site, Abbott and Marjorie Spear; Dedication of the monument, Author's collection; 15th Alabama Reunion, from Oates, *The War...*; Oates' sketch, GNMP; Chamberlain (1905), Pejepscot HS; Oates (1898), Alabama Dept. of Archives and History.

Chapter Six

> Battlefield road construction, GNMP (Tipton photos).

FOREWORD

"Wouldn't it be nice to know what *really* happened?" How often have we asked ourselves that question when thinking about some legendary event of the distant past or even some relatively recent happening such as the fight at Little Round Top on July 2, 1863. This action has been particularly difficult to analyze and comprehend. It was fought by irregular formations of men among rocks and trees amidst thick smoke and under conditions of terrible stress. Understandably, the survivors came out of it with many different versions of what had taken place—each version perhaps true as far as it went but not all-encompassing as a portrayal of the battle.

With the passage of years, the search for truth in such matters becomes even more complicated. True, more versions of what happened become available, and that helps. But the failings of human memory also begin to enter the equation in a way that is not always so helpful.

Taking all this into account, Thomas A. Desjardin has completed the most penetrating study yet made on that part of the Little Round Top battle in which the 20th Maine was engaged—one of the most famous small unit actions in the history of warfare. And while this book centers on this engagement, he also describes in comparable detail the experiences of the involved Maine and Alabama troops throughout the Gettysburg campaign and the effect these experiences had on veterans' lives in the years after the war. His research has taken him to Alabama, Virginia, Maryland, Washington, D.C., and many times to Gettysburg. He has collected more than seventy recollections by some twenty survivors, both Union and Confederate. For preparation of maps and diagrams, he even took his own measurements and compass readings around Little Round Top. All this is in addition to exploring dozens of manuscript repositories and talking with many authorities on Gettysburg and related subjects.

As to what really happened at Little Round Top, is this book the final answer? I would be loath to see that seal placed upon it. More information is bound to be discovered, more views expressed. This battle will be the subject of much discussion and some disagreement for years to come. But I think it safe to say that Tom Desjardin has dug deeper into this event than anyone else to date. Moreover, the result has literary quality. It is not just a mass of information that someone has strung together and called a book; it is *written*. And that makes a difference in the ease and pleasure of reading.

The author was born June 10, 1964, in Lewiston, Maine, and grew up in that area. His whole family was interested in the Civil War. He recalls, "While other families were going to Disney World, we took our vacation to Gettysburg, Antietam, and Fredericksburg (Mom, Dad, and three kids in a car for five days)." He was doing reports on the 20th Maine as early as the fourth grade. He did his undergraduate work and took his master's degree at Florida State University and at this writing he is a candidate for a Ph.D. in history at the University of Maine.

In the now far-reaching community of Civil War enthusiasts, Tom Desjardin is widely known as a speaker, instructor, and reenactor. Several years ago, because of his knowledge of the Civil War as well as the Maine speech and character, he was called upon to assist in the research leading up to the film *Gettysburg*, and he worked closely with Jeff Daniels, the actor who played Joshua Chamberlain, in his preparation for that role.

In gathering information for this foreword, it came as a shock to realize that my own book about the 20th Maine was published seven years before Tom Desjardin was born. Much has been accomplished since then in the way of archival development, research, and study. Tom's book represents one of the most noteworthy results of this progress; it places him in the front rank of Civil War scholars and predicts further success as a writer and teacher.

John J. Pullen
Brunswick, Maine
May 1995

PREFACE TO THE FIFTEENTH ANNIVERSARY EDITION

I fear you will never know all about it. Nobody does, and nobody ever did or ever will. It was a very mixed up and extensive affair.
                                                                    Ellis Spear, 1910

When Ellis Spear penned these thoughts in a letter to his granddaughter Mildred he was expressing what had become a continuing frustration for him in the years that followed the turn of the century. As a young man, Spear served in the 20th Maine infantry regiment during the Civil War and was second in command during the regiment's famous participation in the Battle of Gettysburg. In the same letter, Spear sarcastically marveled at how young Mildred might be the only person who did not claim to have been at Gettysburg. "So many people were there," he mused, "I do not fully understand how you missed it."

Such was the renown that the American public attached to the largest battle ever fought on the North American continent that it inspired awe, exaggeration, and more than a few tall tales. Among all of the stories about Gettysburg that rose to the status of legend, the battle for Vincent's Spur on Little Round Top has become one of the most well known. It is perhaps the most studied and written-about small unit military action in history. Indeed, the U.S. Army still uses the actions of Joshua Chamberlain, the regiment's commander at Gettysburg, as a model of military leadership.

In the half-decade or so prior to the publication of the first edition of this book, the story of Little Round Top had flourished, achieving a legendary status all its own. But while interest in this event grew, so did the myths surrounding it and the desire to uncover new information about it. The culmination of twenty years of interest and research, this work is an effort to build the story from scratch relying entirely on the accounts of the men who, like Spear, fought the battle and spent the rest of their lives trying to understand and explain it. So far as I have been able to determine, having examined nearly eighty of these accounts written by dozens of veterans of the three regiments, there is no one account nor one participant that can be considered the most accurate. They all contribute to the larger picture in their own way. The two commanders, Joshua Chamberlain and William Oates, provided numerous accounts and even exchanged their thoughts on key elements of the fight, but all of the men, from colonels to privates, had equally significant experiences and recollections. All of them, regardless of rank or education, misunderstood some portion of the event and contradicted themselves from one account to the next. The narrative contained herein is a synthesis of these accounts, perhaps a consensus.

In the nearly fifteen years since this book first appeared in print, much has happened in the relationship between the American public and the 20th Maine Infantry Regiment, particularly their Gettysburg commander Joshua L. Chamberlain.

While doing the research that resulted in this book, I was fortunate enough to meet five different people who remembered their grandfathers who fought in the 20th Maine. The most helpful of these was Abbott Spear, a native of Warren, Maine, whose grandfather was Ellis Spear, the acting major of the regiment at Gettysburg and the man who commanded the unit in the field longer than any other officer. At the time, Abbott still lived in his grandfather's home and shared with me many of the belongings that Ellis had left behind with his family. Among them was the photo on page 138 of the 20th Maine's Gettysburg battleflag taken in 1882 in the same position on Little Round Top that it had occupied during the battle nearly twenty years earlier. I shared a copy of this photo with the staff of the Maine State Archives and several years later, the staff of the Maine State Museum compared the photo to a fragile, largely shredded flag stored in a wooden box with a glass window on the lid. By matching up the few remaining pieces of the flag with those shown in the photo, the museum could finally identify the flag as the one that the 20th Maine had carried at Gettysburg. That flag was restored in 1998 and is now in the Maine State Museum's collection.

The restored flag is not the only artifact that has survived from Little Round Top. The boots that Joshua Chamberlain wore that day, including the right boot with its instep repaired where a bullet punctured the leather, are on display at the Chamberlain House Museum in Brunswick, Maine. Likewise, the scabbard of Chamberlain's sword, which was damaged by an enemy bullet, is part of the collection of the Bangor (Maine) Museum and Center for History, and the pistol that an Alabama lieutenant fired at close range toward Chamberlain but missed is also among the items in the Maine State Museum. Each of these important artifacts has been rediscovered in the last twenty years.

Since 1995 two life-sized statues of Chamberlain have been created and dedicated; the first, dedicated in 1997, is in his birthplace of Brewer, Maine, and the other, erected in 2003, is in the town of Brunswick where he chose to live out most of his life. The surge in interest in Chamberlain and his regiment also brought about the establishment—or rather reestablishment—of another monument, this one at Gettysburg. Since the 1960s, as near as anyone can remember, the stone that marked the left flank of the regiment on Little Round Top had been missing. Since this small monument also marked the left end of the Union line of battle, its absence had been well noted in the 1990s. In 2001 a group of

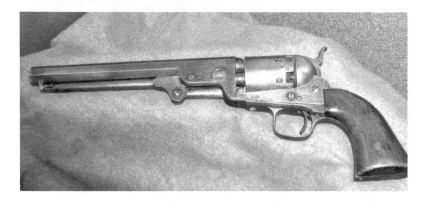

Chamberlain's Gettysburg Mementos

Top: The sword (with a brass "field repair" that cracked again) and boots (with a patch on the right instep) were hit by enemy bullets. Bottom: The Navy Colt revolver was fired by Alabama Lieutenant Robert Wicker at Chamberlain's head—and he missed—all on Little Round Top.

New Memorials

With the help of a photo that first appeared here (see page 138) the Maine State Museum was able to identify the 20th Maine's Gettysburg Battlefield and have it restored in 1997. Also shown here are two new statues of Joshua Chamberlain: one near his birthplace in Brewer, Maine, and the other in front of the home in which he lived out his adult life in Brunswick (right).

Maine citizens raised the money to purchase a replica of the flank marker, which was set in place and rededicated on the one-hundred-thirty-eighth anniversary of the battle.

In 2001, artist Dale Gallon released limited edition prints of his painting "20th Maine and 15th Alabama" that depicts the death of Private William Holloway from page 65 of this book. Two years later, the William Britain Company released three sets of miniature soldiers replicating the painting. The story contained herein made its way from printed pages, to painted artwork, to miniature recreations, and then to film. In 2005, the History Channel aired the one-hour documentary "Chamberlain at Gettysburg" based on this book.

Any author of historical work struggles with the challenge of knowing when to stop writing and send the book off to the publisher despite the fear that within weeks of doing so some new, enlightening, even thrilling piece of information will surface that would have contributed greatly to the book. Nearly always, this fear is realized in the months and years that follow when the author stumbles upon one nugget after another. In the course of nearly fifteen years this book has proven no exception to this particular subsection of Murphy's Law.

Among the most compelling stories of the 20th Maine's Gettysburg Campaign is that of Sergeant Andrew Tozier, who enlisted in the 2nd Maine Infantry Regiment in 1861 and who was among those transferred to the 20th Maine in 1863. Since his service predated the existence of the 20th Maine, Tozier was promoted by means of his seniority to Color Sergeant just before Gettysburg when his predecessor turned up drunk on the march. Decades later, his regimental commander recalled the fight on Little Round Top and saw to it that Tozier received a Medal of Honor for his service there. As good as that story is, the postwar relationship between these two soldiers ran much deeper, a fact that this author failed to learn until well after the critical stop-writing-and-publish date had passed.

Tozier's story had become a favorite of mine when researching the book since he had settled a few miles from my family's summer home on a small farm that I had frequently passed as a child. Nearly a full decade after this book first reached bookshelves, one of Andrew's descendants, William Tozier, was building an impressively thorough catalog of his family's genealogy and added some fascinating depth to the Tozier story.

When he finally completed his service having been shot three times in battles—one injury was in the head, one cost him a finger, the other disabled a shoulder—Andrew returned to Maine a veteran with limited options. As a result, he turned to crime when his cousin brought him in on a robbery he was planning in Mechanic Falls, Maine. With another partner, the two robbed—of all things—a clothing store, stealing more than a thousand dollars' worth of men's coats. Andrew drew the task of waiting outside the store while his two companions rounded up the goods inside. Since his part of the project didn't require use of his hands, Andrew held onto the gun they had brought to the robbery so that when they were caught some time afterward, he was charged with the more serious crime of armed robbery. Fortunately for Andrew, the governor took an interest in his case and issued him a full pardon, including a release from the Maine State Prison. The governor not only freed Tozier from his imprisonment but also took him into his home, helped him improve his reading and writing skills, and set him on the path to a postwar life free of crime.

The piece of information that explains why a governor would take such an active interest in a convicted criminal is the identity of this particular governor: Joshua L. Chamberlain, the former army officer who commanded Tozier at Gettysburg. In 1898, Chamberlain strengthened their relationship when he successfully lobbied the War Department to award the Medal of Honor to his former color sergeant.

Five minutes after the shooting stopped on Little Round Top in 1863, it was already too late for anyone to entirely understand what had happened. Such is the difficulty with which chaotic crises are processed by human memory. In this light, no one will ever really know exactly what happened on the southern slope of Little Round Top on July 2, 1863. This book is as much as we know today, but we hope it is not as much as we will ever know. Keeping in mind that the study of history is a fluid rather than a constant science it is my sincere hope that this is the real story of the 20th Maine at Gettysburg as we know it today and that more will be discovered, determined, and concluded about the fight on Vincent's Spur in the years to come. In this sense, perhaps the greatest contribution this volume could make would be to stimulate further study and discussion of these highly significant events.

ACKNOWLEDGMENTS

If ever a book was written as a group effort, this volume *must* be it. The material upon which this story is built comes from a collection of sources enthusiastically provided by literally dozens of people. The bulk of this material is held in the Maine State Archives within the Civil War Adjutant General's Records. Sylvia Sherman of the Archives provided timely and thorough advice through years of research and months of writing. Sylvia, along with the rest of the Archives staff—Patti Lincoln, Dave Anderson, Jeff Brown, and Art Dostie—gave tremendous support to the research for this book and the state of Maine should consider itself fortunate for having a collection and staff without equal.

Abbott Spear, the late grandson of Ellis Spear, provided enormously valuable material as well as encouragement to the work and the author. Julia Oehmig and Erik Jorgensen were enormously willing and supportive with the Pejepscot Historical Society's collections. Scott Hartwig opened the collections of the Gettysburg National Military Park to me and helped direct me to the most important material. In the same way, Mark Palmer and Ricky Brunner of the Alabama Department of Archives and History contributed significantly, as did Susan Ravdin in the Special Collections of Bowdoin College's Hawthorne-Longfellow Library, Jeff Flannery at the Library of Congress, and Mike Meier at the National Archives.

John Pullen, James McPherson, Harry Pfanz, Jeff Hall, Sylvia Sherman, Julia Oehmig, Bob Crickenberger, and Scott Hartwig each read the original manuscript and provided invaluable advice and criticism. Kathy Kleinman, Robert Krick, Peter Dalton, Bill Boyden, and Robert Donovan provided important contributions to the research material as well. Tom Schaefer and Darryl Smoker shared helpful insight regarding the topography of the Little Round Top area. Edward G. J. Richter has done a vast amount of research on Gettysburg casualties from both armies and graciously provided both information and advice, particularly with Appendices Four and Five. Also, Larry Bulger and Jim Foster provided important and hard-to-locate information about their ancestors in the 47th Alabama Regiment.

Paula Petrik and Marli Weiner have guided my education as both a researcher and writer, and their impact on this work as well as all future work bearing this author's name, is significant. In addition, Eugene Mawhinney, John Battick, and Richard Judd all contributed greatly to the author's transformation from hobbyist to scholar. Fern Desjardin surrendered the family den to a chaotic filing system, while Mark Nesbitt and Dean Thomas provided helpful guidance and support in moving the volume from manuscript to published book.

Finally, and farthest from least, is my gratitude for the enduring imprint that John J. Pullen has made on this work. John's own work, *The Twentieth Maine*, stands monumentally among the literature of the Civil War and military history in general. The gracious and generous manner that he extends toward all who seek his advice was of great help to me and I consider his aid and counsel irreplaceable. Had he not written his book in 1957, and then provided such abundant aid to this work, the pages that follow, had they been written at all, would pale in comparison to what his contribution has helped make them.

Stand firm, ye boys from Maine, for not once in a century are men permitted to bear such responsibility for freedom and justice, for God and humanity as are now placed upon you.

—Private Theodore Gerrish, 1882

1 North From the Rappahannock

The weather was stormy and the traveling has been very bad. But it was not so hot as we had it on the march from the Rappahannock...We have not had a mail for the last two weeks and have seen but very few papers in that time so we have but little of what is going on in the world outside the army and not much that is in it.[1]

Sgt. Hezekiah Long, June 1863

"Who's fault is it?" Sam Keene grumbled to his diary. "The fault of government. Poor management, imbecility, etc., etc." As the captain of Company F of the 20th Maine Regiment, Keene probably felt he had good cause to complain about the state of things in June 1863, and he would have been hard pressed to find a Union soldier who would disagree with him. Marching through the hot summer was wearing patience thin in the army, and the absence of a mail call in Keene's regiment for more than two weeks was taking a further toll on morale.[2]

Samuel T. Keene was an attorney in Rockland before the war. He had not volunteered with the hot-blooded youngsters and enrolled militia who rushed off to fight in the summer of 1861 because at 29, and with a wife and a successful law practice, it was best to leave the fighting to more high-spirited young men with less to lose. By the summer of 1862 however, he felt that horrible mismanagement of the war had caused it to drag on in an endless train of lost battles and young soldiers' graves. That spring Keene and a few of his equally well-educated friends could stand no longer what they viewed as the stupidity of the government.[3]

1

Capt. Sam Keene   Lt. Holman Melcher

Feeling that the war effort required successful men of means to make sacrifices and contribute to the war, they each set out to recruit soldiers from the area around the middle of Maine's coast and helped form companies of volunteer infantry. They succeeded, and for their work they were each commissioned captain of the men they had recruited. So it was with a heavy dose of cynicism—a trait many say is inherent in Down Easters—that Keene started his army adventure, and in the nine months since he left Maine, management of the army had given him no reason to feel better about things.[4]

Keene's first lieutenant, Holman Melcher, echoed his captain's frustrations in a letter home. He blamed the army's woes on "bungling blunders that have transferred the seat of war to our borders, that [are] now destroying the property of good citizens and that have caused these tedious marches that kill more men than the battle-field of the Rappa-hannock." Melcher, too, had waited a year before joining. Though single and eight years younger than Keene, he also had some college education and worked as a teacher in Topsham. He had earned his commission, rising from corporal to lieutenant for his brave and efficient soldiering, particularly at the Battle of Fredericksburg six months earlier.[5]

For the most part, virtually every man in the 20th Maine had reason to be in a state of general unhappiness on the first official day of summer 1863. Their Army of the Potomac was moving north through Virginia in a direction quite opposite that which they had expected to march when the regiment came together nine months earlier in Portland. The men had gathered at the state rendezvous camp the previous September and their

2

mustering in as a formal military unit was a tribute to their state's patriotic fervor. In the summer of 1862, when President Abraham Lincoln called for 300,000 more troops to put down secession, Maine's quota was four regiments. In response, the governor and adjutant general of the state put out a call for the 16th through 19th Regiments, to serve for three years or until the war's conclusion. So many Maine men responded to the call for volunteers that there were enough left over for an additional regiment. The state collected these extra men from various regions and formed them into the 20th, the last of Maine's three-year volunteer infantry regiments. As a result of its unexpected formation the 20th was something of an orphan regiment. While the other Maine units consisted of men from roughly similar areas, the 20th came from all over and claimed no single county or region as its home.[6]

In late 1865 Joshua Chamberlain wrote a tribute to the regiment, describing the circumstances surrounding its formation. "It was not one of your favorites," he wrote to the people of Maine. "It was made of the surplus recruits drifted together, the last of a call for 300,000 more. It was without local pride. No county claimed them. No city gave them a flag. They received no words of farewell on leaving your state. No words of welcome on their return."[7]

Barely a handful of the men in the new unit had any military experience at all, and these were soldiers from other regiments already in the field who had gained transfers in order to receive promotions. As a group, the 20th's officers at least were well educated, if not in military matters, then in academia. No less than ten of them were graduates of Bowdoin College and more had attended other schools, but the rank and file were no strangers to hard laboring, having been mostly farmers and lumbermen before the war.[8]

Just two weeks after leaving their camp in Maine, army leaders held the untrained regiment in reserve with the rest of the Fifth Corps during the Battle of Antietam. They spent the winter near Shepherdstown Ford learning military drill and tactics from their harsh commander, whose strenuous adherence to military discipline clashed with the volunteer spirit of the raw recruits.

Their colonel, Adelbert Ames of Rockland, had recently graduated from West Point and would later receive the Medal of Honor for his actions at the first Battle of Bull Run, where he had remained at his post with an artillery battery despite a severe leg wound. As a young man, Ames learned the usefulness of harsh, strong-handed discipline while serving as a cabin boy on the ships his father captained out of Penobscot Bay, and his years at West Point did nothing to diminish his belief in the

Brig. Gen. Adelbert Ames

strict approach. In the summer of 1862 he accepted the governor's offer of command of the 20th Maine Regiment, and returned to try to make some semblance of a fighting unit out of the thousand raw recruits who answered the first roll call. It was far from easy. Tom Chamberlain, a non-commissioned officer in the regiment, described Ames to his family. "Col. A. takes the men out to drill," he wrote, "and he will d[am]n them up hill and down. I tell you, he is about as savage a man you ever saw…I swear the men will shoot him the first battle we are in."9

Despite their hatred for his approach, many of the soldiers respected the man. One soldier echoed the mixture of respect and dislike that most of the men had for Ames when he wrote, "I wish he would be promoted or resign although he is the best and is called the handsomest field officer there is in Porter's Corps. He is handsome [of] form and straight and [has] handsome features and he has an eye like a hawk." In May 1863 the wish came true. Ames left the regiment with a promotion to accept the command of a brigade in the corps of another Maine man, Gen. Oliver Otis Howard of Leeds.10

Ames' departure should have brought great relief to the men who had suffered under his tight rein through the long winter camp. Months before, they had even plotted to have him removed by the governor, but there was too much to be grumbling about now for them to dwell on any silver linings. The "bungling blunders" to which Lieutenant Melcher attached so much importance and contempt had come to be known by the Union soldiers as Fredericksburg, the Mud March, and Chancellorsville. Fredericksburg was a town in Virginia near which occurred some of the most horrible fighting of the war. Line after line of soldiers in blue marched to their death against an impenetrable Confederate position just twelve days before the Christmas of 1862. The 20th Maine Regiment entered the battle late and suffered fewer casualties than the units who went forward in the main assault, but having to spend the night clinging to the frozen hillside battlefield etched a gruesome experience into their memories. During the long night hours after the futile Union assaults had ceased, the Maine men crouched low behind hastily built earthworks and listened as Rebel bullets thumped into the flesh of the dead bodies in front of them.[11]

If Fredericksburg had not dimmed their patriotic spirit, then the second attempt to shove the Confederates from the heights did the trick. Stung by his defeat in December, Union commander Ambrose Burnside ordered the army up and on the march in late January. Despite an apparently good plan to cross the river above Fredericksburg and attack the Southerners in their flank, incessant rain turned the maneuver into the infamous "Mud March." The 20th avoided the muddy roads that seemed to swallow artillery pieces whole, but they did so only by marching through a swamp that swallowed men's legs, often relinquishing all but the shoes. After a few days of this misery the soldiers could only dwell on the fact that the march was a miserable waste, and they were back where they had begun.[12]

In early May, under the command of another new general, the army again tried to confront the Rebel host near Fredericksburg. Joseph Hooker, the new commander, took the army out on drier roads and across the rivers to meet the enemy at Chancellorsville. Had the 20th been in that battle they would probably have been just as unhappy with its outcome, but army medical personnel gave them an even greater reason to count their woes, injecting it directly into their veins. A rampant case of smallpox kept the men of the 20th out of the fight while an enemy force half its size beat Hooker's army so badly that he retreated north again in the aftermath of yet another Confederate victory. Catching the disease by chance was a cruel enough fate for a soldier, but an errant vaccine supposedly intended to prevent it had caused this outbreak. The 20th Maine's only casualty of the battle was young Moses Warren, the drummer boy of Company A, who accidentally blew off both hands while unwittingly holding a loaded rifle over a camp fire. The pox, meanwhile, took at least three lives and forced three dozen more men to hospitals.[13]

As the soldiers had come to view it, their government had marched them incessantly, caused the wasteful death of their comrades, even injected them with a contagious disease and they had absolutely nothing to show for it. What was worse, nine months in the field had depleted the regiment to half its original strength and those who remained were shaking off the effects of the pox, nursing sore feet, and marching north toward Pennsylvania instead of south toward Richmond. Moreover, the effects of the heat had never been worse in the Fifth Corps. The heat was so bad that eighteen men of the 25th New York Regiment, including their colonel, died of heat stroke the day before the expiration of their term of service would have sent them home. As one soldier in the same

Home: Towns in Maine from which many of the 20th Maine men enlisted.

division as the 20th wrote, "At every semblance of a spring crowds of men swarmed...Men, horses, mules, all rushed pell-mell into the warm, disgusting pools and puddles, and drank the filthy fluid to quench their thirst, sifting sand enough as an old veteran said, to build a fortification."[14]

In the ranks of the 20th Maine, the problems of the army were making themselves known in many ways. James Nichols of Brunswick, the normally reliable lieutenant of Company K, was a week in arrest after getting drunk while serving as officer of the day. In arrest, he joined Addison Lewis of Waterville, a lieutenant in Company A, who was under punishment for returning three days late from furlough. Then Joshua Chamberlain, Colonel Ames' replacement at the head of the regiment, passed uncomfortably near death when heat stroke took him from the march and soldiers carried him to a nearby house. The loss of their new commander made the Maine men uneasy as the reality of impending battle closed on them. Cpl. Nathan Clark of Company H recorded the general feeling of the men in his diary. "Our Colonel is off duty," he wrote, "and we dread to go into action without him."[15]

Corporal Clark was a typical example of the enlisted men in the regiment. In fact, in just about every way, he was the average. He was 24 years old, five feet, eight inches tall, a farmer from a small Maine town, and he had received enough schooling to be able to write with some clarity and grammar—at least all of it that farm work required. He was also among a quarter of the soldiers who had left a wife back home to come and fight, and he wrote to her in both his diary and in letters home.[16]

Listening to these men swapping stories and opinions on the march, one might discover that the sound was sometimes a veritable melting pot of accents. While the vast majority of them were English-speaking natives, two were natives of Italy, a half dozen were Irish-born, and one hailed from Denmark. In addition to those born across the ocean, a large number of the troops were second-generation Americans and still spoke under the influence of their parents' native tongue. A soldier's roots outside of the country were not the only factors that adjusted his accent, however. The sound of a Mainer's words varied from one region of the state to the other, particularly between coastal folks and those who lived back from the Atlantic Ocean. As a corporal from well inland put it, "I can tell a Down Easter as quick as I hear him talk."[17]

At the forefront of this chorus of accents was a professor of speech and rhetoric who was himself fluent in a number of languages. Lt. Col. Joshua Lawrence Chamberlain had taken command of the regiment in

J. L. Chamberlain: from professor in 1860 to lieutenant colonel in 1862.

May when Colonel Ames moved up in rank. The changes made Chamberlain the newest and most inexperienced regimental commander in the brigade, but what he lacked in military experience and training he made up for in intelligence. With three college degrees and a comfortable salary as a professor at Bowdoin College before the war, Chamberlain seemed an unlikely candidate for the military but, in this all-volunteer army, soldiers respected him both as a prominent citizen and a solid commander. He learned what he could of tactics from Colonel Ames in long late-night sessions by candlelight, and he fell back on his college training for the rest. In 1862 he explained to his wife, "I study, I tell you, every military work I can find."[18]

Experienced or not, the men of the regiment admired him. William Livermore, a corporal in the color guard, echoed the feeling of many of the men when he wrote, "Our Lieut[enant] Col[onel] is one of the finest men that ever lived." Despite the respect that Chamberlain could take for granted back home from both students and townspeople alike, he did not consider himself too far above his men and they revered him for his attitude. "He is full of military," they said, "brave but considerate and treats the men like men not dogs...He don't say go boys but come. Why! would you believe it he had some breastworks to throw up and what did he do but off his coat and into it himself." Still, two things loomed quite large when command of the regiment fell to the fighting professor. He had virtually no military experience at all and even if he had, there was not much even the best commander could do while laid up and away from his unit.[19]

8

Making the top of the regimental chain of command even more unstable was the man who was perhaps its weakest link. Maj. Charles Gilmore was a politically connected Bangor native who used his contacts to gain a transfer from his post as a captain in the 7th Maine Regiment into the 20th, with the rank of major. During the Battle of Lee's Mill in the Peninsula Campaign of 1862, Gilmore had come far too close to a serious wound for his own comfort, and from that point on had difficulty stomaching the idea of combat. Consequently, he had a habit of developing a certain illness, quite likely of a gastrointestinal nature, whenever combat loomed. As June 21 came nigh, the outbreak of combat seemed virtually certain, and Gilmore fell out of the march all the way to a hospital in Baltimore.[20]

As if all of this were not enough to give the soldiers pause when considering the strength of their command, they had to consider that the next man in line, Ellis Spear of Warren, was then a captain serving as acting major until Chamberlain returned and the appropriate promotions could be worked out. Spear, a master of subtle Down East dry wit, had been a student of Chamberlain's at Bowdoin before the war. He was teaching in Wiscasset when he joined Sam Keene and another friend in the work of recruiting new soldiers. Rewarding the work, a commission from the governor made him captain of Company G. Now he was acting major, mostly for the purposes of getting duties assigned and paperwork submitted, and was hardly ready for combat command. Spear, too, was ill on the march but could not bring himself to follow Gilmore's path. Years after the war, he described his plight saying, "My malarial fever was accompanied by diarrhea and I was barely able to ride and, after dismounting to rest, it was almost impossible to remount, but going to the hospital in such an emergency was not to be thought of. Gilmore had monopolized that resort as usual, and rendered it impossible for a really sick man to go to the hospital without discredit." With the command structure in such disarray, Atherton Clark of Waldoboro, the captain of Company E, was the senior officer on duty and served as the *de facto* commander.[21]

Sensing that contact with the enemy was becoming more imminent and realizing that the chain of command had reached four deep into the 20th, the commander of the brigade, Col. Strong Vincent, looked for temporary relief outside the regiment. He asked Lt. Col. Freeman Conner of the nearby 44th New York to take command of the Maine regiment until he could make better arrangements. This bolstered the Maine men's confidence. As one corporal put it, "[H]e is one of the finest fellows I ever saw. Perfectly cool, brave and careful of his men." Anoth-

Capt. Ellis Spear

Capt. Walter Morrill

er soldier, a private, wrote that "the boys have grate [sic] confidence in him and feel joyous over the matter." In the third week of June, Conner got a chance to test his mettle as a combat commander in a skirmish that the soldiers remembered as the Battle of Middleburg, Aldie, Ashby's Gap, Upperville, Atoka, or Rector's Crossroads.[22]

☩ ☩ ☩

In the weeks just prior to the Battle of Gettysburg the Union and Confederate armies marched north from Chancellorsville on either side of the Blue Ridge mountain range in western Virginia. Robert E. Lee led his Confederates down the Shenendoah Valley toward Maryland on the western side and, to the east, Union commander Joe Hooker shielded Washington while giving chase. Occasionally, cavalry units from one army or the other would poke their heads through a gap in the mountains to see what their adversaries were up to. On June 21 the First Division of the Fifth Corps, including the 20th Maine, left the rest of the corps on a mission to shove the Rebels back through Ashby's Gap, about a dozen miles west of the town of Aldie. As a result, the brigade was on its feet for fourteen hours chasing Confederate cavalry and artillery in a series of sharp skirmishes from Aldie, back through the gap. They stopped to fight at several places whenever the Southerners found favorable ground, and the name of each place seemed to stake its claim to the battle in the memories of at least one of the soldiers.

By June 21, Sam Keene had endured one "blue lonesome day" after another, and each day that passed seemed to show no promise of improvement. At three in the morning an orderly rode into camp with orders for the First Division to prepare to march. The Maine men drew three days' rations, left their tents, knapsacks, and other gear behind, and headed through a gap at Aldie toward a town called Middleburg. Rumors had been circulating that Southern cavalry was nearby attacking Union supply trains, and the brigade's orders were to chase them back toward the Shenandoah Valley. The men in the 20th got their first look at the 1st Maine Cavalry, some of whom had been neighbors back home. The 1st Maine, fresh from a surprise attack on their Southern counterparts at the Battle of Brandy Station, was part of the skirmishing force. The Union detachment passed through Middleburg at 5 o'clock and turned left into the woods just south of the town toward the enemy.[23]

At 8:30, Union artillery lobbed a few volleys toward the Confederates and, hearing no reply, Colonel Vincent formed the Third Brigade in line of battle with the 20th Maine on the left. They advanced out of the woods to a field where Rebel pickets—dismounted cavalrymen—opened fire on them. Deployed as skirmishers in front of the regiment, the men of Company E drove the Confederates off as the brigade charged across the field. When the Federals came into view, Southern artillery opened fire. Neither shells nor high stone walls checked the advancing blue line before it reached Goose Creek, just below the enemy battery. There, the order was to lie behind a fortuitously thick, high stone wall. The enemy battery tried canister on the wall with surprisingly little result, given the close range. One Southern shell, a solid shot, found its mark and impolitely removed the leg of Cpl. John West in Company G, wounding several others. When a Federal battery came up to answer the fire, the Confederates skedaddled. Watching them fall back, the Union soldiers realized that they were facing only cavalry and artillery, no match for a large force of infantry, and the chase began.[24]

The battle turned into a running skirmish as the Southerners retreated to the safety of the gap. Hezekiah Long of Company F described the day in a letter to his wife:

> We pitched into them about 10 o'clock and after a hard fight for about an hour they commenced to run and we after them. They would make a stand when they would come upon ground that suited them and then we would have to stop and maneuver and fight awhile when they would start again. We followed them that way until 5 o'clock when we were relieved by another Brigade.[25]

By 6 o'clock the division had successfully driven the Southerners back through Ashby's Gap and another brigade replaced Vincent's men, relieving them after fifteen hours on their feet. They fell back a mile and

Theatre of War, June 21–July 10, 1863
Region in which the 20th Maine marched and fought.

rested for the night. As the Union men rounded up Southern prisoners, organizing them for their march out of the war, Capt. Walter G. Morrill of Company B saw a familiar face in the group. The face belonged to a captured lieutenant with whom Morrill had worked on the Penobscot River back in Maine before the war. Having found each other hundreds of miles from home and on opposing sides in battle, the two took a moment out of the war to reminisce.[26]

Morrill was one of the officers in the regiment who had received on-the-job training with another unit in the first year of the war. He was a young a laborer in the slate quarries around Brownville, Maine, before the war began. During the first summer of the conflict he volunteered with the 6th Maine, serving as a first sergeant with that regiment through the Peninsula Campaign and Fredericksburg. Working in the quarries and campaigning with the army had matured him beyond his 21 years, and he had become a tough, dependable soldier. Just after the Battle of Antietam, Morrill arrived with his transfer to the 20th, taking a commission as second lieutenant. Only two months later, the captain and first lieutenant resigned, and Morrill took command of Company B. Meeting a former workmate on the fields of Virginia was just one of many new experiences that he had encountered in the army, and he took greater pleasure than most at finally seeing the Rebels run.[27]

Once the tired soldiers got a chance to rest and make use of the three days' rations they had drawn, a few of the men of Company E detailed themselves as skirmishers and outflanked a detachment of Rebel hogs. The "enemy" lost six killed so that a number of soldiers had fresh pork for dinner. John Lenfest, a private in Company E, marveled at the skirmish party's efficiency. "[S]ome of them," he wrote, "hed it cooking in twenty minets from the time tha was a running."[28]

When the regiment finally halted for the night—hogs and all—they bivouaced at a farm known as "Atoka" near Rector's Crossroads, about one mile from the Middleburg Bridge. Unknown to the Maine men, a bit of history had occurred there just eleven days earlier when, on June 10, a group of local men formed Company A, 43rd Battalion of Partisan Rangers. By war's end this new Rebel unit would ride to Southern glory as some of "Mosby's Rangers."

⊕ ⊕ ⊕

"A very pleasant day," was Sam Keene's description of June 22, the first day of the new week. Keene's mood had undergone a warm transformation since he and his comrades had finally gotten a look at the backside of a Confederate uniform. For the first time in the miserable ten

John Chamberlain

months since leaving Maine the men of his regiment had seen Rebels skedaddle from the field and there was general agreement among them that, even though it was a small one, victory was a very satisfying feeling. Despite soreness from the previous day's march, the men of the 20th were "All well and in good spirits," an unusual but welcome feeling.[29]

Shortly after dawn the men rose and prepared to fall in for the march back to their camp near Aldie. During one of the halts Ellis Spear performed an uneasy task. When the cannon shot came bounding through his company behind the stone wall the day before, it had wounded three of Spear's men. Two of them were friends whom he had recruited for the company. Now it was his unenviable duty to bury one of them. With a squad of men, he took the body of John West, the corporal who lost both his leg and his life to a cannonball, to a peaceful site above the stone bridge near Goose Creek and laid him to rest. Though he had lost a man to disease months back, this was the first time that one of Spear's recruits had died in battle and under his command. The proper burial did little to diminish his lingering feeling of responsibility.[30]

When the march resumed, the column moved slowly, making long pauses to see what the enemy had in mind. Some of the Rebels followed along at what they thought was a safe distance, occasionally testing the Union rear guard. Apparently some of them misjudged their safety, since rumors among the infantry had it that Union cavalry flanked and captured five hundred of the enemy.[31]

Once the First Division reached its camp east of Aldie in the late afternoon, the men found that there was still no mail or newspapers to read, but they welcomed the chance to get off of their feet. Ellis Spear retired to the vacant headquarters tent to rest from his fever and complete the day's paperwork but he did not get the time to do so. Presently, a civilian who had been asking around camp came through the tent flap. Spear stood and looked at the visitor in mute astonishment as he recognized the face of an old friend from his days at Bowdoin College. It was John Chamberlain, Joshua's younger brother, who had come all the way from Maine at Joshua's request. In addition to its other woes, the regiment was currently without a surgeon, and Joshua had asked John to pay a visit as a representative of the U.S. Christian Commission and help out where he could. Having had no mail for two weeks there was no way of knowing that John was on his way, so his arrival was a complete surprise.[32]

John Chamberlain reached the Fifth Corps after a dangerous journey through a countryside infested with Confederate raiding parties, and had carried with him a cocksure attitude. Having completed his education at Bowdoin and two years at the Bangor

Lt. Tom Chamberlain

Theological Seminary, he was anxious to see what the army and the war were like. John inquired about his brothers—younger brother Tom was a lieutenant in the regiment and Joshua had appointed him as his adjutant—and Spear explained that the colonel was sick and Tom was in Aldie. As the two headed toward town in search of the Chamberlain brothers, they passed a sorry-looking horseman cantering up the street. Recognizing the rider as his brother Tom, John Chamberlain shouted out, "How are you adjutant? Take off my pants. What will you go for them, a five spot?" After a brief reunion on the road, the group rode on to where Joshua was recuperating from sunstroke. They found him looking poorly but out of danger.[33]

Tom was the only one of four Chamberlain brothers who did not attend Bowdoin College and in the years prior to the war he struggled to find his niche in life. In 1862 he decided to volunteer with his older brother and the army seemed just what he needed. While other soldiers lost weight, Tom gained it, and he took to military thinking quickly. It was true that his brother had appointed him adjutant of the regiment, but he had earned it, and the men respected him despite the family ties.[34]

The next day Tom took the new visitor on a riding tour of the surrounding countryside that included some of the previous day's battlefield. There was a lot for the adjutant to tell his brother that letters home could not fully explain. Among Tom's explanations was a description of the commander of the Third Brigade, Col. Strong Vincent. The Pennsylvania native and Harvard graduate had previously commanded the 83rd

15

Pennsylvania, another regiment in the brigade. Though he began the war as virtually the lowest-ranking soldier in the Union—he was a private in a three-months regiment—by age 27 he had risen to become the youngest brigade commander in the army, but his youth did not diminish his ability. On the contrary, Gen. George B. McClellan, when in command of the entire Union army, once noted that the 83rd, thanks to Vincent, was the best-drilled regiment in its division, if not in the whole army. If McClellan's endorsement was not enough—and to the soldiers it most certainly was—then Vincent's first go at commanding the brigade in combat two days before definitely settled the matter.[35]

Thanks to Vincent's work near Middleburg the Confederates were back on the other side of the Blue Ridge, and the diminished threat of impending attack allowed Lieutenant Colonel Conner to return to his own regiment where he noticed some unfamiliar faces. While camped at Aldie, eighty men from the 14th New York reinforced Conner's 44th. The state of New York had organized its fourteenth regiment as a two-year unit and the two years had expired. Unfortunately for these four score men, they had either enlisted some time after the regiment's mustering in or signed enlistment papers that required three years of service. Even though the regiment's term was up, these men had more time left to serve in Uncle Sam's volunteer army. To refuse meant a court martial for desertion, and the penalty for desertion was death. So, the transferred men begrudgingly fell in among the ten companies of their new unit.[36]

If Conner and the other New York officers had sought a short walk over to the next regiment. Just a month earlier, the 20th Maine had undergone a similar infusion of malcontents, and the experience had been just another reason for morale to be setting record lows. Over the course of three weeks in late May and early June, an irregular flow of enlisted men in groups from one to sixty-nine came straggling into the 20th's muster rolls. These were men of the recently disbanded 2nd Maine, and two score of them came to their new regiment under guard at the points of bayonets. The 2nd Mainers were big, tough, seasoned veterans who had been in the field since July 1861, and they had fought in just about every battle of the war since it began. When they enlisted back in Maine, no one expected that the war would last more than a few weeks, paperwork was new, and orders from the government were difficult to understand. In the confusion of those first months of the war, some men signed three-year enlistments but joined a two-year regiment. Since their regiment's term was up, most of the 2nd Maine men were going home and the three-year men felt that they had a right to go as well, no matter what the enlistment papers said. Others, who had enlisted well after the regiment mustered in, felt that they deserved a discharge, even though some of them had served little more than six months.[37]

This unhappy lot arrived just as Colonel Ames departed, leaving the whole mess for Lieutenant Colonel Chamberlain to deal with, and he did the best he could under the circumstances. He treated them with respect and divided the men up among the various companies to dilute their resistance. By late June there were less than a dozen still under arrest for

Cpl. William Livermore

refusing to take up rifles and perform their duty. The paperwork showed that more than 170 men thus transferred, but in reality, only a little more than a hundred men actually made it into the ranks. Nonetheless, their presence raised the rolls of the 20th above 500 men, making it the largest regiment in the brigade, and despite the circumstances, their combat experience was an asset that outweighed their sour attitude.[38]

✠ ✠ ✠

On June 23 the soldiers got a break. They had a chance to dwell on their first victory, however small, and spent the day doing very little. A refreshed Sam Keene "[l]aid still all day feasting upon cherries, sleeping, eating, etc. Nothing transpired to create much excitement." As far as they could hear, the war was all quiet and the men washed their clothes and their bodies. In the evening they even had time for a dress parade and some band music. Cpl. William T. Livermore got his soldierly duties accomplished and sought some way to pass the time.[39]

Will Livermore was a farmer in his early 20s before the war. He volunteered with a number of other local men, and a few who were still boys, from the area around Milo in the center of the state. When he left home for war, he had no idea that it would keep him away this long. In October 1862 he reminded his brother and father that if they went fishing in northern Maine that winter he wanted to go along, fully expecting he would be home by then. As the war dragged on he made the most of it, becoming a fine corporal and religiously making full and insightful entries in his diary.[40]

Without much else to do in camp that day, he decided it was a good time for a stroll, but in this hostile region wandering away from camp without permission was forbidden. So he obtained the required pass from his commander and set off in search of some cherries. As soon as he had gathered a supply, Col. Alexander Webb of Gen. George Meade's staff ordered him to fall in with a squad of men that he had gathered outside of the army's picket line. Livermore presented his pass to the colonel, but Webb was having none of it, and ordered him to fall in anyway.

The squad marched to the brigade headquarters and Livermore was sent back to his tent and, though Webb did not place him under guard, the actions of the colonel galled him. Livermore had prided himself on being a good soldier and his conduct had earned him a place of honor in the regimental color guard. The indignity of the slight, though harmless to his military record, grated on him. That evening, he reminded his diary that "[t]his was the first time I ever was picked up or pulled out of camp and I had a perfect right out then."[41]

For everyone except the hapless Corporal Livermore, nothing happened that was out of the ordinary—at least what passed for ordinary in a war—and the soldiers enjoyed a typical day in the monotonous life of the infantryman. They even got a chance to buy the local paper which already contained an account of the recent skirmishing. It seems the only thing raising concern in the regiment was that there was still no mail, and that John Lyford was still missing. Lyford, a private in Company B, was the oldest man in the 20th and had been missing for a number of days. For some reason, the absence of this one soldier caused a great deal of concern among the men.[42]

On June 24 the campaign seemed to come to a halt. The soldiers laid out their tents in rows by company (called "streets") and returned to drilling twice a day. Colonel Ames had impressed upon them the importance of keeping their tactical skills sharp, and frequent drill was essential to success in battle. Keeping the army safe and protected while in camp was also essential, and the soldiers took regular turns, sometimes as a whole regiment, serving guard duty and manning the line of pickets that surrounded camp. These duties returned that day as well. In the afternoon the men got another sign that their luck was changing for the better; there was still no mail to the regiment but the chaplain had agreed to take some out.[43]

The next day, the soldiers discovered that their camp was within a mile of the mansion where James Monroe had once lived, a few miles south of Leesburg. The current owner was Maj. John W. Fairfax of

Confederate Gen. James Longstreet's staff. With her husband and six brothers away in the army, Mrs. Fairfax did not have a guard on the property and after morning picket duty the Maine men got a closer look at the largest, most elaborate house that many of them had ever seen.[44]

Also on that Thursday signs began to indicate that the army would be marching soon and with greater purpose. After the adjutant recorded the official morning roll call, he packed the regiment's papers in mule-drawn wagons to be left behind. On that last roll, he recorded that eight men were under arrest within the regiment, seven of whom were the last of the holdout transfers from the 2nd Maine.[45]

The next morning reveille sounded at 4:30, and the troops broke camp and set off north on the Leesburg road at 6. In addition to most of their baggage, including their shelter tents, they left the good weather behind as the rain turned the roads back to mud. Creeks swelled enough so that the regimental pioneers—men detailed to wield axes—had to build makeshift bridges at points, and an occasional team of horses knee deep in mud forced the column to halt. Lieutenant Colonel Chamberlain was with the regiment but, despite three day of rest, his health was still poor. His brother John tried in vain to convince him to travel by ambulance wagon but he refused. He would ride, he said, "like a man." To lighten his responsibility, Col. James Rice of the 44th New York watched over the 20th for him on the march.[46]

After fording Goose Creek—the same stream over which they had fought the Rebels on the Ashby's Gap Turnpike—word came that Chamberlain was to go ahead to Leesburg, make himself comfortable, and recuperate. He and John rode on ahead of the army and rested in the town at the house of a Confederate surgeon. Despite the fact that the occupants were confirmed secessionists the Chamberlains got a warm meal and "polite usage" during their stay. John repaid this Southern hospitality by stealing a small Rebel flag from the house.[47]

On the whole, the town of Leesburg had boarded itself up as the army approached. John remembered that the village seemed to display its dislike of the bluecoats. "All the windows, shutters closed," he wrote, "and everything bespeaking contempt for the Yankees." All of this was not surprising since about half of the Army of the Potomac had already passed through the area. Despite the coolness of the town's reception, the brothers felt refreshed by their meal and a good rest, and they returned to the march when the Fifth Corps came up three or four hours later.[48]

The remainder of the Maine men arrived in Leesburg at 2 o'clock in the afternoon and they also got a break and a meal, though not as luxurious as the Chamberlains had enjoyed. Afterward, they marched

19

east toward the river from which the army took its name, and crossed pontoon bridges at Edwards Ferry near sunset. This was the ferry that a portion of the Union army used when it crossed the river to attack Confederates above Ball's Bluff in 1861. That battle had seemed to inaugurate a recurring nightmare for Union soldiers, as they were badly and embarrassingly defeated by the Rebels. The soldiers got a glimpse of the now infamous hill as they crossed out of Virginia and into Maryland. A few miles beyond the Potomac late evening arrived, so the army halted near Poolesville and bivouacked for the night, having marched more than twenty miles.[49]

Not long after the soldiers settled down for the evening, a team of mules pulled an army wagon into their bivouac. Their arrival solved a week-long mystery as the missing John Lyford was aboard. It seems that the popular private had become separated from the wagon train several days earlier and, in the confusion of an army on the march, he had taken nearly a week to catch up with, and then find, the regiment. Realizing that Lyford had not fallen prey to Confederate guerrillas was a great relief to the men of Company B, not because of his personal charm or wit but because he was driving the company supply wagon which was full of equipment, rations, and soldiers' personal items. Unfortunately, Lyford had not come across any of the regiment's mail but, knowing that the wagon's contents were safe after all, the men undoubtedly passed a more restful night.[50]

✠ ✠ ✠

On the morning of June 27 reveille roused the men at 4 o'clock and by 6 they were on the march again. After slogging through thick mud in light rain for several miles, they reached a ford on the Monocacy River below Buckeystown. The river was running quickly at the ford, but it was not more than three feet deep and a few dozen feet across in most places, so they did not need pontoons. In order to save time, the entire First Division crossed at once, creating a remarkable if not unusual sight.[51]

Infantrymen in every war have always maintained a deep dislike for wet feet on the march and the blisters that all too frequently result. In this trait, the men of the Army of the Potomac were no exception, but at the Monocacy they took the practice to an unusual extreme. Perhaps the march had raised an odor that the division commander found unpleasant, or it just seemed like a novel idea at the time but, whatever the reason, the entire division stripped and crossed over. It is impossible to say whether any of the local inhabitants witnessed this unique event but, if any did, it is likely that never before or since has a sight instilled more concern in a Maryland farmer for his daughter than that of three thousand naked men with weapons swarming across the river, holding their belongings over their heads. The contrast of bronzed hands and faces against alabaster bodies usually shaded under uniforms made the scene all the more ridiculous and the soldiers, at least, enjoyed the adventure immensely.[52]

"I never saw a field of wheat til today," William Livermore recorded that afternoon. "We passed thousands of acres. Some is cut and in the shock." For a number of the Maine men the sight of a field of wheat was another in a long line of new experiences in the continuing adventure of army life. As farm folks, many of the men noticed that the flora and fauna of the South held a certain charm that was different from back home. Along the rivers in Virginia and Maryland they marveled at great sycamores which bowed over the water, walnut trees that grew five feet wide, and grape vines as thick as half a foot.[53]

With great envy they had come to admire the fertile fields of Virginia and Maryland. Farmers in Maine would swear at times, and with some accuracy, that the crop most often yielded from their fields was rock. Moreover, Maine was hilly country where, with exhaustive effort, families carved out a small farm from a forest that seemed to forever close in on them. By the looks of things around them, these Southern farmers had life pretty easy, at least when the war was not destroying the fruits of their labors. Long, wide, flat fields that went on for dozens of acres were a luxury back home. Here, the people thought of these as just another wheat field.

The fertile farms of Maryland and the "Sacred Soil" of Virgina were like nothing they had ever seen. One thing did remind them a bit of home, however. In some parts of Virginia, the war had ravaged the countryside and hardly a tree had survived the soldier's need for firewood. Most Maine farmers at that time supplemented their income in the winter months by working in the vast lumber trades that drove the state's economy. For the men who had spent so many winter months felling trees and driving them down river to saw mills or waiting ships, the sight of an area picked clean of timber was not unfamiliar.

While the natural beauty of the region made its mark on their memory, the sights created by people elicited their own sense of awe and wonderment. After fording the stream (and presumably making better use, once again, of their clothes) the regiment passed another of the majestic estates that brought to mind the enormous wealth of which they had only read before the war. For John Chamberlain this, and the Monroe Mansion, "...filled my idea of old fashioned Virginia elegance." [54]

After another twenty-mile day, the troops passed through Buckeys-town and at sunset the entire Fifth Corps lay together in the same field for the night. There was still no mail and, given the hasty movements of the army in various directions, the prospect of getting any soon was only dimming. But, they were now within a few miles of Frederick City and its rail line, and they thought perhaps their luck would turn. One hopeful sign came with an order for some of the men to fall in and draw clothing. If some supplies had made their way to them, perhaps the mail would follow.[55]

On June 28 the Fifth Corps observed the Sabbath by resting, but it was anything but a quiet day. In the morning, some of the men of the 20th attended religious services performed by the chaplain of the 44th New York. Their own chaplain, like their colonel, lieutenant colonel, major, and surgeon, was no longer with them. Others cleaned their weapons and themselves, preparing for the inspection at noon. A bath and a chance to boil clothes always brought a measure of relief to army life, for it helped curtail the lice that often seemed as plentiful on a soldier as fleas on a farm dog. Missing a chance at the boiling kettle often meant a long night. The experience, lived through once, was not easily forgotten. "I had a restless night," a Maine man once recalled, "for the lice were aware of my designs and they seemed to rally their whole force, and they were drilling a skirmish drill except when they were falling in for rations."[56]

Sgt. Hezekiah Long of Company F, formerly a guard at the state prison in Thomaston, took advantage of the free time to describe the regiment's recent activities to his wife. "The weather was stormy," he wrote, "and the traveling has been very bad. But it was not so hot as we had it on the march from the Rappahan-nock...We have not had a male [sic] for the last two weeks and have seen but very few papers in that time so we have but little of what is going on in the world outside the army and not much that is in it."[57]

If the soldiers had offered a prayer at Sabbath services that they would soon receive news from home, they finally got a long-awaited answer. After a sixteen-day hiatus, the bugler sounded mail-call in camp, and the regiment finally got the letters, papers, and packages that had been trying to reach the elusive army. Many of the men got several letters and newspapers, both from Maine and other places, such as Washington. With the influx of information came the usual flood of camp rumors, and one of the stories going around had it that President Lincoln had replaced Hooker with Gen. George Gordon Meade. The change of their army's commander on the eve of what they believed would be a great battle should have caused deep concern among the soldiers. For the men of the 20th, however, the change, assuming the rumor was true, meant that they would serve under their fourth new commander in just six months of campaigning since they left Maine. They might have paid little attention at all to such gossip had the scuttlebutt not been that President Lincoln had promoted the commander of their own Fifth Corps to lead the entire army. So many difficulties had befallen them since the war began that the men had adapted and seemed to take news like this in stride.[58]

Included in the mail were the regiment's official papers, and when a weak and sick Ellis Spear read them his spirits fell a bit further as he found that they did not include his name among the promotions. The leaders in Maine and Washington had managed enough paperwork to promote Joshua Chamberlain to colonel and Charles Gilmore to lieutenant colonel but that was all that they had done. Moreover, neither of the men promoted were at that time present for duty to receive their new rank and responsibilities.[59]

For many days now the soldiers had known that a large battle was closing in on them, but early in the afternoon they began to understand how large it might become. Throughout the camp officers and aides were making requisitions to prepare their units for an extended march and campaign. Shortly after inspection, two brigades of Pennsylvania Reserves marched past the 20th which told the Maine men that something was brewing since these men had previously manned the defensive works near Washington. They reckoned that if the War Department had allowed the depletion of the defenses around the capital then it was a good bet that things were about to get very serious. Another sign of the growing tension surfaced in the camp when a unit of U.S. Regular Army troops made an example of one of their own. As the men of the rest of the division looked on, the regulars forced a soldier to walk through camp with his head shaved and a board across his back that read "coward" while the band played the "Rogue's March."[60]

If the overdue mail had not lifted the morale of the troops high enough, then the next morning's march through Frederick must have finished the job. As they approached the outskirts of town the commanders ordered the men to march "in column by platoon" with colors unfurled so that the army made a wide imposing column as it moved through the streets. The good citizens of Frederick showed their strong Union sentiments in return, hanging the Stars and Stripes from nearly every house while women waved handkerchiefs and gave water and food to the passing troops. John Chamberlain remembered the scene in his journal. "This city made the strongest demonstrations of Union sentiment of any city I have found in the Union South," he wrote. "Flags were flying from every window and everybody honored our troops with a smile or at least a look." Albert Fernald gauged the effect on morale in three words: "Union feeling strong," and even Sam Keene's previously sour disposition seemed to turn around.[61]

Ellis Spear was feeling only a little better as he rode with the column and he was mindful of what lay ahead. Decades later he remembered the march in his memoirs when he wrote:

> The country was fresh and beautiful but we were on no picnic, but on the very serious business of hunting for the enemy, with reasonable certainty that they would make themselves very disagreeable when found. We marched through Frederick on the 29th, the same old Maryland town which we had visited in September of 1862. As we had made no acquaintances on the former visit, we had no social duties here. There was no time even to pay a visit to the poultry houses, where we might claim acquaintance with more reason. Occasionally, with deep regret, we passed a cherry tree, but no straggling was permitted.[62]

Beyond Frederick, the corps sped up a bit and men pulled out their rubber blankets to help shed the rain that had begun to fall again. At sundown they passed through Liberty and after two or three more miles, they stopped for the night. The halt gave Color Sgt. Charles Proctor a chance to sober up and return to the regiment. On the march, Proctor let his patriotic fervor and a little too much alcohol get the best of him and, after cussing out the officers, they relieved him of his position of honor and took the regimental flag from him. Proctor fell out, and three men in the rear guard could not keep him up, so they left him behind and listed him A.W.O.L. The honor of bearing the flag then passed to the next sergeant in seniority. William Livermore, one of four other men in the color guard with Proctor, had little sympathy for his drunken comrade. To his diary he admitted, "I hope he will be broke and probably will."[63]

The new color bearer, Andrew Tozier of Plymouth, was one of the 2nd Maine transfers and a seasoned veteran. The son of an abusive alcoholic father, he was no stranger to hard living. At 27 years old he enlisted in Company F of the 2nd Maine and, a year and two days earlier at the Battle of Gaines Mill, he lost the middle finger on his left hand, broke at least one rib, and received a painful wound in his left ankle from a bullet that went in but not out. In the year since, he had recuperated after spending time in two Confederate prisons in Richmond.[64]

With the flag over his shoulder, Tozier endured the evening's march while the rain fell hard and the troops got soaked, having been ordered to leave tents behind on the march. If they had cursed the heat the week before, it was the rain that drew their wrath now. Even in the rain, the Maryland humidity stifled men who were used to cool Atlantic breezes back home. The bugle sounded reveille before daylight, and at 4:30 the march began again with even greater vigor. During the day the regiment passed near or through the towns of Unionville, Union Bridge, Uniontown, and camped at Union Mills, reminding them that they were marching in a friendly region. Later, an order from General Meade confirmed the rumor that he had taken command of the army, and his instructions required in a sense, that they pick up the pace. All commanders were to send away excess wagons, baggage, and animals, and put the long blue column "into lightest possible marching order." For the 20th, this meant saying good-bye to the few luxuries that might still have been within reach, and that the threat of encountering the enemy at any moment had become very real.[65]

Getting any more distance or speed out of the Fifth Corps was an almost impossible task as many had already reached the limit of their endurance. The heat had subsided to some extent but the rain made marching almost as miserable, particularly when wet feet yielded to blistering. A soldier in the First Brigade of the 20th Maine's division later wrote, "Men became ragged, foot-sore and chafed. Many were marching in their drawers, and with handkerchiefs of many colors tied about their heads or necks certainly presented anything but a martial appearance. Some were marching in their stocking feet, while others were bare-footed."[66]

Wet, sore and worn out, the Fifth Corps marched past another portion of the army about midday and reached Middleburg, Maryland. A stream known as Big Pipe Creek ran past the town and as they crossed it the soldiers expected a fight shortly. The 20th was at the head of the column where they viewed what they supposed were signs of Confederate cavalry so that a company had to march as skirmishers on each side of the regiment making the march more tedious and slow. Later in the afternoon the 44th New York went ahead to take over the skirmishing.[67]

At 6 o'clock they halted at Union Mills, where relieved villagers told them that seven thousand Confederates had been there just seven hours earlier. The gray-clad cavalrymen had taken about everything they could carry and occasionally offered to pay their victims in Confederate scrip which the Marylanders considered worthless. As they left the area, the Southerners had warned the citizens that the Yankees were coming, and that the soldiers in blue would burn their buildings and kill their children as they had done in Virginia. Ignoring the warning, the people met the Union troops with smiles and sold them all of the food that they could spare at reasonable prices. William Livermore wrote, "There is lots of guides. Citizens that go with us. It is a sport to hear the old people talk about the rebs. One old lady 70 years old came out to the road to day said the rebs had cavalry and two artillerys and right smart of men with guns."[68]

When the troops finally bivouacked for the night, they reckoned that they had marched at least twenty-five miles that day, and perhaps as much as fifty since leaving Frederick the day before. Now only four miles from Pennsylvania, they began to hear cannonading off toward Hanover. With the sound of battle a few miles to the north, they had one very good sign to consider. Professor Chamberlain had returned to duty with his new colonel's eagles on his shoulders and, though still a little weary from his fever, he again assumed command of his regiment.[69]

As Chamberlain sat atop his mount and observed his unit in column, he must have noticed that it had become considerably smaller than he had left it. Ever since the forced marches brought the army out of Frederick toward Pennsylvania, the speed and duration of the movements were too much for many of the men and straggling took its toll. Stragglers, as a group, could be separated into two different classes. The first, men who were at the mercy of sore and worn-out bodies, were truly unable to continue the march. Most of these men fell out with permission and needed only for the army to halt for a time so that they could catch up and return to their places. The second class of stragglers were soldiers with no intention of enduring such great exertion, especially when risking life and limb in a battle was their likely reward. A large number of these men from various parts of the army gathered in Frederick, the largest city on the route of march, and they made life miserable for the citizens who had welcomed the army's march through their streets. Whitelaw Reid, a news reporter who followed the war making regular dispatches to his readers, described the havoc stragglers were creating in Frederick.

"Frederick is Pandemonium," he wrote. "Somebody has blundered frightfully; the town is full of stragglers, and the liquor-shops are in full blast. Just under my window scores of drunken soldiers are making night hideous; all over the town they are trying to steal horses or sneak into unwatched private residences or are filling the air with the blasphemy of their drunken brawls." For the most part, these were not men who had fallen out with a commander's permission when their feet, legs, or both, finally gave out. As Reid described them they were, "The worst elements of a great army...in their worst condition; its cowards, its thieves, its sneaks, its bullying vagabonds, all inflamed with whiskey, and drunk as well with their freedom from accustomed restraint." Reid's dispatches continued to reveal similar scenes all along the march north to Gettysburg.[70]

To the soldiers who remained in the column, it was becoming clear that General Lee had moved his invasion all the way into northern territory, and that the men would soon fight their first major battle in their own region. This, however, was about the extent of the soldiers' knowledge of the situation. Years later, Ellis Spear observed, "It was curious afterwards to remember how ignorant we were (I mean, we of the regiments) of the position, or movements, of the other corps of the army. Even Army Headquarters were not swift in finding out the positions and movements of the enemy. We knew only that Lee's army had crossed the Potomac and was hurrying up the valley behind the mountains." As the 20th prepared to cross Maryland's northern border they had no way of knowing that the lead elements of the Confederate army had already done so 35 miles to the west a week before, and were now threatening the state capitol at Harrisburg.[71]

At about 7 in the morning on the first day of July, the regiment marched out of Union Mills toward Pennsylvania under intermittent rain. As they marched north, they encountered more signs of war and moved slowly, with skirmishers out, expecting that at any minute they might meet the Rebels. Near noon, they passed a stone monument that marked the border into Pennsylvania and the enthusiasm of every soldier grew. They unfurled their flags and beat drums, the bands played, and the troops voluntarily took up the regular marching step as they had when passing through Frederick City. With each step, the intensity seemed to grow.[72]

Sometime during the march on the first of July, three of the 2nd Maine men who were marching in Company D apparently decided that they had endured enough, and they fell out from the march never to return. Their complaint could not have echoed many of their fellow transferees who felt that a two-year enlistment was sufficient, since only one of the three had been in the army more than a year. Nonetheless, their departure left only a handful of transferred men still in arrest for refusal to do their duty.[73]

At 3 in the afternoon the regiment marched into Hanover and realized that the war was very close by. Confederate cavalry had been in the town the night before and left behind burned carts, wagons, and dead horses. By now, the Fifth Corps was marching in serious campaign style, and there was no longer time for prolonged bivouacs, but the troops had endured hard marching in mud and rain for days and they could push no further without rest.

In Hanover, the regiment halted and stacked its rifles hoping to bivouac, while men scattered in every direction in search of water and fence rails for cooking fires. As they halted, some of the forage wagons pulled up with a harvest of rations from the fields of local farms and men gathered at the backs of the wagons for a chance at them. Shortly after they lit fires and took out their rations rumors began to flit through the camp that boded poorly for the Union cause. The enemy had struck a part of the army at a town called Gettysburg, fifteen miles to the west, and the First and Eleventh Corps—the latter under Gen. Oliver Otis Howard of Maine—had barely held on against overwhelming numbers. The fight had apparently cost the Union one of its best commanders when a bullet killed Gen. John F. Reynolds, a Pennsylvanian considered one of the best commanders in the army. Given the blindness with which they had seemed to be groping the countryside, and the lack of any information about the enemy at all in recent days, the men found it difficult to believe that the rumors were true.[74]

At sunset, just two hours after they had halted, intense activity and orders from above seemed to confirm the rumors. Joshua Chamberlain remembered the activity. "Staff officers dashed from corps, to division, to brigade, to regiment, to battery—and the order flew like the hawk, and not the owl. 'To Gettysburg!' " The Fifth Corps rose to its feet and prepared to march again, and Chamberlain remembered the effect on the mood of the soldiers. "The iron-faced veterans were transformed to boys. They insisted on starting out with colors flying, so that even the night might know what manner of men were coming to redeem the day."[75]

Virtually every man in the regiment recalled that the march from Hanover toward the sound of battle was the most memorable of the war. At a reunion years later, Howard Prince recalled that "[N]one who made that night's march will ever forget it." It was a warm evening and they were marching in friendly territory. Crowds gathered along the route and cheered as the blue column passed. Women and children stood at the front gates of their homes and gave water and milk to the men as they went by. Some women sang the "Star Spangled Banner" and other patriotic songs to which the soldiers responded with cheers. These scenes raised a sense of pride and enthusiasm in the troops, who had grown accustomed to marching through the hostile towns of Virginia, where the local people despised their presence. For the first time since joining the army they found themselves marching to a fight amid strong reminders of what they were fighting for, like gladiators marching to the coliseum before a cheering crowd.[76]

Corporal Livermore, marching with the colors at the head of the regiment, remembered the scenes as they marched. "The troops felt nicely and I never heard such cheering. Cheer after cheer ran along our line of march. Every man, woman and child was out to see us as we passed. The [R]ebels had just gone through the town and the people gave us a hearty welcome."[77]

The soldiers got a great boost from the outpouring of good will that the women provided along the route. Howard Prince, the quartermaster sergeant, remembered that the men, three-fourths of them unmarried, "were only too ready to take snap-shots at flirtation, and put in practicearts almost forgotten amid the sour faces and averted heads of a hostile population." At least one of them, however, had reserved his devotion for women of different stock, and he had expressed his wishes to his diary months back. "Once in a great while," William Livermore wrote, "I see a woman but they are not like our M[ain]e girls. When I get a woman I shall get her just as near Katahdin as I can, for the farther south I go the more inferior the inhabitants are."[78]

Despite his preference for women of more northern climes, the Maine corporal was probably as appreciative as the rest of the men for the sentiments expressed by the women of Pennsylvania. It was no wonder they expressed them. Many of these women were alone and unprotected, trying to be both parents to their children as they worked the fields and conducted the business of farming while their husbands and sons were away in the army. For the soldiers, the images kindled a sense of manhood, bravely marching to defend the noble women of the North against the invading Rebel horde.

As they marched through the moonlit evening, a wave of cheering drifted back from the front of the column toward the Maine men. They soon learned that the source of this enthusiasm was a story that their beloved General McClellan was again commanding the army and riding with them toward the battle. There was great confusion about who started the report. Joshua Chamberlain got it from a staff officer at a turn in the road who reported it to each colonel as he passed, while his brother John, who was riding beside him at the time, thought the report had come from Gen. James Barnes, the division commander, through Colonel Vincent. Many soldiers also had difficulty understanding whose job McClellan had taken. Some thought he had replaced Meade, others thought Gen. Henry Halleck, the commander of all Union forces in the war, and still others thought Hooker, whom Meade had replaced two days before.[79]

Whatever the source, and despite the confusion, the news created even greater enthusiasm in the blue column. John Chamberlain marveled at the effect of the news on the Maine men. "Shout after shout rang upon the air. Everybody said 'it is as good as 50,000 men. It gives new impulse to the army.' The men said now we will fight. Col. Vincent catching the enthusiasm rode along and with a wave of his hand said, 'now boys we will give 'em hell tomorrow.' "[80]

The rumors about McClellan were so pervasive that they even reached over into the Confederate Army. As late as July 2, General Lee and his staff were questioning prisoners as to who commanded their army and where McClellan was. A private in the 3rd Maine whom the Confederates had taken prisoner that day told Lee that McClellan had gone to the rear to bring up fifty thousand reinforcements. Years later, the Maine prisoner said that he hoped his disinformation had helped with the battle, perhaps encouraging Lee to push his attack.[81]

The news of McClellan's reinstatement, however, was just another army rumor of unknown origin, for at that moment McClellan was nowhere near Gettysburg, nor even a command position in the army. It was not the only rumor of a change in command, however, as yet another wave of news swept the column about a commander who was even farther away from the army than McClellan. Reports trickled in to the troops that someone had seen Gen. George Washington himself riding among the hills of Gettysburg that afternoon. The ethereal mood of the evening was so intoxicating, that even Colonel Chamberlain, one of the most educated men in either army, had to resist the thought. "Let no one smile at me!" he wrote years later. "I half believed it myself,—so did the powers of the other world draw nigh!"[82]

To speed the corps along, the units divided up and marched towardthe fight on separate roads in order to prevent the clogging up of any one ute. The 20th passed through McSherrytown and Bonnaughtown before turning south off of the Hanover Road within several miles of Gettysburg. They then marched until they reached the Baltimore Pike below Rock Creek and halted after midnight, having covered more than thirty miles since sunrise.[83]

The forced marching finally slowed when the army arrived just southeast of Gettysburg, and some of the men who had been straggling and falling out caught up with their units. The 20th seemed to have a slow but steady stream of tired, footsore soldiers wandering in, especially after they reached the battlefield during the night of July 1. If they had awarded prizes for the most persistent straggler, it would have probably gone to Cpl. John Morin, and his story would have shamed the shirkers who were wallowing in Frederick City. Morin had floundered in the hospital system around Baltimore and Washington since he developed a bad fever in camp near Antietam the previous November. In June a surgeon told him that he could no longer endure campaign life, and he would be transferred to the Invalid Corps. Morin figured that he still had some fight left in him, so he struck a deal with the transportation officer at the docks in Alexandria and made his way back to the regiment. Meanwhile the hospital, discovering his absence, listed him as a deserter. He managed to keep up until after the fighting at Middleburg, when he could not make the forced marches. Undaunted, he convinced the driver of a supply wagon to let him ride along and, bypassing the stragglers' festival in Frederick, he made it to Gettysburg and took his place in Company F.[84]

Near sunrise of July 2 the men woke and managed a hasty breakfast before falling in. Officers inspected the soldiers' weapons to be sure that they would serve their intended purpose in the coming fight. Under the stifling heat of a fiery red sun, they marched the remaining few miles toward Gettysburg and reached the hills southeast of the town at about 11 o'clock. At first, they halted south of Wolf's Hill with the Twelfth Corps, but later, the entire division crossed over Rock Creek, halted at a crossroads near the McAllister mill, and took a reserve position in a peach orchard. The men stacked arms and rested as more complete news of the battle began to reach them. Some cooked coffee and others spoke, but only in subdued undertones. The sounds of battle were growing louder and stronger, while white puffs of smoke appeared from shells exploding over the hills in front of them.[85]

Later that afternoon, Corporal Livermore took his regular place in line with the color guard after jotting an entry inside the back cover of his diary. "In line of battle before Gettysburg, Pennsylvania," he wrote. "First, 5th, 6th, 11th Corps are here. There will probably be a great battle tomorrow." He was right about the battle, but it would come much sooner than he thought.[86]

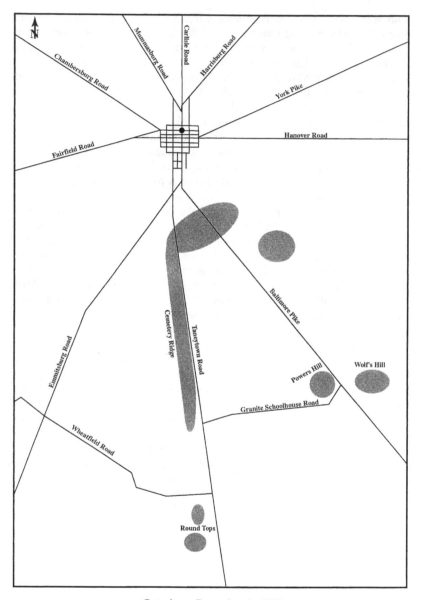

Gettysburg, Pennsylvania, 1863

2   The Death-Strewn Slope

No, I never expected to leave that hill alive. At one time it looked as though we all must perish and so far as I have been able to learn, there was not a single man in the 20th Maine but got hit in one way or another.[1]

Joshua Chamberlain, 1912

Most of the afternoon on July 2 the 20th remained safely nestled between the other regiments of the Fifth Corps along the Granite Schoolhouse Road. The First, Eleventh, and Twelfth Corps occupied the ground around them. Aware of his own shortcomings as a military commander, Joshua Chamberlain fretted over the apparent lack of information or strategy that seemed to consume the army around him. "But what much more impressed my mind," he later wrote, "was the great calm, the uncertainty of overture, and seeming lack of tactical plan for the tremendous issue. We were aware that other troops were coming up, on one side and the other; but we had no means of knowing or judging which side would take the offensive and which the defensive or where the battle would begin."[2]

The only official word that Chamberlain received was an order to hold his men ready to take part in an attack on the army's right. What little information the men received through the soldiers' grapevine told them that the army was forming a defensive position. This deepened their confidence in Meade who, by now, had managed to succeed both McClellan and George Washington as the real commander of the army.

The Round Tops and the Valley of Death. This Matthew Brady photograph was taken July 15, 1863, from the first position of Vincent's Brigade near the Wheat Field. The brigade twice passed over the farm lane in front. The 20th Maine fought on the opposite side of Little Round Top between the two hills.

The men drew 20 extra rounds of ammunition, stuffing them into their pockets and cartridge boxes with the 40 rounds already there. Those who did not sleep or otherwise rest focused their attention on a hill to their right and front. The locals called it Culp's Hill, and the Maine men thought that they would surely be sent toward it at any moment. Before an order could deliver them there, however, Confederate artillery altered the plan. Behind and to the left, in a direction opposite their expectations, the battle opened and the familiar rattle of musketry followed the booming of the cannons.[3]

The bugles sounded and the whole Fifth Corps, the Third Brigade in front, pushed to its left. Without time to make proper use of the road, some of the men marched through a swamp and over stone walls and hedges while the earth shook as they moved toward the sound of exploding shells. After crossing the Taneytown Road many of the men realized that the corps they were rushing to support was not where reports had said it would be. Somehow, Gen. Dan Sickles' Third Corps had moved forward almost a mile and was desperately trying to hold off Confederate troops in its front and on its flank.[4]

As the First Division crossed a road before halting on the edge of a wheat field, Colonel Chamberlain sat upright in his saddle awaiting orders. To his right, he saw the other two brigades of the division move forward into a wooded area beyond the wheat field where they immediately joined the battle. To his left, he could see the far end of the Third Corps near a boulder-strewn corner of the valley that he later learned was called the Devil's Den. Had he been able to see over the ridge to his left and make out the battle flag in the center of that thinnest of lines, he would have recognized it as the banner of the 4th Maine, stalwart men from the Maine coast. Presently, the 4th was getting the worst of the fight in the Den trying simultaneously to protect a battery of artillery while holding off an ever-growing swarm of Alabamians, Texans, and Georgians. They did all of this in slippery army shoes amid boulders the size of a Maine barn, but what Chamberlain could not yet know was that the work that the 4th was now doing would help save his own regiment within a half hour.[5]

But now, the Third Brigade was about to form into line of battle on the edge of the field, and Chamberlain prepared to pass along the necessary orders. When they completed the maneuver, the 20th would be positioned between the 16th Michigan, on its left, and the 83rd Pennsylvania, then the 44th New York, on its right. With his brigade commander in sight and a regiment on either side of him in an open field, Chamberlain could breathe a bit easier about his first go at commanding his regiment in battle. He would have plenty of support and all in the open where he could see the fight and react.[6]

In front of their line the Mainers could see blue troops falling back through waist-high wheat at the far end of the field. They did not know it then but it was the outnumbered 17th Maine, the regiment with which they had shared a rendezvous camp near Portland the summer before. A good portion of the men of the 20th's Company K were originally recruited for the 17th, and the men now falling back toward them were neighbors and relatives back home around Brunswick. From behind them, the soldiers could hear a battery firing, lobbing shells, they presumed, into the woods beyond the field.[7]

A few hundred yards over Chamberlain's left shoulder a bald-faced hill known as Little Round Top dominated the whole area. The western face was exposed by a receding treeline, leaving rocks and bushes to contend for the steep slope. Boulders and rocks were everywhere. As Chamberlain described it, "Even the smooth spots were strewn with fragments of rock like the playground or battle-ground of giants." The eastern half of the hill was wooded and the trees reached around the southern end before giving way to scattered scrub oak and then the open face. Beyond that far end was a larger hill known as Big Round Top which was covered from top to bottom with trees.[8]

Only a few men, some with signal flags, were looking out from the top of the smaller hill. One of them was Gen. Gouvernor K. Warren, General Meade's chief engineer. Warren had arrived on Little Round Top at Meade's request in order to examine the ground on the Union left and offer any advice he could as to placement of troops and artillery. Beyond Devil's Den, Warren saw the right of Longstreet's assault moving in strong force against the left flank of the Union army, which was then near Devil's Den. Warren did not need the use of his West Point education to realize that the Confederates were about to flank the Union left and that the loss of Little Round Top and its commanding position would result. Startled, he sent messengers in various directions in search of troops who could occupy the hill.[9]

One of these messengers reached Gen. George Sykes, commanding the Fifth Corps, who forwarded the message through a staff officer. Before Colonel Vincent had gotten his brigade into line of battle in the wheat field, Sykes' staff officer came galloping up to him shouting and asked where he could find General Barnes, the division commander. Demanding to know the rider's orders, Vincent quickly understood the crisis that would befall the army's left if Little Round Top were not defended. The young commander took responsibility for his actions, deciding to move his brigade to the hill and defend it. He ordered Col. James Rice of the 44th New York to lead the column to the summit, and he rode ahead to study the ground and decide where to place his regiments.[10]

The brigade followed a farm lane over some rudely placed logs bridging a creek known as Plum Run. As they neared the northern end of Little Round Top they circled behind the hill to climb its eastern slope by way of an old lumbering trail. As they did, shells from enemy artillery sent tree limbs down upon the column

Capt. A.W. "Pap" Clark

as they burst overhead, or sent deadly shell and stone fragments flying as they exploded against the rocks. John Chamberlain had been surveying the area with General Howard's brother Rowland, and he rode up to the brigade to shake hands with his brothers before they went into action. The three were riding together when one of the shells hit nearby. "Boys," said Colonel Chamberlain, "I don't like this. Another such shot might make it hard for Mother." Having explained his reasons, he sent Tom back to be sure that the men in the rear of the column kept up, and he asked John to ride ahead and begin the work of preparing for wounded.[11]

Chaplain Luther French was riding with the regiment when the same shell hit, killing the horse of an officer in the brigade. This greatly unnerved the chaplain, who galloped over to Capt. A.W. Clark, excitedly trying to explain the effect of the shell. The captain cut him off, and in a manner and language that the men had come to expect from "Pap" Clark, he retorted, "For Christ sake Chaplain, if you have any business attend to it!" Shortly afterward, Colonel Chamberlain asked the troubled Chaplain to assist his brother John and Granville Baker, the hospital steward, in setting up an aid station for the men who would shortly be wounded.[12]

The effect of the shells forced the column to move below the crest of the hill, where the bursting missiles brought more tree limbs down on them, wounding some of the men. As if this were not enough as they neared their destination, exhaustion was still taking its toll and men continued to fall out. While some men gave out and scrambled for safer cover, others, who had been following behind as stragglers, finally managed to catch up with their unit.[13]

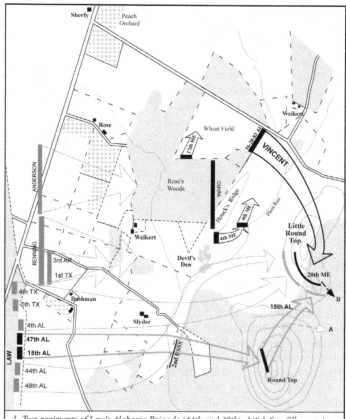

1. Two regiments of Law's Alabama Brigade (44th and 48th) shift left to fill a gap in the division battle line.
2. All four regiments of Vincent's Brigade march to the edge of the Wheat Field, then up Little Round Top.
3. Though ordered to the left, the 15th and 47th Alabama turn right and ascend Round Top.
4. Members of the 2nd Regiment of U.S. Sharpshooters harass the Alabamians as they pass the Slyder farm.
5. Oates detaches Company A of the 15th Alabama.
6. Chamberlain detaches Company B of the 20th Maine.

Left of Hood's assault and arrival of Vincent's Brigade.

By now it was clear to Colonel Chamberlain that a fight was very near at hand. He released the pioneers and provost guard, sending them to their companies and when he confronted the last of the 2nd Maine holdouts, all but three took rifles as well. He also detailed the drummer boys as stretcher bearers and allowed the cooks and servants, at their own request, to take up rifles. "Others whom I knew to be sick and footsore," he noted, "and had [been] given a pass to 'fall out' on the forced marches of the day and night before, came up, now that the battle was on, dragging themselves along on lame and bleeding feet, finding their regiment with the sagacity of the brave."[14]

✠ ✠ ✠

Less than a mile away, on the right of the enemy battle line, the assault that would fall on Little Round Top within a few minutes was struggling from a slow and confused start. Near the left of the brigade of Alabamians that began advancing east toward Big Round Top from the Emmitsburg Road were two regiments, the 15th and the 47th. The 15th was the larger of the two—at 450 men it was twice the size of the 47th—and it was the pride of several counties in southeastern Alabama. Unlike its relatively untested younger brother, the 15th Alabama was one of the most battle-hardened regiments in the Army of Northern Virginia. Organized in July 1861, the men of the 15th fought at Bull Run—both times—and in eighteen other battles and skirmishes. They fought under Stonewall Jackson in the legendary Valley Campaign, were actively engaged on the Peninsula and at Antietam, and had never known defeat. In two years of war, the 15th had developed a reputation as a collection of gamblers, drinkers, jokesters, and fighters and, as it had with most of their comrades in gray, the invasion of the North boosted their morale to its crest. They began the march into Pennsylvania more than 650 strong, but the hard marching, the last twenty hours of it covering more than thirty miles, had deducted a third of the men from the rolls.[15]

The new colonel of this group of veterans had taken command in May. He was a large, rough man whose men counted among his best traits the fact that he slept warm, which was no small compliment in an infantry regiment used to hard campaigning and crowding together under blankets to sleep. At 29, William C. Oates had lived a harsh but full life, though it had settled considerably in the years just prior to the war when he worked as a teacher, published a small newspaper, and passed the bar exam after only four months of study. He opposed secession, but was among many men who rushed to volunteer when the state sided with the

Col. William C. Oates

Confederacy. In an unbridled youth, he had outrun the law in several states, believing he had committed at least one murder, and had a way of trying to gouge his opponent's eyes when caught in a fight. In most things, Oates was ambitious and aggressive, often to a fault, and with the help of both of these traits his life was about to take an unexpected and unwanted turn.[16]

As he straightened his line for an assault, Oates noticed his brother John lying on the ground behind his company. John, first lieutenant in Oates' old Company G, had been sick all day with a high fever and had fallen out on the march. The two men were very close, having grown up together with an alcoholic and abusive father, and it had been John who went to Texas a few years before the war to bring Bill home where he finally settled down. Not long before reaching Gettysburg, the colonel had sent a horse back to bring the younger brother up. Seeing his condition now, Colonel Oates told John to remain behind when the men went forward. "No brother," he snapped back as he raised himself up, "were I to do that it would be said that I avoided the battle and acted the coward. No sir!" That moment, when John rose and the assault march began, remained etched in the mind of Bill Oates forever.[17]

The regiment on the left of the Oates brothers was the 47th Alabama, a small regiment and one of the first of those formed after the Confederacy implemented conscription. It received its baptism of fire at the Battle of Cedar Run and, of the 115 men who went into the fight at Antietam, only seventeen came out, commanded by a sergeant. The march to Gettysburg had reduced its numbers as well, to the point that barely 230 men remained in line to step off with the rest of the brigade now closing on the left of the Union army.[18]

Lt. Col. Michael J. Bulger, the man who had organized the regiment, had only recently taken command. A 57-year-old goateed planter from Dadeville, Alabama, Bulger was from an old Southern military family. His grandfather migrated from Ireland to fight in the Revolutionary War, and his father was a veteran of the War of 1812. He owned nearly two dozen slaves but, when secession rose, he opposed his state's separation

from the Union, served as a national delegate for Stephen A.
Douglas in the election of 1860,
and even led the "cooperationists"
in his county. Once Alabama decided her course, however, Bulger stood with his native state and
sided with the Confederacy.
Knowing of his anti-secession activities, the men of the regiment
did not elect him as their first
commander. Since taking to the
field of war, however, Bulger had
proven his loyalty, in part by
virtue of two wounds at Cedar Run
which nearly cost him an arm and
a leg. His service had helped him

Lt. Col. Michael J. Bulger

politically, as well. While recu-
perating from his wounds in bed at home, Bulger was elected to the
state senate in Alabama, where he served until well enough to
return to his regiment.[19]

General Lee's orders for Longstreet's attack were to move in a
direction in line with the Emmitsburg Road and attack the left flank of
the Union army. Poor reconnaisance and the forward movement of
General Sickles' Union Third Corps forced Confederate commanders to
chose between the two parts of the order. Attacking up the Emmitsburg
Road meant they would not hit the Union flank, and striking the flank
meant moving in a direction more eastward than the angle of the road.
As a result, Gen. Evander Law's five Alabama regiments with two
regiments from the neighboring Texas brigade (the 4th and 5th Texas)
moved straight in the direction of the Round Tops seeking the new
Union left flank, while the rest of the division followed Lee's route up
the road. This maneuver meant that, after only a short distance, a gap
opened between the two parts of the division which widened as they
moved onward at slightly different angles. To offset this effect, Law
moved two regiments from his far right (the 44th and 48th Alabama)
around behind his brigade to the left, and placed them in line filling the
gap. With this corrective measure, Law left Oates and his men on the
extreme right of the Confederate line, with the 47th Alabama on their
left, both facing squarely toward Big Round Top as they marched.
Shortly, however, Law rode up to Oates with an order for the right of
the brigade to wheel a little toward its left. He wanted Oates' men to
pass between Big Round Top and a rise of ground called Houck's Ridge

running north from Devil's Den where the neighboring Texas brigade had just begun to trade volleys with the enemy.

This set of movements proved critical for both Oates and Bulger because three companies of the 47th Alabama had been deployed in front of the brigade as skirmishers, effectively reducing by one-third the men that Bulger had with him. Unfortunately for the rest of the brigade, the skirmish companies were each commanded by captains who had not been informed of the correct line of attack. As a result, when the brigade moved toward the left, the skirmishers continued forward, ended up on the south end of Big Round Top, and never fired a shot during the assault that occurred on the opposite side. While the moving of regiments from one side of the brigade to the other and the loss of a group of skirmishers took its toll on the Alabamians, their northern counterparts from Maine were about to have a similar experience, but with significantly different results.[20]

☩ ☩ ☩

When the head of Vincent's brigade reached its dismounted commander on the southern end of Little Round Top, he had already taken stock of the ground and determined the best positions for his regiments. The 44th New York began to form the line of battle on the open face of the hill while the rest of the brigade uncurled from marching column to fighting order, one regiment after another. Arriving last in line, the 16th Michigan formed in the valley between the Round Tops, poised to thwart any attempt by the Rebels to pass through the vital corridor. The 20th Maine was next to the 16th about twenty feet up a spur of the hill, its left flank resting in an open level space while the the rest of the brigade formed in line to its right, hugging the hill well below the summit. The 83rd Pennsylvania, next to the 20th, filled the space between the spur and the main hill in a bent line so that its center jutted out a few feet, owing to the shape of the ground. The line of the 44th New York then ran up the slope toward a higher part of Little Round Top, resting its right in an open rocky area with a clear view of the valley below.[21]

While his men moved into position, Colonel Chamberlain listened to a somber Vincent explaining the situation. He surmised that a desperate attack would probably try to turn the position and seize the hill that the brigade had just occupied. Vincent's order was clear and in a language that even the newest regimental commander in the brigade could understand. He explained that Chamberlain was to "hold that ground at all hazards." As Vincent walked off toward the right of the brigade, the Maine colonel could only guess at the intentions and location of the

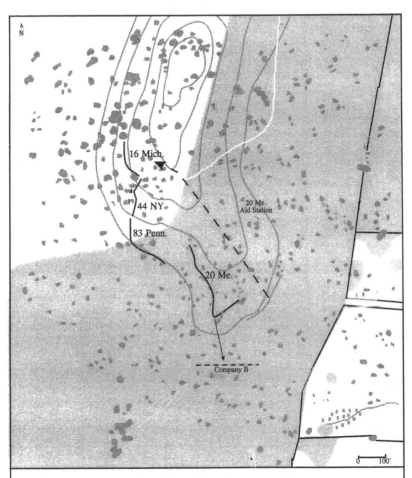

Using an old logging path for access to the hill beyond artillery range, Vincent's brigade took its position on the southern end of Little Round Top, making use of the boulders for protection. Shortly after the brigade went into line, the 16th Michigan moved from the left of the brigade to the right, and Company B (20th Me.) went forward in a skirmish line.

Original placement of Vincent's Brigade

Confederates, but he would soon learn that while the order seemed simple enough, obeying it would become hazardous indeed.[22]

As he watched his men form a roughly straight line of battle he fell back on all of the military books he had read and knew that he must send out a line of skirmishers so that he would have some advance warning if the Rebels came in front of him. Vincent's orders required that each regiment send out a company of men as skirmishers and Chamberlain chose his most reliable captain, Walter Morrill, to carry out the assignment. Morrill was a thorough fighter who made a habit of taking a musket with him into battle so that he could both shoot and command at the same time. He was the most experienced man in the regiment and by most accounts he was, in an emergency, also the coolest. At Chamberlain's request, Morrill's Company B formed a skirmish line in front of the regiment and moved down the slope toward its left, in order to hook up with the skirmishers of the 16th Michigan. When they reached the foliage of the saddle between the Round Tops, they disappeared from view, leaving the regimental line forty rifles thinner.[23]

Between the time that Morrill reported to Chamberlain for orders and disappeared with his company in front of the regiment, Colonel Vincent moved the 16th Michigan behind the brigade from the vale on the 20th's left to the far right of his line. If Chamberlain was aware of this movement, he did not inform Morrill, and Company B wandered off into the woods in search of skirmishers from a regiment that was no longer there. While Company B was smaller in numbers than the three Alabama skirmish companies, and the 16th Michigan similarly smaller than the two Alabama regiments which moved behind its brigade, in percentages, the losses affected the two sides equally.[24]

✠ ✠ ✠

Several hundred yards to the west, Oates' Confederates were struggling to cope with circumstances that seemed to make it impossible to follow a relatively simple order from General Law, and presently, the general rode up again to be certain that Oates understood his mission. He told the colonel that his regiment was now the extreme right of the entire Confederate army and that he was to hug the base of the larger hill in his front, go up the valley between the hills, find the Union line and attack it, doing whatever damage he could. Before leaving, Law told him that Bulger was to keep the 47th close to the 15th and, if the two regiments got separated from the rest of the brigade, Bulger would act under Oates' orders. Within moments after Law rode away from Oates, the Alabama colonel found it impossible, in his view of things, to follow these simple orders.[25]

44

As he crossed Plum Run and approached a stone wall where he was to turn his men to the left and "hug the base" of Round Top, a sharp volley of musketry exploded to his right, doing little harm. Before Oates could react, however, the breech-loading rifles of the 2nd Regiment of U.S. Sharpshooters fired another volley, this time with great effect. The second volley hit Isaac Feagin, the 15th Alabama's lieutenant colonel, in the knee, taking him out of the fight before it started. It also killed two privates and wounded another. The volleys and the uneven ground disrupted the line of march, and Oates' regiment was no longer correctly aligned with Bulger's seven companies, creating confusion and effectively blocking the direction in which Oates was supposed to turn. Realizing this, and feeling that the sharpshooters would threaten his right flank if he turned left as Law desired, he instead ordered his men to "Change direction to the right," swinging toward the enemy who had just fired on him. As soon as Oates' regiment began this move, Bulger tried to respond in kind with the 47th, but his right overlapped the 15th and the two regiments mingled together in the middle. Behind the left company of the 15th, 42-year-old Sgt. William Holley tried, under fire, to keep his line straight. Finally frustrated with the effort, he exclaimed, "Colonel Oates, make Colonel Bulger take his damned concern out of our regiment!"[26]

The sharpshooters fell back firing while the Alabamians returned the fire, all of it with little effect. By now, Oates was in thick woods and ascending a steep hillside with large boulders scattered in his path. This broke up his line of march and gave the sharpshooters good cover. Oates remembered, "In places the men had to climb, catching to the rocks and bushes and crawling over the boulders in the face of the fire of the enemy, who kept retreating, taking shelter and firing down on us from behind the rocks and crags which covered the side of the mountain thicker than grave-stones in a city cemetery." About halfway up the slope, the sharpshooters split into two groups and fled around either side of the hill, some of them firing a few last shots at the Southerners. Oates sent his Company A around the right of the hill to follow one group, while he kept his semi-brigade moving forward toward the summit.[27]

Before the Alabamians had stepped off from the Emmitsburg Road on their assault, Oates had detailed two men from each of his eleven companies to take canteens to a nearby farm and get water from the pump behind it. While these twenty-two canteen-laden privates were gone, however, the order came to move out, and all of the changes that took place on the march caused the canteen bearers to lose track of their regiment. Oates did not yet know it, but these men were at that moment wandering around the south end of Big Round Top directly into Union troops—probably some of the same sharpshooters he was chasing from the hill—and the men and canteens were soon captured.[28]

The loss of twenty-two men was a blow, but the loss of the water they might have carried was, at this critical juncture, an even greater calamity. As the Alabamians reached the summit of Big Round Top some of the men fainted from exhaustion and thirst, and with good reason. Oates later called it, "that awful hill," and argued that "but few men at this day are able to climb without accoutrements, rifles, and knapsacks…" Moreover, the ascent was just the last leg of a march that would have weakened the hardiest of troops. Even their corps commander, General Longstreet, testified to the exertion of the Alabama brigade that day. "Law completed his march of twenty-eight miles in eleven hours," he later wrote, "the best marching in either army, to reach the field of Gettysburg." Including the countermarch, it was actually more than thirty miles, and for Oates' men it ended with this steep hill.[29]

Realizing that he could push his men no farther without at least a short pause, Oates ordered a halt on the summit and they lay down to rest. While recovering from the climb, Oates wandered about, trying to take stock of the ground he had just occupied. When he walked to the eastern portion of the rock formation that crowned the hill, he realized he was in the most unassailable position he had ever seen. Below him, the rock dropped straight down some thirty feet in the direction of the enemy, and beyond the base was another formation which acted as a perfect defense for the first. If the enemy attacked him, they would have to come up the steep slope and then over these two enormous ledges, all the while being fired upon by his men who would have a clear view and solid shelter. Oates later described the position saying, "Within half an hour I could convert it into a Gibraltar that I could hold against ten times the number of men that I had." He was not exaggerating.[30]

Barely five minutes had passed since the halt, when Capt. Leigh Terrell, one of Law's staff officers, somehow rode up to the summit by way of an old logging trail he had found on the south slope and inquired why Oates had halted. The Alabama colonel soon learned that things had gotten worse in the fight raging below. Hood was wounded and borne from the field, and Law had taken command of the division. Apparently Terrell did not inquire how Oates surmised he could "hug the base" of the hill from its summit, but he did remind him that Law's orders were for the Alabamians to attack the left of the Union line on Little Round Top, turn it if possible, and to lose no time. Oates tried to persuade the staff officer that the summit of the bigger hill was too valuable to pass up, and Terrell agreed that this could very well be the case but, neither he nor Oates had the authority to make that decision. What Oates did not realize at that moment was that the Confederate attack had just landed on Vincent's brigade below, and the absent Alabamians were a key element in that attack. Finally, Oates relented, and abandoned his hope of securing the Gibraltar. He turned the regiments to the left to march around the precipice before reforming in line and passing down the northern slope of the hill at a slight angle to the left.[31]

On his way down the mountain, Oates caught a glimpse of wagon covers that he thought revealed Union supply and ordnance wagons. Though he had no orders to capture these or any wagons, and the orders that Law had given him were clear and specific—engage the left of the enemy on Little Round Top as fast as possible—he again detached his Company A, this time with orders to surround and capture the wagons. He did so despite having no knowledge either of the size of the force in front of him, or of how well entrenched it was. The move was a grave error. When the more than three dozen men disappeared down the slope to his right front, he had seen the last of them until the end of the fight. Company A went off into the woods and heard the sound of the battle, but never rejoined the regiment until after the fight was decided. Oates continued on with his men, with no skirmishers out, until he reached the base of the hill.[32]

✠ ✠ ✠

Back among the Maine men, from his place in the second row of the color guard, Pvt. Elisha Coan watched the men of Company B start forward on their skirmish duty. The 18-year-old private could not see much of his surroundings on the hillside except that it was covered mostly with small oak trees. Years later, he described what little he saw. "Our reg[imen]t was formed in an open level space comparatively free from rocks and bushes but in our front was a slight descent fringed by ledges of rock [and] our side of the hill was covered with boulders. Beyond this line of ledge and other rocks at that time the eye could not penetrate on account of the dense foliage of bushes." In front of them, Coan and others were aware that a larger hill loomed above theirs, and between the two peaks was a thinly wooded hollow or vale which stretched far to their right. In that direction they could hear heavy musketry and artillery but it had not yet reached far enough into the vale to affect them.[33]

Pvt. Elisha Coan   *Lt. Henry Sidelinger*

Not far from Coan, Professor Chamberlain glanced at his line and worried. The regiment had never before been in a real stand-up fight. Only six of his ten companies had captains in command, and that only because he had juggled his personnel to make it so. Henry Sidelinger, a 19-year-old, freckle-faced farm boy, commanded Company E, on the right. Lt. Addison Lewis whom Vincent, perceiving the crisis at hand, had just released from arrest, commanded Company A at the center. The regiment had no field officers, so Chamberlain sent Atherton Clark to watch the right wing, and Ellis Spear the left. His brigadier was gone, out of sight, never to return. He could barely see the 83rd Pennsylvania on his right. The rest of the brigade was somewhere farther beyond, around the ledge. His men were tired and largely untested, some still falling out just minutes before. The 16th Michigan was gone from his left, and now only the rocks, trees, and Company B could hold the enemy back if they attacked from that direction. While the haze of his fever still lingered in his head, he worried about two brothers and more than four hundred neighbors who now looked to him for guidance, for survival. He was stuck out on a rocky ledge in the Pennsylvania woods, and for all he knew the entire Rebel army was about to pounce on him.[34]

As he contemplated the foreboding woods in front of him, thinking trance-like the thoughts of a professor working out a difficult problem and wondering if he had done enough to prepare, he was interrupted by a visit from Colonel Rice of the 44th New York. The experienced Rice had wandered over to see if the rookie commander would join him, for a minute, near the open part of the hill. Chamberlain agreed, and they walked behind the brigade to a point from which they could see the approaching battle. The view struck the Maine colonel deeply.[35]

"The enemy had already turned the Third Corps left," Chamberlain remembered, "the Devil's Den was a smoking crater, the Plum Run gorge was a whirling maelstrom; one force was charging our advance batteries near the Wheat-field; the flanking force was pressing past the base of the Round Tops; all rolling toward us in tumultuous waves."[36]

The Plum Run valley was like a coliseum; high ground on either side and a low middle, seething with a fire that had descended on it from literally every direction. Being witness to Fredericksburg had been horrible for Chamberlain, but it had at least been orderly; men marching in military form to their slaughter. The death here was as great, but also chaotic. They watched as if from the balcony seat of a macabre theater. "It was a stirring, not to say, appalling sight: here a whole battery of shot and shell cutting a ragged chasm through a serried mass, flinging men and horses like drift aside; there, a rifle volley at close range, with reeling shock, hands tossed in air, muskets dropped with death's quick relax, or clutched with last, convulsive energy, men falling like grass before the scythe." Down in the Devil's Den the 4th Maine was badly cut up, two of Chamberlain's Bowdoin students among them. Their stand helped slow the advancing Confederates and allowed Vincent's brigade time to organize and prepare.[37]

Near the Den, Chamberlain saw a small group of men kneeling over a slain officer, his saddled but riderless horse continuing to bear down on the enemy. A blue regiment, "broken, slaughtered, captured; or survivors, of both sides crouching among the rocks for shelter from the terrible cross-fire where there is no rear! But all advancing—all the frenzied force, victors and vanquished, each scarcely knowing which—surging and foaming towards us; death around, behind, before, and madness everywhere." Remembering the horror they had somehow survived, soldiers later named the place the Valley of Death and the Slaughter Pen. Chamberlain and Rice looked at one another, unable to find words, and returned to their commands.[38]

Ten minutes had not passed since the 20th had formed its line when the shelling off behind them stopped. The newer recruits, those who had not yet "seen the elephant," may have taken solace in this development, but the veterans knew otherwise. Behind an artillery bombardment there was always infantry. The shells simply cleared the way, softening the enemy before the foot-soldiers took to their work. Shelling usually stopped only when the attackers were too close to their goal for the artillery to safely fire at the enemy without risking the lives of their own. Then the infantry followed, and presently the Southerners did just that.[39]

Capt. Joe Land

The Maine men heard the sound of yelling moving toward them from the right. It was not long before they recognized it as the Rebel yell and they braced for the shock. Early in the war, Union soldiers made fun of the falsetto "ki-yi" yelp, calling it effeminate. Having gotten too many good looks at what Rebel soldiers could do while making the sound, however, they had learned to respect and fear it. They were not completely without lightheartedness, however. Capt. Joe Land, commanding Company H, with a voice that his friend Ellis Spear said was "like the bulls of Bashan," buoyed the sprit of his men by cracking jokes right up until the bullets gave him reason to quit.[40]

When the assault finally reached its goal, it was, thanks to the confusing approach maneuvers, "en echelon," meaning that it struck a point and then rolled toward its right. It was like a wave on the Maine coastline, thundering toward the flank as it broke along the rocks. The enemy struck first in the brigade's center, squarely on the 44th New York. The wave, breaking slowly past the 83rd Pennsylvania, came crashing in on the Maine men and, before long, they were awash in the fight.[41]

"It did not seem to me that it was very severe at first," Chamberlain remembered. "The fire was hot, but we gave them as good as they sent, and the [R]ebels did not so much attempt at that period of the fight to force our line, as to cut us up by their fire." This was the seven companies of the 47th, barely 150 men who hit the brigade in such a way that they faced most of the 20th Maine and the 83rd Pennsylvania. As soon as they hit, the Maine men sought cover, transforming their formal battle line into an uneven collection of men among the rocks.[42]

By this time, John Chamberlain, Chaplain French, and Granville Baker had prepared a makeshift aid station in a "sheltered nook" of the woods on the east side of the hill about one hundred yards behind the regimental line. From there, all that they knew of the fight was what they could hear. John remembered his first and only experience with battle. "[T]he clatter of musketry became distinct for a time but it was soon drowned in the terrific roar of cannon—on every height, on right and left and the front was one continuous roar and mass of smoke." The cannons

50

he heard were from a battery which had literally dragged four guns to the summit a few hundred feet away. The men of the battery, commanded by Lt. Charles Hazlett, had to run the ammunition up the hill since there was no room for horses and caissons on the crest.[43]

On the Spur, Elisha Coan was with the colors in the center of the 20th's line when the 47th arrived, and he described the scene. "Soon scattering musketry was heard in our front. Then the bullets began to clip twigs and cut the branches over our heads and leaves began to fall actively at our feet. Every moment the bullets struck lower and lower until they began to take effect in our ranks. Then our line burst into flames, and the crash of musketry became constant."[44]

A few feet from Coan, on the other side of the colors, Cpl. William Livermore had a similar experience. "By this time," he later wrote, "we heard terrible musketry on our right which rolled along, coming nearer and nearer. We were ordered to come to a ready and take good aim, when the enemy appeared; soon scattering bullets came singing through the trees. Then I saw a rebel and fired at him. The same instant a sheet of fire and smoke belched forth from our line." Down the hill just to his right, Livermore saw that he was closer than he had ever gotten to a Confederate in action. "They came to within four or six rods," he remembered, "covering themselves behind big rocks and trees, and kept up a murderous fire."[45]

From this moment on, Joshua Chamberlain put in practice a lesson that he could not have learned from books, but for which Adelbert Ames had served as a solid example. Ames was always cool under fire, and Chamberlain keenly observed the effect that the West Pointer's confidence had on the men in their one experience in battle at Fredericksburg. They had looked toward Ames for certainty in the past and now they would look to their new colonel. Chamberlain realized that, in spite of his inexperience, fever, and fatigue, he had to maintain his composure and encourage his men, holding back his own fears and uncertainties. "Boys," he said simply but firmly, "hold this hill!"[46]

As soon as the first volleys were exchanged between the depleted 47th Alabama and the two left regiments of Vincent's brigade, Walter Morrill realized he was in trouble. Chamberlain trusted Morrill, and his only orders to him were "to keep within supporting distance of us, and to act as exigencies of the battle should require." Now, just minutes after heading out as skirmishers, Company B found itself cut off and something very much like being lost. "Having advanced across the flat and just commenced to ascend Big Round Top," Morrill wrote, he "was somewhat surprised to hear heavy volleys of musketry in our rear, where we had just left the regiment." It was the sound of the 47th Alabama arriving, and Morrill had to act quickly. He ordered his men to march to their left, taking cover behind a stone wall more than four hundred feet east of the rest of the regiment. It seemed a relatively secure spot given the circumstances as it left a wall to their front and a field at their backs, where they could see the enemy if they were to attack from any other direction.[47]

The spot seemed so secure to wayward troops that it also attracted a squad of sharpshooters who had just been chased from Big Round Top by the men now cutting Morrill off. There were about a dozen of them under the command of a sergeant who asked Morrill if they could remain with his company until the fight subsided. Morrill agreed—who would have refused the aid of a dozen expert shooters with faster firing, breech-loading rifles?—and the group took position behind the stone wall facing the Confederate rear.[48]

Up on the spur, nervous men called Colonel Chamberlain's attention to many directions at once while a commotion seemed to be stirring near his center. Just then, Lt. James Nichols, commander of Company K, ran up to his colonel and told him that something unusual was happening behind the Rebels down in front of his company. Chamberlain followed Nichols back to his men and hopped up on a large boulder in the middle of his company line to get a look. At the same time Ellis Spear came over from the left and suggested that he bend back two companies on his wing to protect the flank. From atop the boulder, Chamberlain could see thick groups of the enemy moving from right to left behind the 47th Alabama. It was Oates, who was finally about to put Law's order into action and turn the Union left. The Maine commander acted coolly and quickly.[49]

Revealing the danger to only a few officers, Chamberlain informed his companies that he wanted the fire kept up on the enemy in front. Whether it had any real effect on them was unimportant, as long as it disguised what he was about to do. With the fire up, he ordered the men to take side steps to the left when they could, so that the regimental line stretched to twice its original front, some of the companies coming into a single rank. While they did this, Chamberlain moved the color guard from the center to the extreme left, where a rotted tree had fallen over three feet up its trunk and a boulder ledge made the position unassailable from the front. Placing the colors about two dozen feet behind the ledge, he "refused" the extending line, bending it back at a right angle so that it formed two fronts; the original one, and another facing the left. As they moved to the new front, the men took advantage of the rocks and trees for protection, disguising their movements from the flanking enemy as the regiment formed a horseshoe around the crest of the spur.[50]

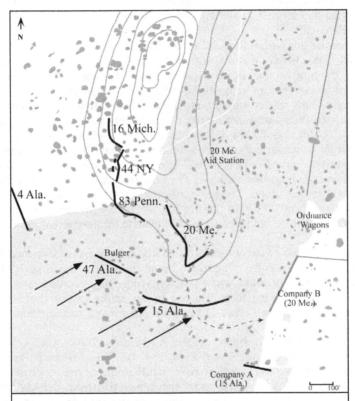

Long minutes after the 4th Alabama engaged the right of the brigade from the base of the hill, the 47th and 15th Alabama finally reached the scene of the fight. Badly cut up in just minutes, the 47th retreated with severe losses, while the 15th moved toward the 20th Maine's "refused" flank. Company B and members of the 2nd U.S. Sharpshooters fled to the wall and wait, while Company A failed to reach the ordnance wagons.

The right of Law's Brigade reaches the spur

Chamberlain later admired how well the men responded to the unusual tactics. "The hazardous maneuvre [sic] was so admirably executed by my men," he remembered, "that our fire was not materially slackened in front, and the enemy gained no advantage there, while the left wing in the mean time had formed a solid and steady line in a direction to meet the expected assault."[51]

When he got within forty paces of the men in blue up on the spur, Colonel Oates began to see a few of them running from rock to rock, and he thought he was in position to attack the rear of the brigade. Where moments before he could have hit the 20th's exposed rear, 250 Alabamians now walked straight into the muzzles of more than a hundred Maine rifles. Years after the battle, Oates remembered that he saw the ledge of boulders and went forward to it. "From behind this ledge," he later wrote, "unexpectedly to us because concealed, they poured into us the most destructive fire I ever saw." The volley from the Maine men on the left tore through the ranks of the horrified Alabamians, and they halted where they stood. The blow inflicted scores of casualties before the Southerners could return the fire but when they did, the Maine men were grateful for the boulders, trees, and the rise of ground that protected them.[52]

A step in front of the color bearer, William Livermore described the effect of the return volley. "Soon we found the enemy flanking us, had got behind a row of rocks under our left wing," he recorded later that day, "and were making fearful havoc in our ranks as every one who dared raise his head was sure of his man, but many lost their brains in the attempt."[53]

On the 20th's right, however, the Alabamians never got as close. On the far left of the oncoming 15th, Pvt. William Jordan pulled up behind a small tree to reload his rifle, while some of the other men in his company rushed forward under the heavy fire from the Mainers. From the tree, Jordan had to bolt across mostly open ground to reach the shelter of a large rock at the foot of the spur. Seeing that he had made it safely, three more men attempted the dangerous run. One made it, but took a ball in the foot in the attempt. The other two fell dead just thirty feet short. Eventually, eight men reached the rock, but getting there hardly meant that they were out of danger. The men in the right companies of the 20th, twenty feet higher and a hundred feet away, had a clear shot and good protection from their own rocks. For the rest of the fight, these eight Alabamians remained huddled behind the boulder gaining sympathy for the plight of fish in a barrel. It was as close to the Mainers as the men on the left of the 15th ever got.[54]

Nearer the center of his regiment, Oates remembered the few moments after smoke from the first volleys cleared. After firing a few rounds he saw the men on the 20th's left scramble back to the shelter of the rocks and he thought they were giving way. He ordered his men forward again but could not dislodge the Mainers, particularly on their right. He later recalled, "that portion of [the enemy] line confronting the two companies on my left held their ground, and continued a most galling fire upon my left." Colonel Chamberlain remembered the first two assaults as well. "We opened a brisk fire at close range," he wrote four days later, "which was so sudden and effective that they soon fell back among the rocks and low trees in the valley, only to burst forth again with a shout, and rapidly advanced, firing as they came. They pushed up to within a dozen yards of us before the terrible effectiveness of our fire compelled them to break and take shelter."[55]

When Oates' men recoiled and recovered, his regimental line extended completely around the base of the spur. Three companies of the 15th engaged the 20th's original front, while the other seven swung around and faced the bent back left wing. This meant that the two opposing regiments covered roughly the same distance, but the 20th Maine, which had bent itself into the shape of a mule shoe, had the advantage of interior lines. A man carrying a message from one flank of the 20th to the other had less than half the distance to travel than his counterpart in the 15th, and the Maine men had rocks, trees, and height in their favor. Moreover, the departure of Oates' canteen bearers and his Company A, along with the casualties inflicted by the deadly surprise volley, evened the numerical odds between the two regiments. If it were not for the men of the 47th, Oates would be nearly outnumbered as well.[56]

✠ ✠ ✠

In command of the left half of his regiment, Ellis Spear steadied his men who had taken cover in an uneven single line along the ridge. Unlike the men on the regiment's original front, their leftward shift and "refusing" occurred too late for them to throw up rocks or breastworks, so the first fire from the Alabamians threw them back among the larger rocks and trees from which they could safely fire back. With the two lines settling in for a prolonged fight, in places less than seventy feet apart, Spear noticed that the roar of musketry drowned out the officers' commands, and the Maine men began to dump their cartridges out and stick their ramrods into the ground, a sign that they did not intend to be driven back.[57]

As he looked down the line from the colors, Elisha Coan could see the effect of the early conflict. "The backward movement of the left wing," he observed, "uncovered many of our men that had fallen killed or wounded. The latter of which were before our eyes writhing in the agonies of their terrible wounds. Over them flew the leaden spray from the two lines, for the storm was raging furiously. The calm of the early afternoon had been succeeded by a cyclone."[58]

Pvt. John O'Connell, one of the 2nd Maine transfers in Company C, looked back behind the line and thought he could see men from the other regiments of the brigade falling. Soon after the line settled in among the rocks, his captain, Charles Billings, took a bullet in his thigh just above the knee and had to be carried to the rear. Lt. James Stanwood had barely taken his place when he, too, was hit in the leg but, despite the wound was able to remain in command.[59]

Around the spur a few hundred feet from the right wing of the 20th, the men of the seven companies of the 47th Alabama were finding it hard to fit in among the other units of their brigade. Half of the 83rd Pennsylvania, in front of their left, and the right end of the 20th Maine, off about a hundred feet beyond, fired at them from two angles. Moreover, the side trip up the bigger hill pushed the 47th beyond the support of the regiment on their left—the 4th Alabama was next in line. Stuck in front of four hundred Union rifles they had nowhere to hide and in moments more than fifty of them were killed or wounded.[60]

When the 47th first began to assault the enemy, before Oates got the 15th engaged, a colonel from Law's staff rode up to Bulger shouting, "Colonel Bulger, charge that line." The old Alabamian found that trying to follow Oates' orders and Laws at the same time had gotten him into a mess and, frustrated, he decided that someone else ought to bear part of his burden. "Tell General Law," he replied, "that I am charging to the best of my ability. For God's sake put in the Fifteenth upon my right and my life for it, we'll drive them when we come to them."[61]

Presently, Bulger was caught in a horrible situation with a small unit and no support. So he tried to lead his men forward in one desperate, if not foolish, assault. Part way to the enemy Bulger mounted a rock and a Federal ball passed through his chest, piercing his left lung before lodging in the shoulder muscle. He staggered back and lowered himself down against a tree, blood running from his mouth and nose. Caught between the hostile lines but sheltered from the fire of both sides, he could only sit with his sword and pistol in his lap and wait for death or deliverance. Oates moved over toward the troubled smaller unit to see what he could do to help Maj. James Campbell, who was now in command. The two officers tried to rally the confused and crumbling line, but it was no use. Enemy fire had taken a devastating toll and the angle of fire made it almost impossible to find safe cover behind the rocks. In a matter of moments the demoralized men were haphazardly falling back in the direction from which they had come, back toward Big Round Top and safety.[62]

Having lost the seven companies that made up his entire left flank— one quarter of his force—Oates made the equivalent of an all-out dash for victory. With every minute that passed his men grew more exhausted and the lack of water compounded their fatigue, so he shifted his regiment to the right, making a move for the 20th's exposed flank. Though it further separated his men from the rest of their brigade, he felt that if he could turn the enemy's left and gain the rear, he could dislodge the entire Federal brigade and, perhaps, win the battle. Working his men toward this goal, he took advantage of the boulder ledge and the steep decline in front of the colors of the 20th to shield his movements.[63]

As the enemy moved around below him, Ellis Spear realized that his scattered line might be in jeopardy. He felt the pressure growing in his front and anticipated Oates' move. The Alabamians had crept forward and were firing from behind boulders and, though many of them overshot their targets, Spear worried that they would overlap his left and do just what Oates was now planning. Understanding the importance of the ground his men held, Spear knew something must be done, so he reported the danger to his colonel, suggesting he send two more companies to the left.[64]

Owing to the departure of the 47th Alabama, Chamberlain's two right companies (E and I), did not seem to him to be heavily engaged, so he ordered them to shift over to the far left wing. The subsequent order caused the two companies to fall back and, in the confusion, they nearly created a stampede for the rear. Fortunately the men of Company K, the third company in line, held their place and, reacting quickly, Chamberlain halted the men, countermanded the order, and decided he had best leave the left to its own devices.[65]

At about that same time Capt. Orpheus Woodward, commanding the 83rd Pennsylvania, noticed that bullets were coming over his head from his rear, so he sent his adjutant to see if the 20th had broken. Chamberlain assured him that they had not, but that he could use the aid of a company if the Pennsylvanians could spare it. Woodward sent word back that he could not spare any men, but he would try to extend his line in the direction of the Mainers and thus provide some relief. In order to accomplish this, he pulled the center of the 83rd back so that the regiment formed a straight, rather than bent, line causing his flank to move leftward a few dozen feet.[66]

From that point, the fight for the spur settled into an extended contest of attacks, withdrawals, and lulls between the 20th Maine and the 15th Alabama. Each time groups of Alabamians surged forward in an effort to seize the spur, the men of the 20th rallied and drove them back down, leaving more dead and wounded in the hostile space between them. These attacks, mostly on the center and left of the 20th's line, often took the form of chaotic brawls, with the two sides coming close enough that the battle became a personal struggle between two individual contestants swinging rifles, bayonets, or even fists. "At times I saw around me more of the enemy than of my own men," Chamberlain remembered, "gaps opening, swallowing, closing again with sharp convulsive energy; squads of stalwart men who had cut their way through us, disappearing as if translated." At one point, he noted that they were forced entirely from their original position, and had nearly gotten out of reach of the rest of the brigade.[67]

As the fight wore on, men of both sides struggled to find the safest place from which to fire without exposing any more of their bodies than necessary. In this environment, a tree, a stump, a boulder, even a slight rise of ground made a useful position. When this happened, calling the two regimental formations "lines" was an exaggeration. Above and below the spur, both regiments lay in scattered groups so that officers could scarcely hear one another or recognize where their company line began and ended. The fight for the spur descended into scattered groups of men doing whatever they could to accomplish a general goal; to seize or defend the spur. In this confusion, and the resultant noise, commands were almost useless and tactics virtually impossible.

During the lulls, Chamberlain sent messengers to the rear and right for ammunition, reinforcements, or both. When none came, the men gathered cartridges from the boxes of the dead and wounded, and dropped their Enfield rifles in favor of the more reliable Springfields among the fallen Alabamians, now lying both in front and rear. They also took the timeto throw up more logs and rocks to provide better shelter. At the same time, the intervals allowed drummer boys and other stretcher bearers to remove the fallen of both sides, carrying them to the aid station in the rear.[68]

In the midst of one particular lull in the fight, Chamberlain walked among the men to gauge their spirits and do what he could for the wounded. He remembered one soldier who had received what looked to

Officers of the 20th Maine. This tintype was made near Rappahannock Station a month after Gettysburg. Left to right, Ellis Spear, William Bickford, James Stanwood, Walter Morrill, William Morrill, Henry Sidelinger, and Atherton Clark.

be a severe wound across his forehead. The colonel had him sent to the rear hoping that, with prompt medical attention, he might be saved or at least die in peace. When the fight resumed minutes later, Chamberlain saw him back among his comrades, firing his rifle with a bloody bandage around his head. It struck the colonel soberly. "I shall know him when I see him again," he later wrote, "on whatever shore!"[69]

In another lull, Chamberlain came upon Pvt. George Washington Buck, a young farmer from Linneus. Buck had been a sergeant through the fall campaign but had been demoted by Alden Litchfield, a cruel bully of a quartermaster, when Buck was too sick to perform a personal service for him. Now, Buck was bleeding badly from a hole in his right shoulder and the amount of blood left little doubt of his fate. Chamberlain reassured the soldier as he kneeled over him. "My dear boy," he remembered saying. "It has gone hard with you. You shall be cared for." The young soldier apparently managed to whisper a reply to his colonel, "Tell my mother I did not die a coward." Moved by his concern, Chamberlian replied. "You die a sergeant, I promote you for faithful service and noble courage on the field of Gettysburg!" With that, Buck was carried to the rear.[70]

Below the spur, there were poignant moments among the Southerners as well. John Nelson, a 24-year-old Irishman in Company K of the 15th, had an intense desire to fight but not for any length of time. As Oates described it, "He would fight any of the men personally, and would go into every battle, then at the first opportunity would run out of it." At Gettysburg, Nelson's company captain ordered Sgt. Pat O'Conner, another Irishman, to watch him and keep him in the fight. The first time Nelson headed for the rear O'Conner grabbed him and held him in his place but the second time he ran a bullet caught him from behind. As the sergeant laid him down dead, he concluded aloud, "Now I guess you won't try to run away."[71]

Throughout the battle, Oates remained near his old Company G where friends from home, including his brother, were in the thick of the fight. In two years of hard campaigning, however, Oates had developed a bond with many of the men in other companies as well. One of the officers he was particularly fond of was James Ellison, who commanded Company C at Gettysburg. Before the campaign began, Oates had given the young man a new captain's jacket trimmed with gold lace. When Oates rallied his men and ordered them forward again, he noticed the jacket and its new owner out in front of his company. Ellison was holding his hand to his ear signaling to Oates that he could not hear the command. The colonel repeated the order and Ellison acted, shouting

"Forward, my men, forward!" As Oates looked on, a ball passed through the captain's head, killing him instantly.

"He fell on his back," Oates remembered, "threw up his arms, clenched his hands, gave one quiver and was dead. I thought him one of the finest specimens of manhood I ever beheld." Ellison's men halted and gathered around him despite being under fire, so Lt. LeGrand Guerry rallied them forward to fulfill Oates' order.[72]

As the Alabamians came on again, the slaughter resumed on the left of the 20th Maine. In front of Captain Land, who was now aiding Ellis Spear on the left wing, Sgt. Isaac Lathrop, the six-foot giant of company H, was hit in the stomach, the kind of wound few soldiers ever survived. Near him, the first sergeant of the company, Charles Steele, staggered up to Land with a severe wound in his chest. "My God, Sergeant Steele!" he exclaimed as he saw the sergeant's grimaced face. "I am going, Captain," replied Steele, and he shortly fulfilled his prophesy.[73]

At the center of the Maine regiment, the scene was growing more desperate. The Confederates at the foot of the spur to their right cut up the two companies on either side of the colors, while their onrushing comrades from the left made repeated assaults. Company A, to the left of the Maine unit's colors, was coming apart. Bullets tore through its ranks from three directions, leaving scarcely a platoon of men on duty. Six of the company's seven corporals were dead or wounded, and half the sergeants. In all, less than a dozen men now made up the company battle line.[74]

Being a non-commissioned officer in Sam Keene's Company F, on the right of the color guard, was just as great a risk that day. Half of the six corporals were dead, the other half wounded. Seven of Keene's men lay dead on the spot, and holes began to open up in what was left of his line. Cpl. John Morin of that company, the man who had made it to Gettysburg on a supply wagon rather than join the Invalid Corps, paid for his eagerness to do duty. A Rebel ball hit him in the left hip, sending him back into the army hospital system that he had deserted a month earlier. Even the trees near the salient suffered greatly, and virtually every trunk was peppered with bullets up to five or six feet high. One tree, about three or four inches in diameter and just to the right front of the color guard, was severed about two feet off the ground.[75]

As the Alabamians struggled up the hill again, Chamberlain noticed the crisis at his center. "In the third fierce onset of the enemy," he later wrote, "through a rift in the rolling smoke, I saw with consternation that our center was nearly shot away, and the color guarded only by a little group, who seemed to be checking the enemy by their heroic bearing and

Alfred Waud, an artist for Harper's Weekly, sketched this first visual image of the battle on Little Round Top a few days after the fight. Chamberlain is shown leading his men in the charge (center) while Oates calls for reinforcements from behind his line (lower right). Considerably more orderly than the actual fight, Waud's sketch depicts the typical Civil War battle; two neatly dressed lines firing at each other from a distance.

not by numbers." The little group he saw had begun the fight with one sergeant, three corporals, and a private and amazingly, three of the five were still on duty, untouched by enemy fire.[76]

The color guard had not weathered the fight without great difficulty, however. Elisha Coan and William Livermore had to step to the front rank when Cpl. Melville Day, standing just inches in front of them, fell dead with five bullet wounds. Cpl. Charlie Reed, the other man in front, took a ball in the wrist. But Reed was not quick to fall to the rear. A place in the color guard was a great honor for Civil War soldiers and one which they did not easily surrender, even to wounds. While the wounded wrist rendered him unable to fire his rifle, Reed did not consider himself totally disabled. Instead, he turned to Andrew Tozier, the color sergeant, telling him that he could at least still hold the flag. Tozier agreed and the two swapped roles, Reed holding the regiment's colors while Tozier used Reed's rifle to fire back at the Rebels. The solution was only temporary, however, as the wound eventually got the better of Reed, and he retired to the rear.[77]

When Colonel Chamberlain looked back toward the center in the midst of the third assault, he saw Tozier, who by now had taken back the flag but was still firing Reed's rifle. Through the smoke of battle, the brief glimpse of the color sergeant struck a sense of awe in the colonel that he never forgot.[78]

"I first thought some optical illusion imposed upon me," he recalled. "But as forms emerged through the drifting smoke, the truth came into view...in the center, wreathed in battle smoke, stood the Color-Sergeant, Andrew Tozier. His color-staff planted in the ground at his side, the upper part clasped in his elbow, so holding the flag upright, with musket and cartridges seized from the fallen comrade at his side he was defending his sacred trust in the manner of the songs of chivalry." From the left, Ellis Spear saw Tozier as well and remembered that he cooly chewed a piece of cartridge paper as he fired.[79]

Initially, there was a roar on the right, but the 15th came again from the left. No Rebel yell this time, just a slow, steady assault. They came on in a solid line and halted, preferring to simply plug away at the Maine line. By a conservative estimate, forty thousand bullets had passed through the deadly space between the regiments, and Chamberlain reckoned that every one of his men had been hit, if not in their flesh, then in their clothing or blanket roll.[80]

With all of this lead flying, it seemed that some supernatural aura kept the Maine commander from harm. Behind a rock below, an Alabama soldier took aim at Chamberlain and fired, but a Maine private passed between his rifle and its target, unwittingly saving the colonel. Not far off, another Southerner who had wedged himself between the rocks leveled his rifle and took careful aim at him. Before he could pull the trigger, however, a "queer notion" came over him. Ashamed of his weakness he aimed again, placing Chamberlain clearly in his sights, but again he could not fire and he finally gave it up.[81]

Time and again fate toyed with Chamberlain's life, and each time it failed. One Rebel ball found its mark on a rock just below the arch of his right foot, a splinter of rock leaving a gash in his boot and a cut in his instep. This hobbled him but did no serious harm. Then another ball caught him squarely in the left thigh, but the bullet hit the steel scabbard of the sword hanging from his belt. The scabbard was badly bent and his thigh bruised but the leg, and perhaps his life, were again spared. Through all of this Chamberlain, on the outside at least, remained stoically calm, walking behind the men on the right wing, providing the confidence and leadership that he had seen in Colonel Ames. If his inexperience and fatigue affected him, his men never knew it.[82]

They kept firing at the stalled Confederates and Oates remembered that it was "so destructive that my line wavered like a man trying to walk against a strong wind, and then slowly, doggedly gave back a little...to stand there and die was sheer folly." After firing into the boulders at the Maine men as long as they could stand it, the Alabamians fell back into the brush to reorganize. This last assault had fallen shorter than the others, and Oates could see that his men did not have much left. There was still no sign of the canteen detail and half of the men remaining on duty had used all of their ammunition, some of them firing until their rifle barrels were too hot to touch. He knew the advantage, if he ever had one, was now lost and he had to make one last desperate attempt to take the hill before his men collapsed from the effort.[83]

Just then, Capt. DeBernier Waddell, his adjutant, came to Oates and asked to take forty or fifty men with him to try to get around the left end of the enemy. By this time, Oates would probably have tried anything, and he allowed Waddell to carry out the plan. The adjutant took his detail around through the woods twenty or thirty steps beyond the rest of the 15th until they got behind a rise of ground. From there, they weakened the 20th's left wing further by peppering it with musket fire.[84]

With Waddell off on his mission, Oates took stock of his situation. His lieutenant colonel was out of the fight before they had reached Plum Run and the major was back with the wagon trains. Now Company A was gone and three captains were down. As he remembered the scene he recalled simply, "The carnage in the ranks was appalling." When his men had gotten a short rest he decided to make another attempt. As he passed through the line shouting, "Forward, men, to the ledge!" few, if any, could hear him with ears ringing from the battle, so he mounted a rock and gestured to them.[85]

Capt. William Edwards of Company E had been lying behind the same four-foot-high rock near the middle of the regiment when he saw Colonel Oates jump up on it, trying to ignite the charge while emptying his pistol toward the enemy not more than fifty yards away. In the noise and smoke, Oates' order went unheeded except by Pvt. William R. Holloway who had been lying with Edwards. Responding to his colonel's bravery, Holloway sprang up onto the boulder, shouting, "Colonel, I can't see them." He dropped to one knee, fired, and had barely lowered his rifle when a bullet struck his left temple and he fell dead. Oates caught him as he went down, took the private's rifle, and fired a few rounds himself. Whether Holloway's act was one of bravery, foolishness, or a combination of the two, it left a widow and ten fatherless children back in Dale County, Alabama.[86]

After watching his seven right companies make charge after charge on the 20th Maine's left, he realized that no one charge managed to throw the full weight of the group forward. The noise and confusion interfered with whatever coordination he had attempted. To remedy this for one last great effort, Oates took more time to try to organize his men and this time it worked. Most of the men in the seven companies followed as Oates' moved up the hill with his brother John at his side. When they neared the crest the Maine men reeled back and holes grew in their line under the pressure. One of these opened at the colors where moments before Chamberlain had admired his stalwart color bearer, and in the urgent moment the colonel sent his brother Tom into the gap. As Tom responded, Joshua realized he would probably not make it to the spot alive, so he sent his orderly, Ruel Thomas, to follow him. The orderly took a bullet in the shoulder, but Tom made it with just a few scratches and managed to pull the center back a bit, closing the gaps. His arrival was timely, for another bullet had just taken down Sam Keene, the captain of the color company. The wound was not mortal, however, since the ball passed through Keene's vest but not his sword belt, and left him with only a severe bruise.[87]

A few dozen feet to the left, the Oates brothers and their men were pushing the Mainers back over the crest to a boulder on the flat summit. Opposing them, Ellis Spear and Joe Land were using both hands against the flat of their swords, literally shoving the backs of their men to hold the line in place. For a brief moment, the charge succeeded and the

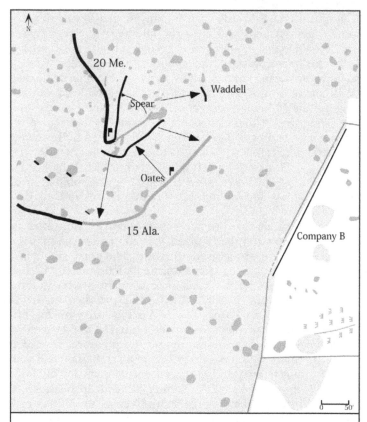

After coordinating one last effort to take the spur, the Oates brothers lead the right wing of the 15th Alabama against the left of the 20th Maine, momentarily seizing the top of the spur John Oates and Bud Cody are mortally wounded at the top before the left of the 20th rallies enough to retake the crest of the spur.

The 15th's final assault

Alabamians broke the line of Mainers and seized the spur. Taking a position such as this is one thing, but holding it in the ensuing confusion is quite another, as Oates soon discovered.[88]

When the assault stalled at the boulder the fight descended into a vicious brawl. Oates looked to his right in time to see a Maine man reach for the staff of the 15th's battle flag. The color bearer, Sgt. John G. Archibald, stepped back to save the flag, and Sgt. Pat O'Conner, whom a Yankee bullet had only recently relieved of his duty watching the runaway Private Nelson, drove his bayonet through the head of the ambitious Mainer. Further over, but still no more than a dozen feet to his right, Oates watched in horror as his brother fell backward with no less than five Yankee bullets in him. Lt. Isaac Parks, who had been his schoolmate as a child, ran to the fallen Oates, dragging him behind a boulder where another bullet removed his little finger. Nearby, 18-year-old Barnett "Bud" Cody, the second lieutenant of Oates' company, fell as well, leaving only one officer in Company G where four had entered the fight.[89]

At that moment, the tide of Alabamian hopes crested and began to ebb. They had fought bravely and under impossible conditions, but they were fighting a regiment that had only marched one-tenth the distance that day, with full canteens. The height of the hill, the boulders near the crest, the delay in getting into place, the loss of Company A, and the flight of the 47th had all conspired to make the task of holding the spur beyond the abilities of even this overachieving regiment. As they slipped back down into the valley below, the fight for Vincent's spur had been decided, but the story was not yet completely written.

When his men rallied again at the base of the spur, Oates realized that this assault was all that his men had left in them. If he had not completely given up hope of some kind of victory before now, he presently did just that. As he looked around at what was left of his exhausted regiment, shocked with grief over the loss of his brother and their friend, he saw a soldier fall when dust flew up from his back. The enemy was in his rear.[90]

It was Morrill. All through the fight, the forty-odd men of Company B and the dozen or so sharpshooters with them had been firing into the Alabamians sporadically from in back of the stone wall in their rear, but Oates had not been aware of them until now. Captains Blant Hill and Frank Park from the right came to Oates with news that the enemy was closing in from behind. He sent Park to see how many and, through some confusion, he returned with news that at least two regiments of Union infantry were approaching from an open field behind them. It was a mistake. The only troops in striking distance out that way were Morrill and his men, but Oates thought he had been nearly surrounded.[91]

In reaction to the startling turn of events, he sent Sgt. Maj. Robert Norris the other way to ask the colonel of the 4th Alabama if he could send relief. Norris was gone but a minute before he returned to inform Oates that there were no Confederates to their left as far as he could see, and that the Yankees seemed to be moving into the gap on that flank. With the enemy closing off all directions except the huge hill behind his left, Oates had no avenue of retreat, and he ordered the two captains to return to their companies, telling them he had decided that the regiment would go down fighting. Hill gave no reply, but Park managed a slight smile, saluted, and said, "All right, sir."[92]

☦ ☦ ☦

As the smoke again cleared from the crest of the hill, Colonel Chamberlain got a look at what was left of his command. From his place behind the right wing he could see that the last enemy attack had been the fiercest and he knew that his line would not hold against another one like it. The enemy seemed to be getting stronger, while half of his own left wing was down and nearly half of the men he had brought onto the spur were no longer in their places. In the same way that Oates' circumstances were going from bad to worse below him, Chamberlain saw his own cause slipping into disaster.[93]

"At this moment my anxiety was increased by a great roar of musketry in my rear, on the farther or northerly slope of Little Round Top," Chamberlain remembered. Bullets from the fight on the other end of the brigade were falling among the already beleaguered men on his left wing, and the Maine colonel surmised that the larger hill behind him was lost and the Union battery there would soon be turned against him from the rear. The men near him on the right were out of ammunition, or firing one last shot before grabbing their muskets as clubs, and he could see the dead and wounded of both sides mingling on the ground in front of him.[94]

In a moment of ultimate irony, both colonels found themselves in much the same position. They had maneuvered their troops to react to each crisis and make the most of whatever advantage they could take. They had both served as solid leaders for their men, risking personal harm in the hottest parts of the fight. They had both ordered a brother into danger and seen a large portion of their commands fall in grotesque ways. Now, they both sensed that they were surrounded, out of ammunition, and that the key to the battlefield was slipping from their grasp. At that crucial moment, they made opposing choices. For each of them, there really was no choice, and for both, their decisions were in keeping with their orders.

Colonel Vincent had ordered Chamberlain to hold his position "at all hazards," and Law had required of Oates that he find the Yankee left and "do whatever damage he could." Both of them had accomplished what their commanders had asked; the Mainers still held the hill, and the parched Alabamians had done all they could. The only difference was that Chamberlain did not realize that he had safely completed his task. He was still holding his ground, but if the enemy attacked again—as he was certain they were about to—his regiment could not hold on, and he would fail to carry out Vincent's order. As Oates had done moments before, Chamberlain also decided to sell out as dearly as possible and save the hill, or lose it, on the offensive. As he watched the Rebels at the bottom of the spur he could see them "rallying in the low shrubbery for a new onset." The Alabamians were rallying, but a new onset was not in their plans.[95]

Having pondered, for a minute, the thought of being overrun by reinforced Yankees, Oates' Southern pride succumbed to the hostile reality around him. He sent Norris with another message. This one said that, when he gave the signal, his men should find any route available back to the summit of Big Round Top, and they would reform the regiment there. Oates never really had time to organize the retreat before the men on the spur above him forced his hand.[96]

Chamberlain had also examined his few options and decided that only one was practicable. He must order his men to charge down into the enemy and hope that they can scatter the Rebels before they charge again. To organize the effort he had to notify the left wing, but before he could, Lt. Holman Melcher stopped him. Melcher had taken over for the wounded Sam Keene in command of Company F, and he came to ask that the colonel grant him permission to advance the center—what was left of it at least—toward the boulder ledge where some of the wounded, unable to move, were calling for help. These men had been cut off in front during one of the Alabamian assaults. Some were virtually helpless and enemy bullets continued to find them while they begged their comrades for aid. Chamberlain admired the lieutenant's bravery and compassion and sent him back to his company, telling him that he was about to order the entire regiment forward.[97]

As Melcher returned to his men, the shout of "Bayonet!" was already working its way down the right of their line, the colonel's order faintly heard above the still roaring battle. Knowing Chamberlain's intentions,

Melcher ordered his men up and organized them. The center had come into the fight eighty rifles strong, but the two color companies (A and F) and the color guard now held their crossfired position with only two dozen. In addition to retrieving the wounded, it was necessary to move forward to the boulder ledge to see what was below and beyond it. Charging over a ledge was dangerous enough but starting a dozen yards behind it was inviting disaster. Before the inevitable order to advance reached them, Melcher started his men toward the boulder ledge with its better view and the suffering wounded.[98]

Out on the far left flank, Ellis Spear and Joe Land were expecting the enemy to resume the work that they had nearly finished on their last rush up the hill. Neither their colonel, nor the order to fix bayonets had reached them, nor had any other word from the right in some time. Pondering their imminent demise, the activity toward the center caught their attention. While the men on the right were aware of an impending movement and had fixed bayonets in anticipation, those on the left could only guess at what was happening. All Spear knew was that the colors were advancing and that, if he did not act, a huge gap would open at the most important and vulnerable portion of the regiment. Any infantry commander with an hour of experience knew that the first rule of combat was to never allow the line of battle to break, so Spear ordered his men to move forward, keeping the line even with the flag. "The left took up the shout and moved forward," he recalled. Starting a forward movement was not difficult for Spear, but, as he remembered, "Stopping such men under the circumstances was quite another affair."[99]

The men on the far left reached the crest of the hill before the flag reached the boulders, and in slippery army shoes they started down. About forty men on the far left of the 20th passed over the hill's crest and half way down the slope. There, they saw Waddell and his detached squad and this pocket of Alabamians fell back in surprise, darting in many directions at once while the Mainers gave chase. Before long these few dozen men on the far left wing were in full pursuit. Spear described the accelleration, saying, "every man eager not to be behind, the whole line flung itself down the slope through the fire and smoke upon the enemy." As they reached the bottom of the steep slope on the left, Spear, Land, and what was left of their companies began to encounter Confederates. Close in front of their line, the two officers lept down over a wide rock and found themselves among a group of Rebels. Fortunately for the Mainers, the enemy rifles were empty and the exhausted Confederates surrendered without further fight. Leaving them to subordinates, Spear and Land led more of their men further forward, chasing the Rebels all the way to the wall that Company B had just abandoned.[100]

Some of the Alabamians ran back along their line in the direction they had come; the rest of the men on the Maine left, still up on the crest of the hill, saw Rebel uniforms in flight, acted on their instincts, and joined the pursuit. Thus, sixty-odd men nearer the center came careening down the slope performing what amounted to a wheeling maneuver as they chased the enemy back toward the direction they had come. Seeing this, Oates knew it was over and he gave the retreat signal he had promised. Probably before, but definitely after he did, his whole line was off in headlong retreat. "When the signal was given," he later lamented, "we ran like a herd of wild cattle." It all happened so fast, and in such chaos, that Oates was astonished to find blue soldiers immediately behind him as his men started to run. He surmised that they were dismounted cavalry who had discretely gained his rear, and some of his men ran right through them. Oates later learned, but never accepted, that it was not cavalry at all.[101]

When the far left of the 20th chased Waddell and his group into the woods, the fleeing Confederates ran directly toward the end of Company B's skirmish line. As the Southerners were scattering in every conceivable direction, Captain Morrill saw them approaching his position, in flight, and he realized what was happening. His men opened fire, shouting "Charge!" in order to fool the Rebels into thinking they were a larger force. Some of the Confederates stopped and surrendered. Others came on, ran right through their line into the field beyond, and kept going. The largest group of them turned and fled toward Big Round Top and Morrill ordered his men over the wall to follow them. While Morrill's men were heading toward the scene of the larger fight, Spear, Land, and the men from the far left were heading in the opposite direction, right past them.[102]

When Oates had given his signal to retreat, Adjutant Waddell and his men were still plugging away at the left of the 20th, and in the roar of the battle, disconnected as they were from the regiment, they did not hear the order. When Spear and his men came down on them, Waddell knew he had to get his men out and he yelled for them to follow him. As he bolted to his left and rear, he noticed that only two of the fifty men had followed, but it was too late for him to stop. With the help of the smoke and confusion, the three men got all the way to Company B's charging line. Waddell and another man made it safely through but their comrade was shot down just as they did.[103]

The other four dozen men either surrendered to the charging left wing of Mainers, or ran straight back into the woods. A few hundred feet in that direction, near the end of Company B's stone wall and the fencing

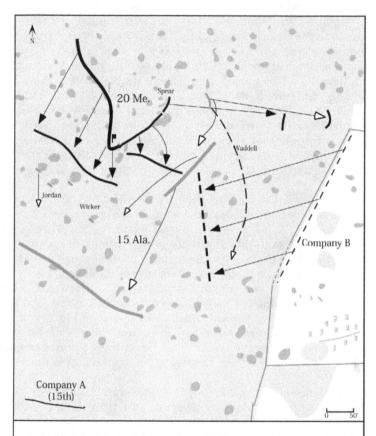

As the far left of the 20th Maine chases Waddell's men through the woods, Company B leaps over the wall and charges toward the retreating Alabamians. The left wing descends upon Oates and his men as they begin to fall back. As the right wing of the 20th joins the charge, the 15th flees in confusion.

Charge of the 20th Maine and retreat of the 15th Alabama

beyond it, there was a farm lane which led directly away from the spur. The lane presented Waddell's men with their only means of escape without having to leap a wall or fence. So a few dozen of them ended up among its muddy wagon ruts nearly surrounded by worm fence. Spear and Land followed, and when the Yankees reached the lane a few of the bottled up Rebels were still not ready to give up. As they climbed the fence to make their escape, Spear's men shot them down and the rest of them, seeing their choices clearly, quickly surrendered.[104]

One of the charging Yankees, Pvt. John O'Connell in Company C, later found it strange that they had literally charged to the rear of the brigade. "The final formation of the reg[iment] was such," he remembered years later, "that where the charge was made it was in a direction directly to the rear from the way the rest of the Brigade were facing and fighting. And the enemy or most of them were driven in their flight at first directly to the rear of the line of Battle of our army and accounts in part for so few of them escaping."[105]

As the men from the 20th's left drove the Alabamians out of the pocket behind the spur, some of the fleeing soldiers ran back toward Big Round Top, the direction from which they had come. When they had gone a few dozen yards, they ran into Company B charging across their path and some of them turned again toward the Devil's Den. This put them out in front of the right wing of the 20th which, by now, was coming down the other half of the spur. Nearer the center, a few feet from Chamberlain, Elisha Coan of the color guard was among the first to reach the Alabamians and take them prisoner. In no time, he was taking five of them to the rear. Decades later, Coan recalled the wild rush down the hill. "The rebel front line, amazed at the sudden movement, thinking we had been reinforced...throw down their arms and cry out 'don't fire! we surrender,' the rest fled in wild confusion."[106]

When the colors reached the boulder ledge the line divided on account of the steep drop, and the color guard went to the right of it, some men stopping to help the wounded that Melcher had worried over. Chamberlain descended the hill beside the flag and, as he looked ahead, he saw a young Alabama officer standing his ground as the Federals came on. His name was Lt. Robert Wicker, and he waited until Chamberlain was within six feet before he raised his pistol, aiming it squarely at his face. Having no pistol of his own, Chamberlain could do little more than brace himself in the split second he had to comprehend the situation. Like those of his comrades before him, however, Wicker's shot was unable to stop the Maine colonel. Despite the close range, it missed him entirely and Chamberlain knocked the pistol away with his sword, drawing the

73

point of it to Wicker's neck. Wicker immediately surrendered the pistol and his sword but Chamberlain, impressed by his bravery, turned him over to a sergeant to protect him from further harm.[107]

Further beyond the courageous Lieutenant Wicker, Colonel Oates was doing all he could to carry his large frame back up the steep hill to his rear. As he ran, John Keels, who had lived not far from Oates back in Alabama, ran past him breathing through a hole in his throat while blood gushed from his windpipe. Through some miracle, Keels made it back up the hill.[108]

As the charge swept toward the 20th's right, the eight Alabamians still huddled behind the large rock had a quick and difficult decision to make. William Jordan, who had bolted from a tree to reach the boulder as the fight began, was still there among them. As the charging blue line came on, he remembered that "some of the men said they would not attempt to escape as it would be death to undertake [it]. The enemy had the drop on us and it seemed impossible to avoid capture." Determined he would not serve out the war in a Yankee prison, Jordan decided to make a run for it. "Without hesitation, I made the attempt, by leaning over slightly, by a left-oblique direction, I escaped a volley, [and] there was not a thread cut on me that I ever knew of, but [I] expected to be riddled with bullets."[109]

Jordan soon found that he was the only one of his group that made it safely away from the rock. When he had gone about a hundred yards he heard a man screaming in pain and he looked back to see Elisha Lane, of his company, who had fled the rock as well, but had taken a bullet in the flesh of his thigh. Jordan stopped to help Lane, who was limping along as best he could and, when he looked back, he saw the other six men behind the rock surrender to the onrushing Yankees. As Jordan later recalled it, he figured that he owed those men his life. "Those that surrendered," he said, "were a protection to the few that made their escape, as the enemy was attracted and jubilant over their prisoners, this giving us a better chance to escape."[110]

Farther to the rear, Captain Morrill and his men continued to push the Alabamians across the vale toward Big Round Top. As they began to ascend the larger hill, the Alabamians put up a stiffer fight. After passing safely through the line of charging Mainers, Adjutant Waddell had come upon the lost Company A, which had also begun to return to the summit of Big Round Top. He halted the company and ordered them to form a skirmish line, which allowed their comrades to pass through but blunted the advance of the bluecoats. With two of his men wounded and four captured, Morrill thought he had gone far enough, and he ordered his men to take cover and hold their ground. Minutes earlier, Capt. Francis Key Shaaff and Company A had come upon Morrill's men in the woods as they tried to carry out Oates' order to capture the Federal wagons. Fearing that he might be leading his men into too much danger, Shaaff had turned back, and did not find anyone from the regiment until Waddell came running at him through the woods.[111]

Back to Morrill's right, the charge was dying out, but not before the Maine men on the 20th's right had done their share of damage. William Livermore remembered the scene as he ran down into the vale. "Some threw down their arms and ran, but many rose up, begging to be spared. We did not stop but told them to go to the rear, and on we went after the whipped and frightened rebels, taking them by scores and giving those too far away to be captured deadly shots in the back."[112]

Seeing the Alabamians in full retreat, some of the men of the 83rd Pennsylvania had moved forward from their position, cutting off Oates' retreat and forcing his men back up "that awful hill." As the men from the right wing of the 20th pursued, some shouted that they were "On the way to Richmond!" Chamberlain thought that Richmond could wait, and that this was far enough. He sensed the Rebels rallying on the hillside and many of the fleeing Alabamians had taken shelter in the rocks on Big Round Top, from where they could do great damage if his men continued. With some difficulty, he halted the men and organized the scattered groups of his regiment, ordering them back into position. The men could hardly contain their enthusiasm. Groups of them "rallied around the colors," and gave three cheers before returning to the spur. For a moment at least, they rejoiced. Having faced the Rebels head-on for the first time, they had whipped them.[113]

The moment of exuberance was short-lived, however. As the smoke cleared and the confusion subsided, the cost of their victory became apparent. The dead and wounded of both sides littered the area around the spur, top to bottom. As they collected the bodies and gathered the wounded who had not already been taken to the aid station, they counted more than 150 enemy dead and wounded. As he stood back on the spot where the colors had been, Elisha Coan reconstructed in his mind what he had just lived through, and the numbers of casualties just among those near him, helped him realize the gravity of it. As he pondered it, he noted that in a circular area around the flag less than thirty feet across, thirteen men were killed and thirty-five more wounded.[114]

The enemy dead were left at first where they lay, so that the men could focus on those who might still be saved. In particular, wandering the woods east of the spur proved a gruesome task. In the area from which Oates had launched his assaults on the left, and where the charging left and Company B had nearly crossed paths, the Maine men discovered a large number of suffering Alabamians. Ellis Spear came upon one of them who was shot through the arm and lying on the ground. He was calling for water, so Spear gave him some from his canteen, cut open the Rebel's sleeve, and poured water on the wound.[115]

During the immediate aftermath of the charge, Colonel Chamberlain passed by Lieutenant Colonel Bulger of the 47th, still sitting under the tree where he had slumped. Bulger was in bad shape, the blood still spilling from the wound and his mouth, but he was apparently holding his own. Moments before, the old Alabamian had refused to surrender to a New York captain because he was not, in Bulger's view, of high enough rank. Actually, Bulger had hoped the ruse would allow him to escape back to his regiment, but he soon realized that he was too weak to move, much less run any distance. Eventually the New Yorkers brought Colonel Rice to Bulger, and the lungshot officer surrendered his pistol and a sword he later claimed was a recently captured trophy from the 22nd Maine.[116]

Taking care of the wounded prisoners presented its difficulties to the beleaguered Mainers, but watching over those not wounded was an even greater task. They counted 308 of both near their part of the brigade, and to organize the exhausted but still mobile Rebels, they took them to the rear in squads. In one instance, two Mainers thus handled eighty-one Alabamians. This, after the enormous effort of the march, then the fight and the charge, was too much for many of the Maine men, and their colonel later remembered that, "Many had sunk down and fallen asleep the instant the halt was ordered."[117]

Fatigue was an even greater factor for the Alabamians now scurrying to the summit of Big Round Top, and even their colonel became a casualty. Oates managed to carry his large frame back up to the Gibraltar that he had unwillingly abandoned little more than an hour before but, there, he reached the limit of his endurance. Near the summit, he tried to reform the regiment, perhaps to hold the enviable position after all, but his men barely noticed. They were too scattered throughout the woods, helping wounded and disabled comrades to the rear while looking after their own safety. Finally, Oates collapsed under the strain of the heat and the desperation of what had just transpired. Two of his men carried him up the rest of the way and found the assistant surgeon, Dr. Alexander Rives, who poured water on his head, reviving him. When he came around, dusk was settling on the battlefield, and Oates turned command over to Captain Hill, telling him to get the men down to the field they had come through on the approach, find out where the brigade was, and report to whomever had replaced General Law.[118]

As they tended to their grisly duties below, the Maine men suspected, but did not know for certain, that the battle for the spur was over. Still, as if saving the smaller hill was somehow not enough, they had yet another challenge ahead of them on the bigger hill.

Musicians of the 20th Maine. At Gettysburg, some of them fought while others acted as stretcher bearers.

3 *The Bigger Hill*

*They were lying on their arms—all but a few pickets—in a
sleep like a swoon. I had not the heart to order the poor fellows
up, but called for the Colors, and for volunteers, and every
man sprang to his feet.[1]*

Joshua Chamberlain, July 1863

The hour or two that immediately followed the end of the fighting
was filled with a mixture of busy soldiers carrying out various duties
and clumps of them lying in a state of collapse. In the falling darkness
company officers, many of them newly promoted by virtue of Rebel
bullets that had found their targets, sent out details of men to bury the
dead, gather discarded weapons, and carry information up and down the
chain of command. Amid all of this coming and going much rumor,
gossip, even an occasional fact passed from one regiment to another,
and the soldiers began to piece together the previous hour or more that
had seemed to pass so quickly. Officers did their best to account for the
men under their command and, when their fatigue waned, soldiers
wandered about in search of mess-mates, neighbors, and kin among the
dead and wounded.[2]

While they sat and discussed what they could recall about the
fight—did you see Frank get hit? I think I shot two of them Johnnies—
word from the rest of the brigade drifted into the ranks of the 20th, and
the news was not good. Col. Strong Vincent, the man who had so gallantly

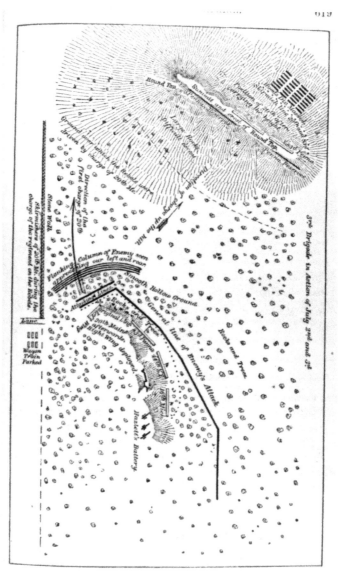

Facsimile of sketch by Col. James Rice which accompanied his official report after the battle on Little Round Top. The sketch includes the "second charge of the 20th Maine" which they made up Big Round Top.

led their brigade through the previous two months, was dead, or gravely wounded, depending on the messenger. Lt. Charles Hazlett commanded the cannons that they had heard above and behind them on the larger portion of Little Round Top. When Gen. Stephen Weed, who had just brought his brigade up to rescue the far side of the hill, was hit with an obviously fatal wound Hazlett leaned and then slumped over him, badly wounded trying to hear what he thought may have been Weed's last words. The stretcher bearers had collected Weed and Hazlett and carried them to a small aid station in rear of the crest, where the 20th's sheltered nook had grown to a larger purpose.

As bad as the Maine soldiers thought their fight on the spur had been, reports of the desperation that had occurred on the right flank of the brigade and beyond seemed equally perilous, if not worse. The casualty lists from the units there were nearly all headed by commanders. Reports had Lieutenant Hazlett, Colonels Vincent and O'Rourke, General Weed, and even Gen. Dan Sickles of the Third Corps, among the dead or severely wounded. All, excepting Sickles, had fallen within a quiet day's earshot of the spur. Around on the open face of the hill, where Vincent, in a moment of remarkable military foresight had moved the 16th Michigan, the flank had fallen into a state of chaos as the Confederates came within steps of seizing the hill and its battery of guns. Just as the small Michigan regiment seemed to break and fall back in flight, Col. Patrick O'Rourke, at the head of five hundred men of the 140th New York Regiment, came charging over the crest from behind the guns, turning back the onrushing Texans in a manner that Napoleon himself would have admired. The bold young Irishman had just led his men into the thick of the carnage when he joined nearly every other Union commander on the crest of the hill, mortally wounded.[3]

Forcing their prisoners to carry some of the wounded to the rear, the men of the 20th began to size up the enemy that had just wreaked havoc in their ranks, albeit unsuccessfully. From a brutal bayonet wound in the head to a harmless bullet hole in a blanket roll, they could not find a single man in the regiment who had not been hit by enemy fire in some way or another. The prisoners claimed to be from four different Alabama regiments but, as Will Livermore put it, "The regiment we fought and captured was the 15th Alabama. They fought like demons and said they were never whipped before, and never wanted to face the 20th Maine again."[4]

Sam Keene struggled painfully to move, yet despite the intense pain in his hip, he was among the fortunate. "Had seven men killed and ten wounded as far as I can ascertain," he recorded in his diary. "Not well by any means." Keene's friend Ellis Spear and Spear's former first lieutenant Joe Land reckoned as they surveyed the carnage on the battlefield that they had survived a day they would not soon forget, and probably not much cherish either. For the second time in two weeks Spear had given orders that resulted in the death of some of his men while he had come through the fight unhurt, at least physically. The psychological scars, however, were painful enough to him.[5]

Joe Land had reason to feel a guiltful sorrow as well. Two of the men under his command in Company H were dead and the life's blood was ebbing out of at least three others. Moreover, Land had himself convinced Albert Cunningham, Andrew Herscomb, and James Knight, all wounded men in his old Company G, to join the regiment the year before, even giving them the papers to sign. Now, Cunningham nursed an arm wound while the latter two appeared mortally wounded, and Land realized that there would be mothers and wives to notify and family members to face back home. Thus did Spear, Land, Nichols, and others become acquainted with the bittersweet collection of guilt, sorrow, joy, and relief that came with desperate victory.[6]

Defeat was no better. Beyond the summit of Big Round Top, the ruptured Alabama regiments had gathered the remnants of their once proud companies in a field near the Slyder house, reforming almost on the spot where the first sharpshooter volley had hit them from behind a stone wall. Dusk had given way to darkness and Oates decided to bivouac for the night. Not long after, the grim reality of the evening's disaster settled on him when only 242 men answered the roll call. Hardest hit was Company B which took forty-two men into the fight on the left flank, never got within a hundred feet of the Mainers, and still came out with only ten men in line. Company A had returned, though too late to do much good, and the lost companies of the 47th were back in line after their useless skirmish march. When Major Campbell made a count of the seven companies of his regiment that had fought, little more than one hundred responded to the roll. Counting both units, Oates had attacked the spur with more than 550 men but, of those, barely three hundred remained and his brother was not among them.[7]

✠ ✠ ✠

One hundred and ninety-eight bayonets. That was all that Chamberlain could count of the Maine regiment that had come into the battle with about four hundred armed enlisted men in line. Going into the fight, captains commanded only six of the ten companies, now they were down to three, and none of the officers in Company C escaped unwounded.

82

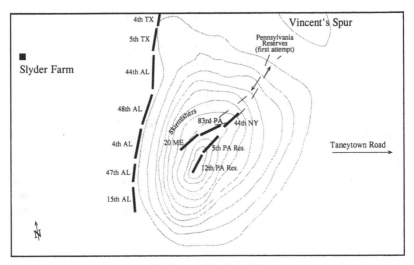

Positions on Big Round Top

Straggling, wounds, and helping others to the rear, all had depleted the regiment to little more than a strong skirmish line, and details sent out to bury the dead or seek ammunition from anywhere they could find it, further depleted the ranks of the regiment. With so little left with which to defend the spur and little hope of gaining any reinforcement from the rest of the tattered brigade, Chamberlain fretted over the intentions of the Southerners somewhere in the dark woods on the huge hill in front of him.[8]

In case the worst might come, he had the wounded prisoners taken to the rear and the dead gathered and laid in one area behind their line. The men instinctively piled up smaller rocks where openings between the larger rocks and trees exposed them to fire. They had scarcely begun preparing to again defend the spur when Colonel Rice, now commanding the brigade in place of the fallen Vincent, sent for the Maine colonel. Rice had brought up reinforcements from another part of the corps—Fisher's Brigade from Gen. Samuel Crawford's division—and three thousand rounds of ammunition. But the welcome news hardly had time to settle in Chamberlain's mind before Rice made a startling request.[9]

The new brigade commander was as uncomfortable as Chamberlain about what the Rebels might be doing up on Big Round Top, so he had asked Col. Joseph Fisher to occupy the hill with his brigade of Pennsylvania Reserves. Fisher declined the assignment on grounds that his men had just arrived, leaving them ignorant of the situation and that, in the dark, the task would be dangerous or worse. When Fisher would not make the ascent, Rice asked for Chamberlain, and presently he suggested that the 20th take on the task. The Maine colonel offered no comment on Fisher's refusal, though he could have made a good argument—this *was*, after all, Pennsylvania they were defending. He was new to command and eager to prove himself, and his first instinct was to respond affirmatively, even when the orders were only suggested. As he walked back to his men, a larger task presented itself; perhaps the biggest challenge of his new command, calling on his best professorial skills. He knew he had to figure a way to tell his men.[10]

"They were lying on their arms—all but a few pickets—in a sleep like a swoon," he later recalled. "I had not the heart to order the poor fellows up," he remembered. Instead, he called for the colors saying, "Boys, I am asked if we can carry that hill in front." To his great relief the weary regiment met his call for volunteers with enthusiasm, as "every man sprang to his feet."[11]

It was now 9 o'clock, quite dark, except for the light of a full moon, and only an occasional snap from the rifle of a sharpshooter or picket interrupted the distant quiet. Chamberlain sent word out to Morrill who had remained on his skirmish line at the base of Big Round Top since the repulse of the Alabamians, and the men of Company B finally rejoined their regiment nearly three hours after they had disappeared into the woods. Spread out as skirmishers in the best line of battle they could form, what was left of the 20th then headed down the spur, across the vale, and began struggling over the boulders and up the steep slope of Big Round Top.[12]

The cover of the trees closed out most of the moonlight, and Chamberlain sent out a squad on each flank, fully expecting they were walking directly into the enemy. Knowing his small group could not overpower whatever force might lay ahead, Chamberlain told his men not to fire, but to use the bayonet if necessary. As they pushed forward, they encountered scattered fire from nervous Southerners who, trying to aim at noises in the darkness, fired over their heads. Most of the way up the hill they captured a half dozen more Confederates including Lt. Thomas Christian of General Law's staff and another officer. Eventually, they reached a position just short of Oates' Gibraltar where noises on the hillside below hinted that the enemy was close by and in force. Chamberlain ordered the men to take cover as best they could while he sent a skirmish line down the hill in front. One soldier, who later won praise for his bravery, remembered that he was never in his life as scared as he was on Big Round Top that night.[13]

If huddling behind the rocks in such an exposed and dark position did not give the tiny regiment reason enough to be frightened, the next five minutes probably did the trick, and the fear closed in from both front and rear. In front, the skirmishers descended almost to the bottom of the hill when they began to see enemy campfires and hear the Rebels talking, so they went part way back up the hill and took their position. Apparently, the Confederates heard something in the woods and sent a squad of men to investigate. As they approached the site of the noise, one of the Maine skirmishers ordered them to halt, inquiring, "Who goes there?" and in reply, one of the Southerners allowed that they were 4th Texas.[14]

"All right, come on," one of the sharp Mainers answered. "We're 4th Texas." The relieved Texans relaxed and went forward only to hear the cocking of muskets as the Maine men got the drop on them. As Ellis Spear later recalled, "The first fire is always recognized as an important advantage, and they surrendered and dropped their muskets." As the skirmishers brought the thirty-odd prisoners back to their main line, one of the Texans inquired what regiment had just duped him into capture. When the Mainers answered the question he good-naturedly remarked at how strange it was for men from opposite ends of the country to meet on a hill, in the dark, in Pennsylvania.[15]

While the skirmishers in front were gobbling up wayward Texans, another threat presented itself from the rear, and the men back up in the regiment thought that they were about to spend the rest of the war in a Southern prison, or worse. They had discovered for certain that the Confederates were close by, and presently, the noise on their right and rear told them that a large force was cutting them off from their brigade. As the Mainers prepared for an attack they were relieved to discover that the noise was actually the approach of some of the Pennsylvania Reserves who had apparently gotten over their initial reluctance. The Mainer's relief quickly turned to confusion and then disgust as they watched Fisher's men try to take a position on the 20th's right.[16]

Through some confusion the Pennsylvanians marched up the hill "by the left flank," which meant that when they halted and faced front on the hill, according to military tactics, their backs faced the enemy. Trying to get their faces, rather than their other ends, toward the enemy became such a noisy mess that the Southerners far below heard the commotion and someone among them shouted "fire!" The resulting volley did no damage but it was all the excuse the reserves needed to make haste back down the hill. Their departure left a noticeably exposed flank on the right of the 20th, so Chamberlain ordered a few men toward the abandoned position to form some sort of picket line while he sent word to their more reliable old friends in the 83rd Pennsylvania and the 44th New York for support.[17]

Meanwhile, there was the matter of three dozen Texans to be addressed. Having prisoners in this precarious situation was hardly a benefit to the already hard-pressed skirmishers, and the Texans refused to be taken to the rear by the small squad that they could spare from the skirmish line anyway. Eventually, two men from Company I took them down the hill in search of the provost guard. Unfortunately, they got lost in the dark woods, finally deciding to stay put until morning, when they successfully delivered the prisoners.[18]

With the shooting and prisoner-taking subsided, the 83rd Pennsylvania and then the 44th New York came up the slope, presumably not by the left flank as their predecessors had, and they took up the line to the right of the 20th. The 83rd brought additional relief in the form of ammunition for the depleted cartridge boxes of the Maine men. Near midnight, two regiments of the reserves mustered the courage to try a return march and they took position behind the 20th on the rocky summit of the hill. With his position apparently as secure as he could make it, Chamberlain ordered the men to lie on their arms, getting as much sleep as possible when not on picket duty. Will Lamson of Company B lay "with my back to the field and my feet to the foe," that night and managed to get some rest, but not before a Rebel bullet came so near his face that he felt it go by.[19]

Still suffering from malarial fever and diarrhea, worsened by the lack of food, sleep, and the exhaustion of the march and fight, Ellis Spear sat against the trunk of a tree and tried to rest. His servant had taken his blanket and horse away from danger before the fight and had yet to return, and Spear woke in the night shaking with a chill. One of the men near him also woke and shared his blanket with him, which gave him some relief. In the morning Hospital Steward Granville Baker gave him a flask of whiskey with quinine pills dissolved inside and his strength returned.[20]

Through the night, the Alabamians at the bottom of the hill stood guard and fired a few useless volleys into the darkness. Some of the men of Oates' old Company G decided to risk an attempt at the Union lines to see if they could rescue John Oates and Bud Cody, assuming they were still alive. They managed to get through a picket line near the spur and even thought they had reached Cody for a time but that was all. The Yankees discovered and nearly captured the bold Rebels before they escaped back to their lines, rescuing Cody's knife and pocketbook but not the lieutenant. While they were unable to retrieve these two officers, there were others not behind enemy lines who would have been glad for their help. In the vale between the Round Tops, somehow undiscovered despite all of the movement, a handful of badly wounded Alabamians, scattered here and there, suffered through the night.[21]

Others among the wounded were more fortunate. After the fight earlier in the evening, Colonel Rice apparently sent Lieutenant Colonel Bulger of the 47th Alabama to a nearby barn to be cared for. Rice gave Bulger some quinine pills and had his men build a shelter out of blankets to make the wounded officer more comfortable. When a Federal surgeon at the makeshift hospital inspected his wound later, he informed the old Alabamian that his chances of survival were one in a hundred. Bulger simply replied, "I will take that chance."[22]

East of the Round Tops, the wounded began to gather as regiments moved their casualties from aid stations and field hospitals to more centralized operations. Dr. John Billings, medical officer from the Second Division, Fifth Corps, established one of these at the stone farmhouse of Jacob Weikert and his family along the Taneytown Road. As he arrived at the house he noticed the Maine men of Company B behind the stone wall out across the field and remembered that a small force of Confederates—probably the lost Company A of the 15th— fired a volley from farther away. When he entered the house, Billings found a fire in the kitchen stove, bread dough ready to bake, and greased baking pans indicating that the family had not been gone long.[23]

Treating more than seven hundred wounded here, most with bullet wounds, Billings and surgeons from two regiments undertook the gruesome task of sawing parts off soldiers' bodies until piles of amputated limbs reached higher than the fence outside the house. Lt. Ziba Graham of the 16th Michigan remembered that the occupants of the house, Jacob Weikert and his family, were less than cooperative. When the fighting near the Round Tops began in earnest, literally in their back yard, the family had climbed down into the cellar of the stone house for safety. In the hours after the battle ended, Graham found two wounded Confederates resting near Weikert's well, unable to get water because the owner had removed the handle of the crank. The Michigan officer went into the house, found Weikert and his family in the cellar, and demanded the handle. Weikert refused, until Graham threatened to shoot him, after which the handle was soon returned to the well.[24]

While the long hours dragged on for the wounded near the Weikert house, those still lying uncared for on the field fared even worse. Down in front of Little Round Top, soldiers North and South were enduring

87

their own difficulty. A New York sergeant recorded scenes from the night in his diary.

> At night of July 2d, our company was on picket in our front at the foot of the hill. The ground was literally covered with dead and wounded. It was the worst picket duty I ever performed. Will never forget it. The rebs were principally Texan troops. They said it was the first time their brigade had ever been repulsed. I spent all my time, while on picket, attending to the wounded, giving them water, fixing them in easy positions, cutting off shoes and helping them in every way I could. It was terrible, some crying, some praying, some swearing and all wanting help.[25]

☩ ☩ ☩

Around daylight, the Maine men heard the enemy down the hill, apparently building up a stone wall for protection, so they built their own from the stones plentifully scattered on the hillside. Not long after finishing it the order came to advance a few feet and build another one, evidently to give themselves a place to fall back to just in case they needed it. About this time Lt. Arad Linscott foolishly decided to take a musket out and see if he could get a shot at one of the Rebels but instead, one of them got a shot at him. The bullet hit him in the thigh and his men had to carry him to the rear.[26]

At 10 o'clock on the morning of July 3, the rest of the Pennsylvania Reserves took over the line on Big Round Top and Colonel Rice brought the Third Brigade together on Little Round Top. On their way there, the Mainers passed by the spur and noticed that the enemy dead still lay where they had left them, but that the dead of the Third Brigade were now buried, twenty-one of them in one grave. On the top of the hill they received another sixty rounds of ammunition and then marched about a half mile toward the Union center. There, they halted behind two other lines of Union infantry and threw up two rows of stone wall in case of attack.[27]

About this time, Colonel Chamberlain sent Pvt. J. B. Wescott of Company I to find and care for the wounded Lieutenant Linscott. Wescott soon discovered that medical personnel, fearing that another attack by the enemy might endanger the hospital operation, had removed the wounded of the division from the Weikert farm. He learned that they were setting up another hospital a few miles to the southeast and set off to find it. When he arrived there he got a first-hand look at what happened to the wounded after a battle. He went into a huge barn filled to capacity with suffering soldiers, most lying on beds of straw with little

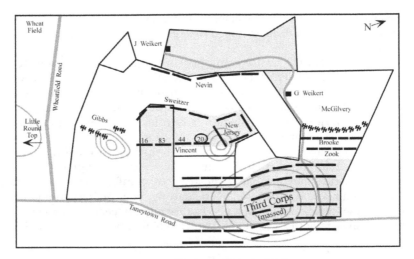

Position of Vincent's Brigade, July 3.

help or comfort. Outside the barn the wounded lay in long lines on the ground with little or no shelter from the elements. The men of the 20th got some aid from nearby surgeons but since the regiment was without a surgeon of its own, many of them had to wait and suffer. Wescott did the best he could for them.[28]

Back at the regiment, a short time after they had settled into their new position behind the stone wall, some of the division wagons moved up behind them on the Taneytown Road and the non-combatants in the 20th came over to check on friends and learn of the previous day's news. At the same time, the butchers drove a small herd of cows up to the same place on the road and began to issue beef rations to the brigade. Except for an occasional shot from a skirmisher or an artillery piece, it had been quiet through the morning up until that point. Then, at about 1 o'clock, Confederate artillery began to fire with enormous force. This sent the butchers scurrying for a safer area, leaving about half of the beef behind. Never inclined to pass up rations under any circumstances, especially fresh meat, each regiment sent out a detail and everyone got some beef.[29]

The shelling that had sent the butchers away from their duty grew louder until the earth beneath the soldiers shook. John O'Connell, one of the 2nd Maine transfers who had experienced the sound of huge artillery barrages at Malvern Hill, Antietam, and Fredericksburg, remembered that "The air was thick with screeching shells, the likes of which we

89

thought we had never heard before." Fortunately for the Mainers, the shells flew well over them or to their right or left, causing no harm in their ranks.[30]

Lying behind the wall nursing his sore right hip as the previous day's events came into focus, Sam Keene's mortality closed in on him. In the midst of this enormous cannonade, he took out a pencil and paper and began a letter to his wife. "Here we are near Gettysburg and one of the most terrific cannonades is now and has been taking place for the last hour or two," he wrote. "I cannot tell you how many reports a minute as I cannot count them suffice it to say it is one continuous roar." Expecting that, at any moment, his regiment would again be thrust into the battle, he tried to comfort his wife while reconciling his soul with God. "Now, darling, your prayers strengthen me. If I die, recollect I die in a good cause and my peace is made with my heavenly father I trust. Good Bye. God bless my very dear, darling wife."[31]

✠ ✠ ✠

No one in the brigade could remember exactly how long the cannonade had gone on. Some thought two hours, others three or four. But after it ended the Maine men learned that the Confederates had mounted an enormous attack, the likes of which had never been seen before in the war, save perhaps Fredericksburg, and the Union soldiers in the center of the line had thrown them back. Reports came in indicating that the Federals had taken 2,500 prisoners and that General Longstreet was among them.[32]

With the exception of Longstreet—it was actually General Armistead who had been wounded and captured in the battle, then taken to a barn several hundred yards behind the 20th—most of these rumors were true. Lee had launched an all-out attack with more than twelve thousand men, aimed directly at the Union center, about a half mile north and a little west of where the Maine men safely huddled behind the wall. Shortly after the repulse, General Meade rode the length of the entire Federal line and as he passed the Maine men, they joined the other troops in giving him a tremendous cheer. At last, the army had a general who could beat Robert E. Lee—and within a week of taking command![33]

At some point during the day, the 20th received another unexpected visitor when Gen. Adelbert Ames rode over to visit his old regiment saying how proud he was of them. Earlier in the day, Ames, whose new command had been badly cut up on the first day of the battle, heard of the part that they had played in the defense of the two hills which now anchored the Union left and he wrote them a letter expressing his pride.[34]

> Head Qtrs. 1st. Division Eleventh. Corps
> Field near Gettysburg, July 3d.
> My dear Colonel Chamberlain;
> I am very proud of the 20th. Regt. and its present Colonel.
> I did want to be with you and see your splendid conduct in the
> field. God Bless you and the dear old Regiment. My heart
> yearns for you; and more and more, now that these trying
> scenes convince me of your superiority.
> The pleasure I felt at the intelligence of your conduct
> yesterday is some recompense for all that I have suffered.
> My love to the officers and men.
> A. Ames, Brig. Genl.[35]

Although the Maine men had hated living through their first eight months under the West Pointer's tight rein and would have reiterated their disdain for him just two days before, the events of the previous twenty-four hours had shown them, better than he could ever have explained, what all of that discipline was about. In a moment of extreme crisis they had remembered their training and put it to good use. Those who survived the fight now reckoned that they were alive thanks in no small part to their training and that, in effect, they owed their lives to Ames. This feeling sealed a strong bond between the veterans and their first commander that never waned.

✠ ✠ ✠

On the far right of the Confederate line of battle, still held by Law's Brigade, one of the men in the 4th Alabama overheard two Yankee cavalry generals—Kilpatrick and Farnsworth—talking loudly in the woods. Kilpatrick was ordering Farnsworth to seize a North Carolina battery in rear of the Alabamians and the piece of intelligence allowed General Law to prepare for the attack. In a wild charge the cavalrymen passed over the 1st Texas lying in a skirmish line behind a wall. They then headed for the battery under fire from some Georgians, a cooking detail, and the 44th Alabama.[36]

Oates received orders to move into the fracas as well, so he threw out skirmishers and headed for the Yankees. As his men approached, one of the guns of the battery fired a shot of double canister and Oates remembered that the sound of the small lead balls passing over their heads reminded him of a covey of partridges in flight. Eventually, the officer commanding the cavalry was knocked from his horse with several mortal-looking wounds and lay on the ground awaiting death. A Lieutenant

Adrian, an officer from the 44th Alabama, was nearby trying to capture a horse and he accidentally found himself commanding Oates' skirmishers when the fuss broke out. He approached the dying Yankee, telling him, "Now, you surrender," figuring he had little choice in the matter, anyway. There were two different versions among the men as to what happened next. Oates said that the Yankee swore he would not surrender, and he turned his own pistol toward himself and pulled the trigger. Another story among the men said that he killed a Confederate who demanded his surrender and was shot by another. Whichever version was accurate, it left him just as dead.[37]

Still exhausted, Oates saw the incident from about fifty yards away and one of his skirmishers after brought the dead soldier's shoulder bars to the colonel, saying "Colonel, don't you want that Yankee major's straps?" The mistake was an honest one—Confederate majors wore one star on their collar—but the dead officer was no less than Brig. Gen. Elon J. Farnsworth. Oates went over to the body where squads of men had gathered to get their first look at a dead Yankee general. He found letters in his coat pocket addressed to "Gen. E. J. Farnsworth," apparently from the general's wife, and destroyed them out of respect.[38]

With the exception of Farnsworth's men, joyous cheering, shouting, and self-congratulation swept along the Union battle line. While the celebration was underway there were still a great many men who could not find the strength or the desire to engage in such merrymaking. Sgt. William N. Johns of the 15th Alabama was still lying severely wounded in the vale between the Round Tops, where he had now lain for nearly twenty-four hours without aid. When a Yankee bullet broke his thigh bone during the fight, he had fallen on his back, unable to move and nearly died of thirst during the night. The next day he went from one extreme to the other when, a few hours after the repulse of the huge Confederate charge, rain began to fall and continued heavily into the night. Johns was barely able to keep from drowning by putting his hat over his face.[39]

Johns, along with many other Confederates found on the field during and after the battle, was taken to the hospitals set up in the fields around a group of farms southeast of Round Top. Actually, hospital was hardly a word that accurately described these pitiful fields, barns, and groves of trees where wounded men of both sides seemed to lie in windrows as far as one could see. John Chamberlain followed the wounded he had cared for from the brigade's aid station to Jacob Weikert's farm and beyond and he never forgot the sights that he later found almost impossible to explain.

"From every quarter, the ambulances were hurrying with the dying, I say dying for those who were not in the most critical condition did not receive the comfort of a ride. The paths and woods were filled with groups of men who were wandering around in the sun searching for their respective hospitals that they might have their wounds dressed. Many of the hospitals I was able to point out to them after getting them water and washing their wounds. Poor fellows!"[40]

The hospitals were organized generally by division and corps, and for days after the battle they lacked everything except suffering. Supplies of food, water, medicine, and bandages, were all completely inadequate to care for the more than thirty thousand casualties of both sides. When the rain did not douse the unsheltered thousands, many of them unable to move, the sun gave them cause to suffer even greater from their wounds. In all of this, John Chamberlain found himself caught up, fully expecting that the next dying man he relieved would be one of his brothers. As he helped pack men into ambulances at the Weikert house, John saw many of the men he recognized from the 20th and heard rumors that his oldest brother, the colonel, was wounded, his regiment badly cut up.[41]

With no medical training at all, and no life experience that could have prepared him for this—"men without an eye or nose or leg or arm or with mangled head or body would constantly attract your sympathy, each one looking a little worse than the one that went before"— John did his best to comfort whomever he could, however he could. At one point, he discovered that Lieutenant Kendall of the 20th was most severely wounded but hanging on without any attention or shelter. Thirty-six hours after the fight, Kendall lay with a bullet still lodged in his neck, apparently left by surgeons who often abandoned such hopeless cases in favor of those they might be more certain of saving. John convinced an assistant surgeon from one of the regiments to do what he could for Kendall, and he managed to remove the ball. The effort was in vain, however. When John checked back again, returning the lieutenant's hat which had been lost on the field, he was dead. "[T]he military symbols," John pondered, "were useless to him now, he had entered on his last sleep. He was a patient man."[42]

While Kendall may have been among the worst of the men from the 20th that day, there were others very nearly as bad. J.B. Wescott continued searching the hospitals for Lieutenant Linscott until he, too, found himself caught up in the service of the wounded and he began to see familiar faces. Sgt. Abner Hiscock of Company G had already lost an arm and Cpl. Frank Ward, of Company F, a leg while the surgeons had already given up on Capt. Charles Billings. The officers got care faster than the enlisted men, but without a surgeon at Gettysburg the men of the 20th languished longer than most.[43]

In the late afternoon of July 3 a heavy thunderstorm came, as if the Almighty sought to wash the blood from the battlefield and quench the thirst of the untended sufferers. Around the hospitals, many reckoned that the rain was probably no worse for the collected but unsheltered casualties than the searing sun had been. For those still on duty with the regiment, the rain simply added to their discomfort, and they hunkered down behind their wall again, trying to sleep and wondering whether this Fourth of July would be worth celebrating.

At the same time, Oates and his men set out on a mission that gave them a taste of the apprehension and silent fear that their opponents from Maine had survived on Round Top the night before. As the heavens opened, Oates received orders to form a line in the woods about a half mile south of the brigade (and the rest of the army) facing east near the base of Round Top. Oates did so, and soon discovered that a strong line of Union cavalrymen waited just one hundred yards in front of him. As night drew on and the rain continued, his intuition made him feel as if something was wrong. "The surroundings presented the most weird and lonely appearance. The dead lay scattered through the drear and sombre woods...not a sound was heard; the stillness was awful." Unable to remain still, Oates rode back toward the rest of the brigade to see what was happening and, undoubtedly, to see if he could either get support or get his men out of those eerie woods.[44]

Having gone about a hundred yards, he heard the cap from a gun or pistol snap closer to him than he would have liked. Oates made an about face and rode back to his old company calling for Sgt. William Holley. Oates' trusted the sergeant who, the evening before, had demanded that Oates tell Bulger to "take his damned concern" out of his regiment, and so he sent him creeping into the darkness to see what was back there. The wet leaves allowed Holley to move quietly and he shortly returned, reporting in a deep cotton belt accent, "A line of Yankees out thar. I went up close to some of them; they are thar sho."[45]

Oates may have cursed his luck, having found himself surrounded by the enemy for the second time in two days in the space of about a half mile, but he knew he was not about to let Yankee cavalry swallow his regiment up. "No orders came, and I was satisfied none would come, except from our enemies, and that would be to surrender whenever they found us isolated from the main body of our troops." As he had the day before, Oates determined to get out and by moving to the right and traversing a circuitous route, the 15th managed to find its regular place in line with the brigade. To Oates' enormous relief, he found that Col. Sheffield, the new brigade commander, had sent an orderly with a message calling his regiment back, but the messenger and the message were captured before reaching their destination. In the face of the enemy, Oates had disobeyed orders and abandoned his post but fortunate circumstances had saved the Alabama colonel a dicey situation with his commanders.[46]

With this last maneuver, the Alabamians settled in for what was left of the night, not yet aware that the Battle of Gettysburg was over. For their Maine counterparts across the way the rainy night passed much more quietly. They could rest knowing that the worst, of this battle at least, had probably passed, but they had yet to learn one more lesson from this remarkable experience. For many of them, the worst memories of their lives lay little more than a day ahead. The newer soldiers especially, were about to learn what it means to be seared by the horrors of war.

4 *Seared by the Horrors of War*

But what a scene before us. Oh how would a man that had not been seared by the horrors of war have felt to look upon the scene…This is a great story and I would not have believed it if I had not seen it myself.[1]

William Livermore, July 6, 1863

The Fourth of July was wet and passed slowly. The rain that began the previous afternoon lasted well into evening and paused only a short while before returning as a torrent. Between the opposing lines the occasional skirmish firing continued, but nothing more. With the confusion waning and the two armies apparently settled in to weather the storm, Joshua Chamberlain had time to wander and have a look around. He returned to the spur where details of soldiers had removed the scenes of the conflict, marking the burials of his men with rough headboards made of ammunition boxes. As he led his horse past the shallow graves, he thought that even the animal bowed his head, "as if recognizing the faces of those who often followed him to battle."[2]

After revisiting the scene of his triumph, he took a few moments to write a letter to his wife, an attempt to share with his beloved the incredible experience he had just come through. As he penned the words to paper on his knee, he swelled with the pride of victory. "We are fighting gloriously," he wrote. "Our loss is terrible but we are beating the Rebels as they were never beaten before. The 20th has immortalized itself." Despite his almost overwhelming expressions of affection and love for his wife, Chamberlain never felt as if her feelings for him were as strong, at least not openly. A few days before, he had become a colonel, and since then he had proven himself in command and in the crisis of combat, with a scar and a bent scabbard to show for it. Surely, this would help to warm her to him. "I am receiving all sorts of praise," he told her, "but bear it meekly."[3]

The pack mules had not brought up their tents and supplies, so the Maine men lay behind the wall all day with only rubber blankets for shelter, getting soaked to the skin. During the day they heard reports that the Rebels were falling back and some of the men found a local citizen who carried mail out for them. As it turned out, reports of a Rebel retreat were accurate. The men of the 15th Alabama, still on the Confederate right, had fallen back with the rest of the army and there awaited an attack by the Federals that never came. If secession had dulled their spirit for celebrating their former country's Independence Day, there was even less to celebrate on the eighty-seventh anniversary of the Declaration. "It was the coldest fourth of July I ever felt," remembered William Jordan of the 15th. "There were some houses between us and the enemy, which obstructed our view, that were set on fire and burned. I remember it was pleasant to get near the burning houses to warm." Thus, the weather precluded any celebratory recognition of the national holiday on either side, and the Fourth passed unremarkably.[4]

In Bangor, Maine, citizens of the world's lumber capital found greater reason to celebrate than their young friends in Pennsylvania. As early as July 3, telegraph wires brought news of a fight at Gettysburg, and not long after the thunderous cannonade finally ceased on the battlefield, headlines in the *Whig and Courier* trumpeted news of the previous day, exclaiming, "The Result Highly Favorable to Our Arms." The *Whig* reported rumors of Longstreet's death and that Confederate Gen. William Barksdale was surely dead. Pennsylvania soldiers buried Barksdale near the Hummelbaugh house in the morning on July 3 and citizens of Bangor read about his death the next day. Thus, the folks at home knew of it sooner than the men of the 20th Maine who lay barely half a mile away.[5]

Farther north into rural Maine word traveled much slower. In Aroostook, an area of Maine called simply "The County," the July 3 *Aroostook Times* brought news that Lincoln had removed General Hooker, replacing him with Meade, of whom it read, "the public know very little indeed." By the time Sgt. George Buck succumbed to his wounds, the people in his hometown of Linneus knew even less of the battle at Gettysburg. In fact, the *Times* included a story on the favorable mortality rate in the army, a rate that was changing dramatically even as the ink dried on its pages.[6]

While their parents back in Brewer read the news of the battle, John Chamberlain confessed to his older brother Joshua that he had lost the rubber poncho he loaned him. When rain soaked the still-feverish colonel during the night, John apologized, swearing that he would replace the poncho the following day if it cost him fifteen dollars. At the time, John worried over how he would be able to find a replacement but the following day he discovered that replacing almost anything would require very little effort.[7]

On the fourth, concluding that Meade had no desire to attack him on this field, General Lee decided to turn what was left of his army around and head for home, if he could get it there. Before the march began on the fifth, Colonel Oates rode to the division field hospital to say good-bye to the men for whom no more could be done except to leave them to the care of the Yankees. His lieutenant colonel, Isaac Feagin, had not even really made it into the fight, but he was leaving a leg at Gettysburg by virtue of amputation, and would go to a Yankee prison where he would endure another. After a few poignant farewells, the 15th and 47th Alabama stepped off in retreat and Hood's division traveled until they arrived near Hagerstown, Maryland.[8]

The following day, Ellis Spear wrote a letter home to his friend Lysander Hill who had recruited Company I of the 20th, and Sam Keene returned to writing the letter to his wife that he began during the bombardment two days before. "My little company," Keene wrote in a fatherly tone, "seems so different from what it did that it makes me feel bad. I have only twenty guns with me now—a few days ago I had forty-three. Poor fellows—they braved the storm of bullets heroically."[9]

A dozen of Spear's men from Company G had fallen on the Round Tops and three were missing but, as yet, only one of them had died. In the sixty-odd hours since the fighting ended for the 20th, Keene, however, learned that the suffering in his company was greater than any other. Eight of his men lay buried near the sheltered nook on the spur, sixteen more were wounded, and another would pass before the day ended. In all, seven more Maine men had died since the fight, joining twenty buried on the spur and five more at the Weikert farm behind it. The rain that seemed to fall in a continuous downpour since the battle ended dampened the jubilance of victory and sporadic reports from the Fifth Corps hospital only foreshadowed the horror that lay ahead.

Many of these reports came from John Chamberlain who, after struggling to care for casualties while enduring the uncertainty of rumors about the well-being of his brothers, finally found the regiment and both brothers by late morning. "If ever I shook hands heartily," he recalled, "I did so then, as I looked on Lawrence and Thomas alive." John brought word that Lieutenant Kendall had died from the wound in his neck and that dozens of Maine men were languishing in the farm-field hospitals a mile and a half to the south. Learning from his brother the fate of Lieutenant Kendall, the colonel faced for the first time the duty of notifying the men of the death of one of their officers. He issued Special Order Number 33, which stated that "It is the the painful duty of the colonel commanding to announce the death of Lieut Warren Kendall...Modest as he was faithful, gentle as he was brave, he has left a bright example for all that becomes a soldier."[10]

If the grisly scenes he had waded through in the rear affected John Chamberlain, he returned to the regiment in time to venture to a part of the battlefield that would impress itself even more deeply into his memory. In the early morning the Third Brigade formed in line of battle and began to advance across the portion of the battlefield where the Confederates had sustained and inflicted thousands of casualties fighting with the Union Third Corps on July 2. Over the two previous days neither army had occupied the area that lay between the hostile lines. As a result, shattered and burned equipment alongside dead and dying men and animals, littered fields which had days before been fertile farmland. "I remember the spectacle," Joshua Chamberlain recalled. "We tried to advance in line of battle but the wrecks of battle so strewed the ground that it was impossible to keep a line. Men and horses, arms and missiles literally blocked our way."[11]

Among the first sights they encountered in this wasteland of warfare were two bodies draped over a fence near the area where the brigade had almost formed in line of battle at the Wheat Field on July 2. One of the men in Company C thought they were from the 17th Maine, which meant that they could be the neighbors or even relatives of some of the men in the 20th. A few yards beyond, they came closer to the scenes where the fighting had been hottest, and the carnage extreme. Near the Abraham Trostle farm Colonel Chamberlain counted nineteen horses among the fragments of an exploded caisson and gun carriage. John Chamberlain also saw the dead horses and he remembered that "some were crouched on their legs with heads up and bodies, they looked lifelike."[12]

As they moved on, John caught a glimpse of a uniform lying just over a rise of ground in front of him. He rode over to the dark bundle and was startled by the sight of the first dead soldier he had ever seen on a battlefield. The body lay on its side and it was so hideous that it startled Chamberlain's horse as well. From atop the rise John could see another body, and then another, and he thought for a moment that he should count them. But, as his eyes scanned further ahead he realized that it would be a futile effort. "The further I rode," he recalled, "the thicker the ground was strewn with dead and dying." Fresh from the hallowed halls of Bowdoin, the young seminarian struggled to find words to describe the scene and pondered the idea that war did not discriminate. "Here were men of every rank and nation and age," he wrote. "Rebels and Yankees, side by side. Just as they fell in

"The further I rode, the thicker the ground was strewn with dead and dying." This photograph of dead Union soldiers on the battlefield, taken the same day the 20th Maine passed over it, shows evidence of looting by other soldiers.

different actions. There were the rough features of the hardy working man and the pale delicate lineaments of the student or the family pet. As I looked on some of these boys, I thought of their mothers and sisters."[13]

Older brother Joshua gave up the thought of counting the bodies as well, and it seemed that the closer they got to the Emmitsburg Road, the more horrifying the scenes became until they reached an extreme just beyond the Peach Orchard. Crossing the road, the brigade halted in line of battle and began throwing up breastworks. The center of the regiment rested in front of the charred and smoldering remains of a barn that shell fragments had apparently set ablaze during the battle. As the men moved to grab the barn's foundation stones to build a wall, they peered over the four-foot-high underpinning and gazed at a scene more startling than most of them had ever experienced.[14]

During and after the battle, wounded men of both sides had crawled to this barn for shelter or comfort, and many of them remained unable to flee as it evaporated into a roaring inferno. When the Mainers reached the edge of the structure they saw the ruins. Some of the bodies were charred to the skeleton or mere ashes while others lay swollen with their clothes burned off. Near the barn, William Livermore saw thirty or forty dead of the 114th Pennsylvania Zouaves, recognized by their red pantaloons, who had defended their home state against Barksdale's Mississippians. "They had lay there three days in hot July weather and I wish I never could see another

"In some places on the bigness of your house there would be eight or ten horses and from three to eight men." Alexander Gardner took this photograph of the Trostle House the day after the 20th Maine passed by it.

such sight. It is nothing to see men that have just been killed. But every man was swollen as large as two men purple and black."[15]

While many of the men found the sights and smells of the barn too grotesque to look upon, others who had long since hardened to such scenes took the opportunity to poke around the dead flesh with their ramrods in search of whatever treasures might present themselves. One soldier thus found success in the form of sixty U.S. dollars, some Confederate money, and a lady's gold ring. Even John Chamberlain overcame his initial queasiness long enough to snip a few buttons from the coats of Southern officers and collect letters from some of the dead. "One was dated Florida," he wrote, "and was bitter on the Yankees."[16]

John's brother Joshua had witnessed the aftermath at Antietam, Fredericksburg, and Chancellorsville but nothing he had ever seen compared to this. "There lay the remnants too terrible to describe of officers and men–rebel and union—half burned or with roasted heads...a number of them being shot through the head still breathing after twenty-four hours. We tried to do something for them but they were past all human wants or human aid. I hold back rather than attempt to describe this scene." Like their colonel, many of the veterans in the regiment remembered that it was the "hardest" battlefield they had ever seen.[17]

Aside from the gruesome bodies, many strange and unexplainable scenes caused wonder in the regiment. Some of the Southern dead had their hands

"Within three rods of a house, nineteen horses lay in the bigness of your barn yard." Gardner also took this photo of the Trostle barn the day after the 20th Maine passed by it.

bound and one a handkerchief tied around his mouth. Inside the house near the barn, the Confederates had left notes on shingles and scraps of paper addressed to the "damned Yankees," In the orchard across from the barn lay piles of loaves of bread that they surmised the Southerners had forced the local women to bake. Nathan Clark guessed that there were five hundred pounds in the two piles he saw. As they ventured farther away, the men came upon a fence behind which they found literally thousands of blankets, knapsacks, rifles, everything the Confederate soldiers had carried toward the fight, but shed before the assaults began. For some strange reason, they had taken time to remove the shoes of the dead but left almost everything else where they had dropped it. From piles and rows the Maine men took what they could find. "It was some sport to overhaul their things," William Livermore wrote his brother, and he added Rebel paper, stockings, and new shirts to his own haversack.[18]

From behind the breastworks at the barn, Sam Keene finally finished the letter to his wife that had now taken three days to write. He, too, tried in vain to put the visions to words adding, "may heaven save you from the distress of such scenes." As the nagging pain throbbed in his side, reminding him how close he had come to the Great Beyond, the fatalistic tone which had covered his writing the day before returned. Sitting just a few feet from the smoldering barn, he contemplated the manner of death that the men had suffered there. "What a fate for a poor soldier, after receiving a fatal or

103

lingering wound to be thus hurled out of existence by the furies of a burning stack of hay and timber is doubly horrible." While the pioneers and other detailed soldiers set about collecting weapons and burying the dead, Keene curled up near the wall and despite the gore a few feet away, "an almost intolerable stench," and even an occasional cannon shot in the distance, he fell asleep.[19]

Not long after Keene awoke from his nap, the brigade started back across the fields toward their morning position. As they passed, again, over the ground that had amazed them that morning, William Livermore tried to put the scenes near the Trostle farm into some framework that his brother could understand. "[I]n some places on the bigness of your house there would be eight or ten horses and from three to eight men. Where their guns stood, one place in particular where the 5th Mass. Battery stood within three rods of a house, nineteen horses lay in the bigness of your barn yard, some without heads, others their legs and some their thighs tore away." In time, he gave up the effort, saying, "After what I have written you have no idea of the scene nor I did not much til this battle. You look at it in too small a scale."[20]

They left the macabre fields at dusk, but the memories stayed with them long after. In the years that followed Gettysburg, the survivors of the regiment would talk and write about the battle and the glorious things that they saw and did there, the images growing more distant with each telling's exaggeration. It is testimony to the horrible side of war, however, that of all the memories the veterans took away from Gettysburg, they seldom wrote in those after years about the gruesome sights and smells of the fifth of July.

Near dark that evening the Fifth Corps followed the Sixth down the Emmitsburg Road, finally beginning their pursuit of the retreating Confederates. The night was so dark that soldiers could not see their hands in front of them and officers carried lanterns to guide their troops. Making matters worse, the road was nearly knee deep with mud and complaining soldiers collided, got lost, or fell against others around them. When the mounted officers and aides were not accidentally trampling their men, their heads bounced off of branches or their legs bruised against the sides of trees. Many even exclaimed that it was worse than Burnside's "Mud March" six months back. The Maine men traveled only about three miles in this mess before someone in command called a halt near midnight and they bivouacked near a covered bridge south of Gettysburg. Halting, however, did not necessarily mean rest since the ground was still wet from days of rain, but the men took solace in the fact that they had left the scenes and the smells of the battle behind them.[21]

On the sixth of July, the rain fell hard enough to fill a mounted man's boots with water. Orders came to be ready to march so the Maine men prepared to move and, after soaking a while in the rain, the order was countermanded. At noon, the Fifth Corps tried again to move but after only a mile turned around, marched some more, and finally gave it up. In the after-noon, the weather cleared but the mud lingered and so did the Fifth Corps. The road had become too jammed with army troops and wagons.[22]

With an afternoon free from the responsibilities of the previous days, the men wrote letters, relaxed, and the daily tedium of military paperwork resumed. While they rested, orders came down from General Meade congratulating the troops on their victory and informing them that Union forces had captured Confederate pontoons at a place called Williamsport. This news, coupled with the daily dousing of rain, meant that General Lee would have great difficulty getting his army back across the swollen Potomac River, if they could cross at all. With a few day's marching, the Federals would be able to squeeze the already weak Confederates against the river, and perhaps put an end to the war altogether.[23]

Before all of that could be pondered, however, Colonel Chamberlain had paperwork to catch up on. The most pressing issue awaiting his attention was the first official "after action" report that the new colonel had ever filed, and it taught him a lesson in army etiquette. It took seven pages for Chamberlain to describe the events of July 2 and 3, beginning with their arrival on the field and carrying it through their departure from Big Round Top, which he mistakenly called Wolf's Hill. Later in the day Colonel Rice, who had ascended to command of the brigade from his post as commander of the 44th New York, asked Chamberlain to revise his report and resubmit it. Undoubtedly, Rice pointed out a few errors to the new colonel from Maine, not the least of which was the omission of the 44th from the late-night defense of Big Round Top. "In compliance with the request of the colonel commanding the brigade," Chamberlain rewrote the report, which now included his commander's old regiment, and sent it back up through channels.[24]

Chamberlain made one other puzzling change in his report before resubmitting it. In his first draft he wrote "As a last desperate resort, I ordered a *charge*," underlining the word charge for emphasis. But by the time he submitted the final draft later in the day he had changed his description of the key moment in the fight. The final official report read, "At the crisis, I ordered the bayonet. The word was enough. It ran like fire along the line, from man to man, and rose into a shout, with which they sprang forward upon the enemy." There is no explanation, even in postwar writings, of why he wrote the first version as he did but, in virtually every account of the battle he wrote after this, he described the second scenario.

✠ ✠ ✠

On the seventh of July the marching resumed early. The Maine men started south at 4 a.m. and passed through Emmitsburg and Creagerstown, covering more than twenty miles along the eastern base of Catoctin Mountain. It rained again "as usual" and another day of slogging through deep, sticky mud ended within a few miles of Frederick. When they reached the outskirts of the city they had come full circle in more ways than one. Only fourteen days earlier they were miserable, ornery, and disgusted with their generals, and ten days back they had passed this same city as their morale surged toward unequalled heights. In the meantime, they had experienced almost everything horrible about war except defeat and finally whipped the seemingly unwhippable General Lee. Presently, however, as they completed their circular route from and to Frederick, things appeared to have returned to what passed for normal before Lee left Virginia and anyone ever heard of Gettysburg. For Pvt. John Johnson, a farmer from Solon who was little more than a boy, it was simply too much to bear up under. He quit the war and the clerk of Company B listed him as a deserter.[25]

As Ellis Spear's strength returned, the health of his colonel and his friend Sam Keene seemed to be moving in the reverse. Spear felt well enough to venture toward Frederick in search of provisions, but Chamberlain returned to the practice of visiting local farmhouses with his brother John to rest and recuperate. Sam Keene found that he could only keep up while riding in an ambulance within which he was thoroughly jolted, his condition only worsening. It was not a totally miserable day, however. As they had when they got the previous mail call, twelve days before and also in Frederick, spirits rose slightly when the second mail in a month arrived.[26]

Five days had passed since the battle on the spur and, though news from home had arrived, there was still no word of Colonel Vincent. A day after their former commander fell on Little Round Top his orderly, Pvt. Oliver Norton of the 83rd Pennsylvania, had found him lying in a room at the Bushman house, one of the farms southeast of Round Top which hospital operations were then quickly consuming. Norton recalled that Vincent was pale and could not speak. Sensing the inquiring look in the fallen colonel's eyes, Norton told him, "The boys are still there, Colonel," and saw Vincent's face light up with a gratified smile. Vincent's wound was clearly fatal. The bullet had passed through his groin on the left side, breaking bone and tearing flesh before it lodged on the right. Lt. Jonathan Clark, his adjutant, and Dr. James Burchfield, the surgeon of his old regiment, the 83rd Pennsylvania, did what they could to keep him comfortable but medically, there was little anyone could do. He succumbed on July 7 but it was nearly another week before Colonel Rice issued General Order number five, which officially announced his passing.[27]

As the eighth day of July dawned over western Maryland the only difference in the rain was that it seemed to be falling even harder, if this was possible. By the summer of 1863, William Livermore had known twenty-one years of rain in Maine timber country and a set of seasons in Virginia and Maryland. From cold, biting rain to fierce summer thunder showers over Moosehead Lake, he had seen his share of torrents. But as he finished his letter to brother Charles that afternoon he testified, "I never saw a more powerful rain."[28]

After Joshua and John Chamberlain got a night's lodging and breakfast at a house nearby, John rode into Frederick to get Joshua's horse shod. The absence of rations and the nauseous stench of the battle's aftermath had kept him from eating anything like a meal for nearly a week. In Frederick, he ate three and a half pies and a loaf cake before his appetite was satiated. On his return to the regiment, the rain fell hard and John was soaked to the skin. In vain, he draped his boots and socks over the saddle to avoid the discomfort of sopping feet. By the time he found the Maine troops again at Middletown he was violently sick, shaking with fever and chills.[29]

While John was on his side trip to "the city of pies" his brothers and their comrades were adding another eight miles to their marching record. Like so many others during the campaign it was a hard march. The rain continued until about noon and the mud gave no relief at all. After crossing over the mountain ridge they reached Middletown where they passed the remainder of the day.[30]

If things seemed a bit familiar to the older veterans of the regiment, there was good reason. Only a few seemed to realize it, but the 20th camped that night in the same field that they had used for bivouac the previous fall just a few days before the Battle of Antietam. With the afternoon free, some of the men washed their clothes in the same creek, got water from the same spring, and straw bedding from the same stack as the previous visit. Will Lamson of Company B noticed how the local farmers lamented that the war had passed over their fields for a second straight harvest season. "I don't know if it was a pleasant sight for the farmers, as it does not improve corn and wheat much!" Lying in the same spot eleven months after their first visit, some of the men must have considered that nearly a year's misery and toil in the army seemed to have made little difference in the grander scheme of things. They were, quite literally, right back where they had started.[31]

✠ ✠ ✠

Nice weather finally broke out on the ninth and it began to seem July hot again for the first time in three weeks, though it would take time for the mud to harden back into roads. As the 20th set out on the march again at about 9 o'clock, they moved off from the familiar campsite, leaving John Chamberlain and Sam Keene behind. With both of them sick and getting worse, the colonel asked John and ordered Keene to stay behind and rest at a local farmer's house where they could get hot meals and restful surroundings for a few days. John took some calomel and went with Keene to the house of the Rev. Doctor Strobel to recuperate. Strobel took the two Mainers to the home of a friend where they rested. Five days later, John rode a sutler's wagon back to Frederick, took a train to Washington, and began the long journey back to Maine.[32]

The regiment, meanwhile, crossed over South Mountain and camped near the town of Boonsboro, no more than eight miles from the old Antietam battlefield. They were still hoping, though with ever-decreasing certainty, that they would have another chance at the Rebels before Lee could escape across the swollen Potomac. Better to have it out now, perhaps hastening the war's end, than to fall back into the strategies of the previous fall which seemed to drag the war out endlessly. "I'm in hopes," wrote Will Lamson, "that General Meade will do better here this year than McClellan did last." Resting near Antietam, wondering if they would attack the Confederates and if their generals even wanted to, orders came down from Colonel Rice announcing the promotion of Strong Vincent to brigadier general of volunteers. While they took brief pride in the elevation of their admired commander, they did not yet know that he had been dead for thirty-six hours.[33]

On the 10th, reveille sounded early and the men got a quick breakfast while the quartermaster sergeant hastily issued new supplies. One would think that the soldiers would have greeted Howard Prince warmly that morning, since he had managed to obtain a wagonload of new shoes for the regiment, especially since a large part of the army was then oozing shoeless through the mud. Despite his success in acquiring the goods, however, he was hardly met with overwhelming gratitude. "[T]he shoes," he remembered, "were the usual collection of misfits, none of them were big enough for Company B, and if adjectives were bullets the Quartermaster Sergeant would have been better off in front of the 15th Alabama."[34]

Clad in their new brogans, the regiment stepped off again on the march at 6 o'clock, shortly passing over Antietam Creek. When they reached the pike that ran between Sharpsburg and Hagerstown, they turned southwest and as they came upon Union cavalry pickets Colonel Chamberlain ordered Company E forward as skirmishers, anticipating the enemy in front. While part of the regiment remained in reserve, the rest of it, along with other parts of the brigade, advanced in line of battle to see what lay ahead.[35]

The sun had passed its crest by now and the skirmishers out in front opened a fire that continued for half the afternoon. It was not much really—

compared to Little Round Top it was nothing—but the capture of a few prisoners and the waste of a couple hundred cartridges cost Company E two lives and six men captured before they bivouacked in the woods for the night with pickets on the pike.[36]

That afternoon, Thomas Townsend, one of four 2nd Maine transfers who continued to refuse to accept their situation in a new regiment, finally took his rifle and his place in the skirmish line with Company E. Since their involuntary transfer, the 2nd Mainers had borne their share of fighting. Sixty-eight of them fought on the spur where four were killed, five others wounded, and one captured. That July 10, Townsend sustained a mortal wound in the skirmish on the pike, and he and Sgt. Gardner Schwartz became the last two casualties of the regiment in the Gettysburg Campaign. Townsend died three days later, and Colonel Chamberlain recommended to Colonel Rice that he drop the charges against him, clearing his record.[37]

✠ ✠ ✠

By practical standards, the skirmish at Sharpsburg Pike signaled the close of the Gettysburg Campaign for the 20th Maine, at least as far as the killing and wounding were concerned. The dying, however, took far longer. When the regiment marched away from Gettysburg it left behind eight men who had yet to succumb to their mortal wounds. The same day the regiment closed out the campaign's fighting on the pike one of these, Willard Buxton of Company K, became the 20th's thirty-third fatality from the fight on the spur. Buxton took a bullet in the left arm while fighting on the right of the regiment eight days earlier and he had languished in the temporary hospitals ever since. On the 10th, he joined comrades from throughout the Fifth Corps in the growing hospital cemetery near the farm of Michael Fiscel.

Working among the wounded immediately after the battle, John Chamberlain had marveled at how well soldiers coped with their condition. Some of them, knowing they could not survive, thought only of their comrades, telling surgeons to give their attention to those who could still be saved. Others bore the agony with the patience of Job. "It is surprising how soldiers bear up," John remembered. "They will never believe their cases utterly hopeless. They think 'it is not so bad as it seems—I shall get well.' I have seen them walking round with broken skulls, with eyes and part of the face gone, with balls in their bodies and through them. Well Bill you got it this time. 'Well I reckon, a scratch or so, how do you come off old chap?' They are all very patient and uncomplaining."[38]

For many, the experience of the first few days was only the beginning of a long and painful ordeal. Their suffering was eased somewhat by an army of care-givers who descended on the field hospitals shortly after news of the

Mrs. Isabella Fogg

battle tapped the telegraph paddles in Washington. Isabella Fogg, a Maine woman who had become famous in the army and whom Colonel Chamberlain labeled an "Angel of Mercy" for her self-devised efforts to care for the soldiers, arrived on the field and was plying her volunteer trade among the wounded almost before the last shot was fired. Fogg had been in Frederick with a load of supplies sent her from the Maine Camp Hospital Association, a Portland aid society she helped establish, when she heard of the carnage in the Pennsylvania crossroad town. Leaving supplies with someone who promised to forward them, she hurried to Gettysburg and began gathering what she could from neighboring farms, putting them to whatever use she came upon.[39]

J.B. Wescott, sent from the regiment by Colonel Chamberlain to render what aid he could to the Maine wounded, remembered having to forage about the countryside in search of food for himself and those in his care. The local citizens were helpful, baking bread and offering what they could, while Mrs. Fogg lit a fire and started an impromptu soup kitchen, cooking and serving farina gruel, beef tea, hot coffee, and hard tack in abundance. Wescott recalled that conditions improved greatly a few days after the battle when representatives of the formal relief organizations arrived and helped reorganize the wounded into more sanitary tent hospitals.[40]

C.C. Hayes was an agent of the state government who focused his energy, and supplies sent from communities, on Maine soldiers in need. Hayes worked through the Maine Soldiers Relief Agency to monitor the distribution of supplies, both private and public, and report back to the governor on the condition of Maine troops. People like Hayes, and representatives of the U.S. Sanitary and Christian Commissions, voluntarily endured the miserable and emotionally draining conditions around these hospitals for a month until the Medical Corps could establish a cleaner more efficient general hospital called Camp Letterman near both the railroad and the York Pike.[41]

One of these relief workers, the Rev. R.J. Parvin, oversaw the work of the Christian Commission at the Fifth Corps hospital. Several months after the war he addressed a national meeting of the commission at the Capitol in

Washington, and he related a sad story which he brought away from his days at Gettysburg. Parvin remembered that orderlies of the Ambulance Corps brought the 20th's Capt. Charles Billings to an old barn along with sixty-five of the worst cases. Billings lay among other men of his regiment and as they began to die around him he became such a "raving maniac" that four or five men had to restrain him. After a struggle, they got him to a room by himself where he calmed, and even improved for a while.[42]

In the hours that followed, a surgeon came to assess Billings' condition and his prognosis was poor. Billings' leg wound was most certainly fatal, though a primary amputation on the field might have saved him days before. Billings gave Parvin a message for his wife and asked him to see that his body was embalmed and sent back to Maine. He then asked Parvin to minister to the other suffering men, sparing a few moments now and again to return and read some scripture to him. At about 11 o'clock on the morning of July 15, Billings died, and a few hours later Parvin sent his body to the embalmers. That night, as Parvin sat writing letters in his tent, Billings' brother knocked and entered, asking for the departed captain. The brother had come all the way from Maine with the captain's wife, so that she could see and care for her wounded husband. Parvin told him the sad news and reluctantly took on the unenviable task of traveling into the town to inform Billings' wife and offer his condolensces. The wife and brother took the body home to Maine where it was buried in the family plot.[43]

✠ ✠ ✠

Confederates who fell wounded into the hands of the enemy also found surprisingly good care and often good conversation among their captors. Before stretcher bearers from the Ambulance Corps could remove the wounded from the aid station in the sheltered nook on Little Round Top, many of the Maine men lay beside Alabama casualties at whom they had been shooting only minutes before. Among these was John Kennedy of Company G, who suffered a painful wound on the inside of his thigh. Lying with the fallen of both sides, Kennedy shared a conversation with Lieutenant Colonel Bulger, whose wound had not weakened him so much that he could not have a word with passing strangers. Bulger assessed the outcome of the battle to Kennedy saying, "I thought I had you, but to my great surprise, you had me." Apparently, Bulger's lung wound did little to diminish his ability to expel hot air. A few days later, Bulger bragged to C.C Hayes, the Maine relief agent, that he had been wounded at Cedar Mountain by the 10th Maine and, mistakenly, that he had met the 20th at Fredericksburg before they captured him at Gettysburg. "He is fully convinced," Hayes wrote his governor, "that the Maine soldiers are thorough fighters and not easily whipped."[44]

Bulger was not the only Alabama officer who found good care in the hands of the enemy. William Oates left his brother John for dead on Little Round Top, but John Oates survived the battle and found care in the hospital of the Second Division of the Fifth Corps, under the supervision of a Doctor Reed, surgeon of the 155th Pennsylvania. Reed's wife, sister-in-law, and a friend took pity on Oates and Lt. "Bud" Cody, who lay beside him in the hospital tent, reading to them and providing what little delicacies they could find in the field hospital regions. On July 23, Cody succumbed to his wounds and, two days later, as the sun set on the fields southeast of Gettysburg, John Oates passed as well. When it was clear that his death was imminent, the women sang two hymns at his request, and with his last few breaths he asked them, "Tell my folks at home that I died in the arms of friends."[45]

Nearly two months after the battle, Colonel Oates and the men of Company G of the 15th Alabama continued to struggle with the loss of their top three officers. In late August, Oates received a letter from another member of the regiment in the same hospital which confirmed that Cody and John Oates were gone. On August 30 Oates wrote a letter of condolence to the Rev. Edmond Cody, the lieutenant's father, expressing his grief. "I feel discomfitted and exceedingly gloomy," he wrote, "even reckless and miserable. I have not only lost my dearest relative on earth, but two of my dearest friends." To ease their grief, and express their feelings toward their departed officers, the men of Company G held a formal meeting at which they passed a resolution praising Brainard, Oates, and Cody. They sent the resolution to two newspapers back home where it was published.[46]

More than thirty years after the war, William Oates received a letter from Dr. Reed describing the last days that his brother had lived. "He says that he died happy," remembered Oates of the letter, "and without regret, except that he was far from home and relatives, and among strangers and enemies in war." While most of the dead were simply buried in unmarked graves with no more than their clothes, the good doctor had Oates and Cody buried in coffins, marking the spot with wooden head boards. Thanks to Reed's careful attention, the bodies were later identified and reinterred at Hollywood Cemetery in Richmond.[47]

Like Oates and Cody, many wounded Confederates who were not able to move found care in Union field hospitals. As soon as they could move, the Medical Corps transferred many of them to hospitals in the North set aside for the care of Confederate casualties. Those who recovered somewhat, but whose wounds had obviously ended their war days, were exchanged for Union prisoners in similar condition. The unwounded Southern prisoners at Gettysburg, or those at least in good enough condition to walk, marched under guard of Union cavalry and infantry to Baltimore. There, they remained at Fort McHenry a few days before transports carried them out to an island prison known as Fort Delaware. Later in the year, authorities transferred a number of them to Point Lookout in Maryland.[48]

James McGuire was a 22-year-old Irishman who had been in the United States only two years when he enlisted in Company H of the 15th Alabama. When the 20th Maine desended upon his retreating regiment, he was among those captured and sent to a Federal prison. McGuire, along with nearly two dozen others from the 15th and two from the 47th, found their confinement in Fort Delaware where soldiers endured an endless number of privations and miseries, including lice, rats, and filthy water which guards sometimes supplemented with sea water. In a postwar reminiscence, McGuire described life in the prison.

> Day after day, from morning until night, (we had) a never ceasing hunger from the lack of sufficient food, and this with an almost passionate thirst for palatable water, our scant clothing, the terrible cold of winter with a single stove for warming hundreds of men, and our nights passed on bunks unimproved with straw, our only covering a single blanket, with the cold air piercing us through and through, making our sleep a matter of fits and starts.[49]

Even daily necessities became an adventure. As McGuire pointed out, likely in a propagandized postwar exaggeration, men who dawdled on a trip to the sinks quite often found a Yankee bullet hurrying toward them on their belated return. "Nearly every prisoner killed at Fort Delaware," he recalled, "was in going to or coming from the sinks."[50]

Miserable conditions did not dampen the Rebel spirit of most of the prisoners, nor did it diminish their dedication to the Confederacy. During their internment, the Union authorities convinced or coerced enough men to desert toward the Federal side that they formed two companies of cavalry, sending them to serve on the plains out west. "No words can describe the utter contempt," McGuire grumbled, "with which all true Confederates at Ft. Delaware looked upon these galvanized Yankees." Inmates viewed with the same sort of disgust men whom they called renegades. When these inmates committed crimes against their former comrades in arms—one North Carolina man reportedly killed eight fellow inmates—prisoners formed kangaroo courts and meted out other forms of prison justice.[51]

Life at Fort Delaware apparently did not dull the fighting spirit of some men, either. Even though the punishment for fighting was hanging by the thumbs for an hour or more, guards could not prevent outbreaks of fisticuffs, or worse. Perhaps the most severe of these scraps took place between two men of the 15th Alabama when John McLeod and Ned Swinny took to each

113

other one day. Swinny, the larger man, was getting the better of his opponent when McLeod grabbed a piece of iron and thumped it against the head of his adversary, who died from the blow a few weeks later.[52]

Escape from the prison was a difficult but not impossible enterprise. Occasionally, the prisoners would receive word that one of their own had strapped empty canteens around himself for buoyancy and had floated out into the bay. According to these reports, some men drowned, others were recaptured, but a few lucky ones found refuge aboard a passing ship whose crew held sympathies for the South.[53]

Escape was also not impossible for the half dozen captured Alabamians imprisoned at Point Lookout, on the southernmost tip of Maryland's western shore. Here, Confederate prisoners were aware that barely eight miles of the Chesapeake Bay separated them from Virginia. From time to time the guards allowed prisoners to go outside of the enclosure on the point and down to the beach to bathe. Occasionally, a barrel or box would drift by and one of the prisoners would seize the opportunity to hide himself, floating beyond the reach of the guards before escaping into the woods.[54]

Of the thirty men from both Alabama regiments who ended up at Point Lookout or Fort Delaware, eighteen died in prison. Only one third that many men from the 20th endured prison life as payment for their participation in the entire Gettysburg Campaign, and at least five of these died in captivity. Alvin Cutler, William Davis, and Lewis Flanders, all privates in Company E captured at Sharpsburg Pike, were among the first Union occupants of the Confederate prison at Andersonville, Georgia. All three died of dysentery, diarrhea or both within a span of ten days in March 1864 and were buried in the cemetery there ahead of six more of the regiment who later followed. Two other captive Mainers died before Andersonville opened. Charles Beadle of Company B and John Lenfest of Company E both died in Richmond prisons.[55]

Lenfest was a 40-year-old farmer when he volunteered in the summer of 1862. He left his wife and children behind in Union to join the 20th but kept in touch with regular letters to and from home. On July 9, Private Lenfest scribbled a short note to his wife, apologizing for its brevity. It was the last time she ever heard from him.[56]

The next day, the Rebels captured Lenfest and five other privates from Company E on the Sharpsburg Pike and sent them down to Richmond. In prison, Lenfest fell ill in the winter of 1863 and developed chronic diarrhea. On January 31, 1864, he was admitted to the Confederate States Military Prisoners Hospital in Richmond, but too late. He died that same day having outlived another 20th Maine captive, George Leach, by two months. The passing of these two prisoners marked the forty-fourth and forty-fifth fatalities that the Gettysburg Campaign had wrought in the regiment. But while the activities of the campaign itself had come to a close, the effect of this three-week period would have a profound impact on the participants for decades to come.[57]

5 In Great Deeds Something Abides

Fighting and destruction are terrible but are sometimes agencies of heavenly rather than hellish powers. War is for participants a test of character; it makes bad men worse and good men better.[1]

Joshua Chamberlain, 1913

The close of the Gettysburg Campaign hardly meant the end of its influence over the soldiers who survived the fight for Vincent's Spur. On the contrary, veterans of the three regiments found that the fight, which lasted little more than ninety minutes, continued to have an impact on their lives for decades. But, in the months immediately after Gettysburg, veterans viewed the battle on the spur as having no greater significance for the cause of either side than any other portion of the battle, and their thoughts turned to engagements yet to come.

The 20th Maine never recovered, numerically, from the losses it sustained at Gettysburg. Though it participated in every major engagement of the Army of the Potomac through the surrender, it was seldom more than half the size it had been before Little Round Top. After helping to thwart Lee's invasion of Pennsylvania the surviving Maine men, sporadically reinforced by recruits, took part in fourteen more battles and skirmishes. When the fighting was done, they stood in formation at Appomattox Court House while their opponents from so many battles lay down their arms, including more than 270 men of the 15th and

47th Alabama. In two and a half years of service, 1,621 men served in the 20th Maine, 147 of them dying in battle or of wounds. One less than that died of disease while fifteen perished in Confederate prisons.[2]

Little more than a month after Gettysburg, Joshua Chamberlain reached the limit of his physical and mental endurance and sought medical treatment for the effects of the campaign, most notably stress and a fever that had lingered since mid-June. Surgeons who examined him in Washington determined that he needed an extended rest at home, so they issued him a fifteen-day sick leave and he returned to Brunswick.[3]

Shortly after his return to the army his division commander gave him command of the Third Brigade when Colonel Rice left for a new assignment as a brigadier general in the First Corps. In the months that followed, Chamberlain's poor health affected him greatly, and he drifted back and forth between sick leave in Washington and brigade command with the army. In June 1864 he commanded the First Brigade of his old division in an ill-fated charge on Confederate works near Petersburg, Virginia, at a place known as Rives' Salient. Realizing the futility of the charge General Meade had ordered, Chamberlain chose to lead the assault himself, and he did so on foot to avoid being too tempting a target. His bravery resulted in a severe wound when a bullet entered his right hip, tearing through him until it struck his left hip bone. The wound very nearly caused his death and he was reported dead in Northern newspapers before he went back to Annapolis, Washington, and eventually Brunswick to recover.[4]

By early spring of 1865, Chamberlain was back at the head of his troops with a promotion to brigadier general, personally authorized by Gen. U. S. Grant while the fighting professor lay, apparently dying, near Petersburg. During the last few weeks of the war a weary and worn Chamberlain made a remarkable record for himself that far exceeded his efforts at Gettysburg both in military leadership and personal bravery. His behavior so impressed General Grant that he chose Chamberlain above all the other generals of the army to command the Union troops at the formal surrender of Lee's army. At the surrender, Chamberlain established himself as both a heroic and sympathetic figure when he ordered his men to silent attention as each Confederate unit surrendered its arms and battle flags.[5]

After the war, Chamberlain returned to Maine where he was elected governor for four consecutive one-year terms and then became president of Bowdoin College. He was an eloquent speaker, seldom passing up an opportunity to address a crowd on matters of religious, civic, and especially war-related issues. After retiring from Bowdoin, he was unsuccessful in a number of business ventures and served as the politically appointed surveyor of the port of Portland, where he died in 1914.[6]

Two months after marching back into Virginia with the rest of Lee's army, the 15th Alabama moved west with two divisions of Longstreet's Corps to relieve the Confederate army near Chattanooga, Tennessee. They fought in the battles of Chickamauga and Knoxville before returning east where they remained, fighting in Lee's army from the Wilderness to Appommatox. In all 1,612 men served in the 15th Alabama, of which 279 were killed or died of wounds. Another 459 died of disease and a few dozen more while in Union prisons.[7]

Colonel William Oates went to Tennessee still in command of his regiment. He led them into a fight near Brown's Ferry in Lookout Valley when, like his Maine counterpart from Little Round Top, he took a bullet through the right hip as well. Two days later, he reached Eufala, Alabama, by train. The wound was still not dressed or cared for, but he found relief at the home of a Colonel Toney. Not only did Oates regain his health, but he became so attracted to the colonel's daughter that he later married her. In March 1864 he returned to his regiment, serving at the head of the 15th another three months before he lost his colonelcy to a political move by an underling and President Davis made him colonel of the 48th Alabama. In August he was wounded again during a fight at Fussell's Mill in Virginia and surgeons removed his shattered right arm. Months later Oates returned home, his service, in this war at least, at an end.[8]

The service of Oates' other Gettysburg regiment, the 47th Alabama, mirrored that of the 15th for the next year and a half in fighting at Chickamauga, Knoxville, the Wilderness, and Spotsylvania. By October 1864 the regiment was no more than a strong company of men and though it retreated with Lee to Appomattox, it was not actively engaged after the fight at Darbytown Road early that month. During the war 969 men served in the 47th, of whom 110 died in battle or of wounds and 256 of disease. Fifty-seven were captured and not exchanged and an unknown number of these also died in service.[9]

Michael Bulger made an unlikely recovery from his Little Round Top wound but remained a captive in several Union prisons before being exchanged while at Johnson's Island in April 1864. Unable to continue service, he went home with a leave of absence later that year, was elected to the state senate, and continued there until the Federal army took the state government back from the Confederacy.[10]

✠ ✠ ✠

Many of the Alabama soldiers did not remain in the Deep South after the surrender. Returning from the war to find their slaves freed and their communities irrevocably altered, a large number moved to Texas or South America. Many of those who remained in Alabama served in public office and chief among these was the colonel of the unit. After the war, Oates not only remained in the state that he had fought for—indeed, given his right arm for—but he represented it in the United States Congress for fourteen years and served one term as governor. His loyalty to his original country and government apparently restored, he served as a brigadier general in the war with Spain in 1898.[11]

In 1905 he expressed the sentiments of a reconstructed Rebel. "It is settled," he wrote. "Let the errors and wrongs of that great conflict and the noble, chivalrous deeds and patient suffering of both sides live alone in history, and let all patriotically join in making and keeping the United States Government—in all the elements of justice, fraternity and durability—the greatest government on earth, and ever remain a blessing to mankind." Years before this he had apparently reconciled himself to the result of the war. In 1897 he wrote to Joshua Chamberlain, explaining that "it looks to me like it was written in the book of fate that the Confederacy was doomed never to become an independent government and I suppose that it was best that it should not."[12]

Unlike Oates, Michael Bulger was unsuccessful in politics after the war. In 1866 he ran for governor with a conservative wing of the Democratic party and lost. It is possible that his war record could not overcome the feelings in Alabama over his refusal to sign the Ordinance of Secession in 1861. He was one of three members of the Secession Convention who would not sign the document which seperated Alabama from the Union, and when he would not, a mob of four or five hundred men gathered outside the hall determined to lynch him. Bulger told the mob that a man who would not vote the wishes of his constituents deserved to be hanged, and that they should do it if they were willing. They did not, of course, but his display of bravery won their admiration. Nonetheless, he was permanently labeled as a man against secession, and he was unable to redeem his statewide political reputation with a glorious military victory, at Gettysburg or on any other field. He was, however, able to gain reelection to the state senate to fill a vacancy and he served in the last session under Reconstruction, which he thoroughly opposed.[13]

While many, like Oates, parlayed their war service into postwar political success, honorable service for the Confederacy was by no means a prerequisite to election. Given the nature of the hardships endured by Confederate soldiers, particularly toward the close of the war, Southern-

120

ers did not always shun men whose military service was below par. On rare occasions, some of these men even managed to win election or appointment to public office. The most outrageous example of a shirker turned public servant may well be Charles Raleigh of Oates' original Company G of the 15th Alabama. Raleigh was a boy of 17 when he enlisted in 1861, and his appearance made him seem even younger. According to Oates he served adequately through the first year of the war but afterward became adept at avoiding battles through one method or another. His luck ran out at Gettysburg when Union soldiers took him prisoner, though no one in the company seemed to remember that he had gone into the fight. Some time later, a letter arrived in the regiment reporting his death in prison. Knowing of Raleigh's cunning and surmising that he had probably written it himself, the captain had the clerk mark him simply as absent.[14]

After the war, he told old comrades how he had remained a prisoner until after the war. He lived in Texas for a time before returning to Coffee County, Alabama, where he took on a new life. Raleigh changed his name to Ben Stevens and assumed the persona of an Irish ditcher. As Oates remembered, "He could tell those people down there all about the bogs of Conenaugh and many good old Irish tales." Raleigh (or Stevens) studied law, passed the bar and was elected county solicitor, then state representative. His work at the Capitol so impressed the governor at that time that he appointed Stevens to fill the vacant judge of probate seat in his county.[15]

Raleigh must have thought the jig was up when the time came for reelection to the judgeship. His opponent in the contest not only found out his real name and past, but also that he was wanted in Texas for horse-stealing. Raleigh hired the old major of the 15th, DeBernier Waddell, as his attorney, went back to face the charges, and was found not guilty. At the next election for judge of probate, he received nearly all the votes. He completed his conversion soon after when he got himself ordained a Baptist minister and, by all accounts, served his congregation well.[16]

While the war may have played a role in setting Raleigh on the straight and narrow—and it certainly mellowed William Oates a mite—other veterans struggled to make the transition from harsh military campaigns to peaceful communities. John T. McLeod of Company H is an example of the latter. McLeod was captured at Little Round Top, and while in prison he fought with, and caused the death of Ned Swinny, another member of the 15th captured at Gettysburg. McLeod was released after the war ended and returned to Dale County, Alabama, where he married and settled on a farm. Some time later, he got into another fight, again causing the death of his opponent, after which he removed to Florida.[17]

✠ ✠ ✠

The experience of Gettysburg, and the war in general, had a great impact on the men from Maine as well. Beginning shortly after the fight ended, relationships between the men took on new meaning as the gravity of the events came into focus. The first and perhaps the most noticeable change took place between the 20th Maine and the man who molded them into soldiers. From the moment Adelbert Ames got word of his former regiment's behavior in battle at Gettysburg the relationship between the Maine soldiers and their first commander became one of fond remembrance. It was a remarkable turnabout for both parties. No more than eight months had passed since a group of officers in winter camp had plotted to have Ames replaced. By summer's end, however, just a few weeks after surviving the great battle, the officers of the 20th gave Ames a sword, belt, and sash as a gift of appreciation for what they now realized he had done for them. Ames replied, expressing his gratitude. "Coming as it does from a regiment which knows no superior either on the battlefield or else-where—from one towards which I entertain the most profound senti-ments of pride and affection—it causes greater pleasure than I can express." A year earlier, Ames had viewed with disgust the collection of green volunteers who crowded into Camp Mason near Portland, calling it a *hell* of a regiment. After Gettysburg, he could accurately make the same remark, but with a decidedly different tone. "[The gift] will ever remind me," he told them, "of the noble deeds of its donors and will recall the battles in which they have borne so prominent parts."[18]

The fondness between them never seemed to wane. A few months after the battle, the 20th's flag had become too tattered for service and when a new one arrived in camp they sent the old one to Ames. Their first colonel cherished the gift for years after the war, graciously returning the tattered national colors to the regimental association when they met in reunion. Decades later, a few weeks before the fiftieth anniversary of the Battle of Gettysburg, Ellis Spear paid a fitting tribute to his first commander in the *National Tribune*, a paper read and written by Civil War veterans. In writing an article called, "The Left at Gettysburg," Spear could not help but take note of a man who, though not with the regiment on the spur, had as great an impact on the outcome as any man. "Adelbert Ames, though young, was a trained soldier, with the original instincts of a soldier, and his firm and made skillful discipline and instruction had made out of the original town-meeting enlisted men of the 20th M[ain]e a regiment which was always ready to charge, and whose line, in three years of active service, from Antietam to Appomattox, never was broken." Ames served as governor and U.S. senator from Mississippi during Reconstruction before settling in Lowell, Massachusetts, with his wife, the daughter of Union general Benjamin Butler. He died in 1933 at the age of 98, the last surviving general on either side in the Civil War.[19]

✠ ✠ ✠

At least one young man found maturity in his war service, due perhaps, in no small part to the fight for the spur. Henry Sidelinger, the freckle-faced farm boy from Union, Maine, who commanded Company E at Gettysburg, compiled a solid record for himself after that battle, eventually rising to the rank of brevet major. Months after Little Round Top, he convinced his brother Jacob to join the regiment and the younger Sidelinger arrived at the warfront in December 1863. Jacob was wounded in the Battle of the Wilderness and met his death at the Battle of Five Forks, just eight days before Lee surrendered at Appomattox.[20]

As many as six Sidelinger brothers served in various Maine units during the war, two at Gettysburg. One of them, Manuel Sidelinger, helped slow the Confederate advance toward his brother Henry on Little Round Top while fighting with the 4th Maine in the Devil's Den. The patriarch of the family, George W. Sidelinger, applied for a postwar pension based on the claim that his departed son Jacob was to have provided him support in his later years. Apparently, he expected the government to believe that the other sons had deserted him in his old age, which they had not. It took many years, but the government finally agreed, and in 1888 he received a pension check amounting to twelve dollars per month. The first payment was retroactive back to the war so that the check totalled more than $2,300. In 1870 the entire Sidelinger farm was worth less than half that.[21]

The war struck hard on many families from the Sidelinger's village of Union. Nearly half of the five hundred men in the town between 15 and 50 years old enlisted in some unit during the war. Their absence left the farming community without a great deal of its agricultural labor force and reduced the town council's ability to collect tax revenues. This was a blow for a town also trying to provide soldiers' bounties reaching as high as three hundred dollars per man. Making their contribution to the war effort drained the resources of small communities considerably, and when the war created even greater demands in the form of widows,

Mrs. Lavinnia Lenfest

orphans, and disabled veterans, the victims found very little left for their needs.[22]

Lavinnia Lenfest and her family were among these victims of war and in her case the workings of the Federal government did not provide as they did for the Sidelingers. Regimental records showed Lavinnia's husband, John, "missing in action" after the 20th Maine's July 10 skirmish on the Sharpsburg Pike. Unknown to his wife or his regiment, Private Lenfest was among the other Union prisoners at Libby Prison in Richmond from which news and correspondence seldom traveled, especially concerning enlisted men. Though it was obvious to the other men in his company, no one could prove with certainty that Lenfest was a prisoner. Without credible word that he was in Confederate hands, the government could not officially list him as such, so Mrs. Lenfest was ineligible for his pay or a pension. Living in a small community already strapped by the war, and unable to work the farm alone or obtain help from the government, she found it impossible to hold her family together.[23]

To keep them clothed and fed, Lenfest boarded the children out to other homes from which they faithfully mailed what money they could spare to their mother. The community helped as well, though she was far from the only woman in need during the war. Townspeople took up a collection for her while women of the community provided some food and second-hand clothing for the children. Even the local Odd Fellows Lodge gave a small donation. In time the state provided aid to families in this condition but it was a small amount and eventually discontinued.[24]

No family was immune from the effects of war, including those which stemmed from the Battle of Gettysburg. In 1865 John Chamberlain suffered a hemorrhage in his lungs which the family attributed to an illness he had contracted while visiting the army in 1863. He recovered from the hemorrhage but his health failed again two years later, and he died in 1867. If the family suspicions were correct, then John was not just the only Chamberlain brother not engaged at Little Round Top but, ironically, he was also the only one to die as a result of the Gettysburg Campaign.[25]

Unlike his older brother Joshua, Tom Chamberlain did not revel in the memory of Gettysburg, though he certainly earned the right to bask in the glow of that triumph, given his courageous conduct there. He was not a regular attendee at regimental reunions and did not attend the dedication of the 20th Maine monuments in 1889. If Tom ever visited Gettysburg at all after the war, he left no record of it. Shortly after the war he moved to Brooklyn, New York, worked a while for his brother John as a clerk and then on his own after John returned to Maine and passed away.[26]

Three years after John's death, Tom married his widow, Delia Jarvis, who had been far better off with the first brother. Tom never found the success and self-satisfaction in private life that he had experienced in the army. After their marriage, he lived in Washington and worked at the Pension Office while Delia stayed in Maine with so little support from her absent husband that she had to seek aid from his family in Brewer. For some reason, or perhaps many of them, Tom never recovered from the war, despite his successful military record. At least he succeeded at nothing afterward. Joshua helped him find work in Florida, but what business associates called "strange and unbusinesslike behavior," coupled with "laziness" prevented his success. Members of the family expressed deep concern in later years for his behavior and health, particularly as he was too often prone to excessive drinking. In the summer of 1896, suffering from heart and lung ailments, Tom died at the age of 55.[27]

Experience in the war, of which Gettysburg was no small part, affected Andrew Tozier in quite the opposite way. Tozier was typical of the men who led a hard transient life prior to becoming soldiers but settled down after the war, perhaps having purged some anger from their system. As a young man, he ran away from home and an abusive alcoholic father and, like so many other wayward boys in Maine at that time, he took to the sea. In 1861 he returned home, enlisted in the 2nd Maine, and served honorably even after his transfer to the 20th Maine. When Joshua Chamberlain tried to replace the officers he had lost on the spur at Gettysburg, he remembered Tozier's bravery in battle and recommended him for promotion to lieutenant. The next day, at Tozier's request, Chamberlain rescinded the recommendation. Two months before his enlistment ran out, Tozier was shot above the left temple at a fight on the North Anna in May 1864. Surgeons removed fragments of the ball months later, but the lingering effects—ringing ears, dizziness, headaches—remained with him for decades.[28]

When his term of service expired in July 1864, Tozier returned to Maine, married, and had a son. Not long after the war ended, he and his new family lived with his former colonel in his Brunswick home during Chamberlain's service as governor. The Toziers named their only other child Gracie, most likely in honor of the Chamberlains' daughter Grace. In time, the Tozier family moved to the area where Andrew was born, settling on a small farm. They grew vegetables, sold a little milk, and lived quietly into the latter part of the century. In 1898, thanks to the belated recommendation of his former colonel and landlord, Tozier received the Congressional Medal of Honor for distinguished conduct at the Battle of Gettysburg. Recommending him for the medal, Chamberlain called his former color sergeant, "An example of all that was excellent in a soldier," and "One of the bravest and most deserving men." In March 1910 Tozier died in his Litchfield home while his passing went almost unnoticed except by his family.[29]

The two men who stood in front of Tozier and his flag on Little Round Top and survived returned home to live relatively unremarkable lives as well. Elisha Coan was little more than a child when he entered the service in 1862, but his years in the war changed his outlook in two ways. For him, Gettysburg was a rite of passage, a test of his manhood in a society that placed great importance on "manliness" and the courage which only military combat could elicit. "[U]ntil then," he remembered, "I did not think it possible that I could stand up in 'open field' under such a fire [and] take deliberate aim, and so it is, we know not what we are capable of until we are actually brought into circumstances that will try us."[30]

With so many Bowdoin men in the 20th Maine, it would have been hard for a soldier not to harbor aspirations of one day attending the alma mater of Hawthorne and Longfellow. After the war, Coan measured this against the gruesome scenes of wounded that he had experienced during and after battles and enrolled at Bowdoin Medical College, graduating in 1870. Dr. Coan was an active contributor to soldiers' debates in both the *Lincoln County News* and the *National Tribune* and around 1885 he wrote a long and interesting account of the battle for Vincent's Spur. At each Gettysburg reunion of the regiment, Elisha Coan posed for photos clutching the battle flag he had defended in 1863.[31]

Holman Melcher, Sam Keene's first lieutenant in Company F, found a vocation in his war service. He became adjutant of the regiment three weeks after Gettysburg and a year later took command of Company F when a sniper's bullet found Keene at Petersburg. Returning from a severe wound at Spotsylvania, Melcher's reputation for efficiency helped him gain appointment as postmaster of the Fifth Corps. In time, he became aide-de-camp on the staff of two corps commanders.[32]

Melcher had nearly completed his coursework at the Maine State Seminary—now Bates College—when he enlisted as a private in Company B in 1862. As it turned out, the war permanently deferred his graduation from the seminary but not to his detriment. Quite the contrary, Melcher's experience at helping move mail, supplies, and paperwork through the Army of the Potomac proved to be a more practical education. In the last year of the war he recorded that he used his spare time, "in reading and studying Bookeeping. I am having a fine opportunity for mental improvement and let me be wise and improve it as I should."[33]

Following the war Melcher settled in Portland where he became a highly successful wholesale grocer, moving produce with the same skill and efficiency that had caught the attention of his superiors during the war. In 1889 and 1890 he served two terms as mayor of Portland, Maine's largest city and a growing industrial center. By the turn of the century, Portland Wholesale Grocers and Flour Dealers Association, formerly H. S. Melcher & Company, served customers in three states from its own five-story building on Portland's waterfront. His comrades in the 20th Maine respected him highly as well, electing him as the first president of the regimental association, a post he filled through most of the organization's existence until he died of Brights disease in 1905.[34]

Not all of the Maine men, however, found that war service could lead to a vocation. Like Coan and Melcher, William Livermore found the experience of the war was a wondrous and horrible adventure but unlike his comrades it turned out to be little more than an interruption of his quiet rural life. The old corporal returned to Milo, Maine, when the war ended and filled his years on a modest farm. He seldom spoke, and never publicly wrote, of his war experiences, attended only one regimental reunion, and died in 1912 with a modest $5,000 to his name.[35]

Not having been with Coan, Livermore, and the rest of the regiment on Little Round Top seems not to have stopped at least one veteran from reaping the benefits of the honor. In 1883 Pvt. Theodore Gerrish, formerly of Company F and then a minister in Maine, included a detailed account of the battle of Little Round Top in a book he published called *Army Life: A Private's Reminiscences of the Civil War*. The story of the 20th's experience at Gettysburg is told in the third person, not surprising considering Gerrish's service record later revealed that he was in Philadelphia when the battle took place. Joshua Chamberlain apparently struggled over the issue of whether to include Gerrish's name among the participants in *Maine at Gettysburg*. In March 1897 he asked Albert Fernald if he knew of any proof that Gerrish had been on Little Round

Top, to which Fernald replied, "Gerrish is not reported in Co. H at Gettysburg. I have just looked over again." Nonetheless, when Chamberlain submitted the final list to the Maine at Gettysburg Commission, the good Reverend Gerrish's name was among those in Company H.[36]

Gerrish's words did two things of significance to the legend of Little Round Top. First, he set a tone for the future writings on the subject when he exaggerated the importance of the 20th's victory. Not only did he elevate the odds to great heights, estimating ten Confederates to every Mainer, he set a tone that raised circumstances on the spur to mythical proportions. "Stand firm ye boys from Maine," he wrote, "for not once in a century are men permitted to bear such responsibility for freedom and justice, for God and humanity as are now placed upon you."[37]

While Gerrish's account may have helped set in motion the building of a legend, it also raised the ire of more than a few veterans of the regiment when it was published. The most controversial statement made in the book suggested that the regiment hesitated when the final charge on Vincent's Spur began. "I do not dishonor those brave men," he said, "when I write that for a brief moment the order was not obeyed, and the little line seemed to quail under the fearful fire that was being poured upon it." He went on to say that it was only the bravery of Lt. Holman Melcher of Company F that initiated the charge. When a portion of Gerrish's account appeared in a Portland newspaper, mostly as a tribute to businessman Melcher, it was too much for some of the survivors of the battle to endure. James Nichols, who had commanded Company K on the right, a few feet from Melcher, wrote for many of them when he fired off an angry retort in the form of a letter to Gerrish published in the *Lincoln County News*.[38]

Nichols did not spare the rod on his old comrade, calling Gerrish's account of Gettysburg, "a work of fiction," respectfully denying the "imputation of cowardice," contained therein. Not only did the men not hesitate, by Nichols' estimation they acted before Chamberlain's command. "[B]efore the completion of the order, it was anticipated by them, and when the order to 'Charge' was given, they were already on the move, and the officer who could get in front of them must have been exceedingly alert in his movements." The article appeared to a national audience in November 1882 on the pages of the *National Tribune*. Half a decade later, the furor over these issues had not completely passed, and Joshua Chamberlain felt compelled to address them in his speech at the dedication of the monument on the spur in 1889. "I am sorry to have heard it intimated," he said, "that any hesitated when that order was given. That was not so...Nobody hesitated to obey the order. In fact, it was never given, or but imperfectly."[39]

Gerrish's "fiction" was not the only topic hotly contested in the pages of the *Lincoln County News* during the 1880s. Samuel Miller, who fought as a private in Company E at Gettysburg, owned the paper at that time and the veterans liked to use it as a sort of gossip fence over which they swapped tales and debated issues, some more significant than others. A typical exchange took place in 1883 over the question of what order the regiments of Vincent's Brigade marched from the Wheat Field to Little Round Top and why Colonel Vincent placed them as he did. It began when a veteran, signing his letter, "Rear Rank," inquired how the 20th Maine ended up on the left of the brigade on Little Round Top, instead of the 16th Michigan which he understood had marched up the hill last in line.[40]

Shortly, a "Reply to Rear Rank" appeared from Elisha Coan, who in later years frequently misstated facts of the battle, once even erroneously listing his own rank as corporal. Coan confirmed the order of march, his memory also placing the 20th Maine then the 16th Michigan in the rear; and he agreed that Vincent originally placed the 16th on the left and moved it to the right of the brigade. Little more than a week later, Holman Melcher offered his thoughts on the issue which further confirmed the order of regiments, but could not offer a reason for the left to right shift of the 16th. Melcher suggested that someone ask his old friend William Livermore, who was known to have kept a thorough diary, to offer his thoughts on the issues, and Livermore's diary entries from Gettysburg appeared shortly thereafter. Even Howard Prince, admitting that he was not on Little Round Top during the battle, offered a theory stating that Vincent probably saw the oncoming Rebel line and felt that his right was more vulnerable. While the order of march and reasons for placements of the four regiments of Vincent's Brigade may seem insignificant details in an event packed with more important elements, it is testimony to the importance of the battle in the minds of the veterans that even these small points generated discussion, if not full-blown controversy.[41]

The *Lincoln County News* also played an important role in creating the final list of participants for *Maine at Gettysburg*. In 1897 Miller published a "List of Officers and Men Actually Engaged in the Battle" at Chamberlain's request to obtain the help of the veterans in compiling an accurate list. Chamberlain did not like the idea of publishing such a roster in *Maine at Gettysburg*, in part, perhaps, because his estimation of the number of men with him on the spur was substantially lower than the list that all of the veterans together compiled. However, Charles Hamlin, the chairman of the Maine at Gettysburg Commission, pressed him to do it, so he undertook the project, working hard to be certain of its thorough accuracy.[42]

✠ ✠ ✠

While Theodore Gerrish prospered, Charles Gilmore may have suffered the most for having not been on Little Round Top with his regiment in 1863. Before the war, Gilmore served as sheriff of Penobscot County, in which the city of Bangor made up the largest portion of the population. He was apparently as well-connected politically as he was unfit for command. In 1861 he went to war as a captain in the 7th Maine Regiment and at the Battle of Lee's Mill on the peninsula an exploding shell injured his head and wrecked his confidence. In May 1863, just before Colonel Ames left the 20th Maine to accept command of a brigade in General Howard's Eleventh Corps, he called a group of officers to his tent to discuss how he would handle the passing of command. Ames had devised a plan whereby he would recommend the promotion of Chamberlain and Gilmore along with the appointment of Ellis Spear as major. Shortly after, by Ames' plan at least, Gilmore would resign, leaving Chamberlain as colonel, Spear as lieutenant colonel, and Sam Keene as major. Ames had not taken one twist to the plot into consideration, however, which was that Gilmore eavesdropped on the planning session from outside the tent and did not carry out his part of the plan.[43]

As a result of his counterplotting, Gilmore found himself in command of the 20th Maine when Colonel Chamberlain succumbed to fever and heat stroke on the eve of the skirmish at Middleburg. Leading the regiment into battle was apparently not in Gilmore's plan, and he relinquished his command, retiring to a hospital in Frederick and then Baltimore. The medical records from the Baltimore hospital show that Gilmore complained that he was suffering from hemophrygia, later defined as paralysis of the left thigh. By Gilmore's testimony, this was the result of the Lee's Mill head injury he had sustained more than a year previous. In the year that interposed, Gilmore had actively sought and accepted his promotion and transfer to the 20th Maine and then refused an arrangement to resign his commission. Either he did all of this while suffering from the paralysis or he seemed to have suspicious relapses whenever a battle loomed. Whatever the case, Gilmore was not with the regiment at Gettysburg and used the hemophrygia to his benefit several times afterward.[44]

Ironically, Little Round Top might have been the greatest event of his life, propelling him to just the kind of political or business success that seemed to draw him into the war in the first place. Since he did not perform his duty heroically on the spur, he did not become one of the glory-covered veterans of the fight, nor did he regain his confidence in himself. Gilmore rose, reluctantly, to command of the 20th Maine when Joshua Chamberlain took his promotion to command the brigade. From that point on, he was seldom with the regiment and almost never in command during a battle. Gilmore's promotion to colonel was contingent on the regiment meeting a minimum size of just over two hundred and, as his regular requests to the governor for recruits and reinforcements went unheeded, so did his official promotion.[45]

While Gilmore retained command on paper he avoided performing his duties by getting himself detailed to Washington to serve on courts martial, or by obtaining leaves of absence. More often then not, the reason for the leave was the old Lee's Mill paralysis, but he had other reasons for his requests as well. At one point, he insisted that he be allowed to return to Bangor to personally contest thirty-six civil suits against him totaling more than $20,000. With Gilmore mostly absent, command of the regiment, but not the corresponding rank, fell to Ellis Spear who seemed continually perplexed with his superior. When Gilmore's eavesdropping thwarted the restructure of command upon Ames' departure, it denied Spear a promotion to lieutenant colonel. When Chamberlain moved on, Spear would have taken command and a new set of colonel's eagles. Thanks to Gilmore's meddling, however, Spear had to do the work of a colonel while retaining the lower rank of major. Gilmore further exacerbated the situation when he resigned, then unresigned again in 1864. Promotions had been made in the interim and Gilmore's return left two colonels in the regiment, squeezing Spear out altogether. Moreover, Spear learned of all this on his return from a recruiting leave.[46]

Gilmore hung on against great odds. In 1865 the War Department sent a terse letter to General Meade asking, "under what authority [Gilmore's] resignation was revoked," and a board of medical examiners determined that his recovery was "remote and uncertain." Nonetheless, he held out until the army finally mustered him as colonel and discharged him at his request, seven weeks after the surrender at Appomattox.[47]

Another man who did not manage to turn a heroic Gettysburg experience into a prosperous postwar life was the regiment's quartermaster, Alden Litchfield, though he did leave his mark on the memory of Little Round Top. Many months before Gettysburg, while in winter quarters at Stoneman's Switch, the regiment was away from camp for several days, leaving behind only those whom the surgeon had excused from duty. Wandering about the camp, Litchfield eyed a sergeant from Company H standing in his tent and ordered him to grab an axe and cut some wood for the quartermaster's personal use. The sergeant, George Buck, was not required to do so, both because he was excused by the surgeon and because he was a non-commissioned officer and thus exempted from such work. When he explained all of this to Litchfield, the quartermaster responded by knocking him to the ground and kicking him. When the regiment returned a few days later, Litchfield reported Buck's disobedience and the sergeant was demoted to private, a rank he retained until Colonel Chamberlain restored his stripes on Little Round Top as his life's blood flowed from a fatal wound.[48]

The incident was not out of character for the quartermaster. As one veteran of the regiment later recalled, Litchfield "was a large, rough, overbearing man, one who disgraced his uniform every day by his brutal treatment of the men; and to say that he was most cordially despised by every man in our company would be putting it in a very mild form." At one time Litchfield might even have unwittingly contributed to the demise of the regiment's first colonel, Adelbert Ames, had it not been for Isabella Fogg, the bold relief worker.[49]

During one of his more unusually abusive periods, Litchfield was bullying his way around camp ordering men to perfom menial or unsavory duties on his behalf, including standing guard over an old nag, despite a driving rain. As Fogg observed, the quartermaster justified all of his abuses by telling the men that he was only carrying out Colonel Ames' orders. Mrs. Fogg seldom pulled any punches, and she wasted no time in bringing notice of the problem to the proper authorities. "I am aware," she wrote plainly, "that many would say that it is no part of the duty of a lady to interfere in these matters, but if I know my duty, I think it is to look after the interests of our sick men and when I know them to be maltreated and abused I feel it is my duty to make it known." Describing Litchfield in her letter, Fogg made it clear that "a more wicked, profane, cruel, unprincipled man I think could not be found in the State of Maine."[50]

Litchfield's demonstrations of his lack of principle did not end with his war service. Further evidence of his flawed character lies in a misadventure that he took part in during 1870. In May of that year, the old quartermaster decided to install himself among the newly rich in his hometown of Rockland where he had become a grocer. To do so, he collaborated with four out-of-town "professionals" to rob the local Lime Rock Bank. Litchfield bribed a policeman to obtain the key to the bank and on the appointed night, two of the hired felons set a gunpowder charge against the safe to blast it open. Before the charge was ready, however, one of the hoodlums accidentally dropped a lighted match into the powder, sending the safe, along with a good portion of the bank, up in the blast.[51]

With the town alarmed, the co-conspirators were apprehended soon after and police implicated Litchfield with little investigation. The old quartermaster finally got his just desserts when the judge read his conviction on charges of larceny, ordering him to serve four years hard labor in the state prison at Thomaston. Some time later, the Rev. Theodore Gerrish visited the prison and recognized Litchfield in a labor gang, despite his convict's clothing. With great satisfaction, Gerrish recalled, "I could not help thinking of the little affair at Stoneman's Switch, and of Sergeant Buck's honored grave at Gettysburg."[52]

✠ ✠ ✠

William Oates wrote two major works on the battle. The first, "Gettysburg—The Battle on the Right," was published in the Southern Historical Society Papers in 1878. In 1905 he revised his account before publishing it in his book, *The War Between the Union and the Confederacy and its Lost Opportunities*, which he also intended as a history of the 15th Alabama. Both accounts contributed greatly to the general public's understanding of the fight.[53]

Oates' first account was primarily designed as an undisguised blow against General Longstreet, stating that his "want of generalship," lost the battle. This was not surprising in light of the long personal conflict with his old corps commander. Their discord was rooted in a feud between General Law, who was Oates' brigade commander and friend, and Longstreet, who even went so far as having Law removed from command and arrested after they transferred to Tennessee. Aware of the relationship between Oates and Law, Longstreet denied Oates' promotion to brigadier general. As Oates put it, "He never mentioned Law's brigade in complimentary terms...[and] did injustice to them because he hated Law."[54]

In arguing Longstreet's incompetence at Gettysburg, Oates laid out a scenario by which the Confederates would have won the battle, thanks of course to Oates' recognition of the importance of Big Round Top, if the corps commander had supported him with reinforcements. The importance of the account was not what it meant to Longstreet's reputation—he had other supporters and detractors too numerous to mention—but rather the foundation that it laid for what became the legendary status of the fight for Vincent's Spur.

In making his case against Longstreet, Oates made the fight for the spur the most important element in the battle he called, "the turning point in the great struggle—'The War Between the States.' " At the same time, using muster rolls dating back weeks before the battle, he overstated his regiment's strength by nearly three hundred men. Having never known the details surrounding their enemy, the account fascinated the men of the 20th. During the fight they had captured men from at least three regiments, two of Alabama and one of Texas, and the Alabama captives admitted that they had charged with a whole brigade of five regiments. If each of these regiments were anywhere near the size of Oates, then the Maine veterans could have made a case that as many three thousand men had attacked them on the spur. Given their underestimated strength of 386, the odds seemed nearly ten to one, which is how Gerrish depicted it in the first major account published. In later efforts his comrades avoided such great ventures into nineteenth-century hyperbole. Acknowledging that they had faced only the 15th and 47th Alabama, they generally claimed a ratio of three to one.[55]

What many of the Mainers never accounted for, because they had no way of knowing at the time, was that the 15th Alabama was more than an average sized regiment in Law's brigade that day—even at 450 men—and the 47th attacked with only seven-tenths of its already depleted strength. In reality, the 20th Maine never directly faced more than six hundred Alabamians, and even then for only a short time before it became a one-to-one slugging contest with the 15th Alabama. Nonetheless, the legend had taken root and, nourished over the years with exaggeration on both sides, it grew.[56]

As the wounds of war, both physical and psychological, healed in the late 1870s, the nation's aversion to many things military began to wane and reminiscences of the war in newspapers and books gained in popularity. The Maine veterans formed the 20th Maine Regiment Association in August 1881 and reunions of the old comrades followed at least annually. These meetings were seldom without a speech or other appropriate reminder of their service in the war and Gettysburg was never far from conversations.[57]

Published accounts helped the legend flourish. Gerrish's appeared in 1882, followed by Spear's "A Visit to Gettysburg," Coan and Gerrish accounts in the *National Tribune*, and a Melcher account in the *Lincoln County News*, later edited and reprinted in *Battles and Leaders*. Inevitably, there was fighting within the ranks when various accounts suggested that credit should fall to, or from, one company or officer, as Theodore

Gerrish discovered when James Nichols pounced on his account in the *Lincoln County News*. But the ranks closed and their focus shifted when forces from without tampered with the legend.[58]

During the 1880s the War Department published the multi-volume *War of the Rebellion: The Official Records of the Union and Confederate Armies*, which contained the official reports of all the regimental, brigade, division, and corps commanders at Gettysburg. The Maine veterans read with great interest the official reports of Colonel Fisher of the Pennsylvania Reserves and his division commander, General Crawford. Both of these reports gave credit for the seizing of Big Round Top to the Reserves who, they well remembered, had skedaddled off the hill at the first sign of trouble.[59]

Unknown to most of the 20th Maine men, this controversy had already been played out between the commanders in the months after Gettysburg when Fisher and Crawford were rebuked by Sykes, their corps commander, for asserting the falsehood. The publication of the *Official Records* which bared the issue for all to see, rekindled the flames. In 1885, not long after Melcher's article on the battle appeared, Fisher wrote a letter published in the *National Tribune* which reasserted his brigade's claim to the capture of Big Round Top, with the 20th Maine as his skirmishers. Elisha Coan spoke for the regiment when he blasted Fisher's account in a subsequent letter to the *Tribune*. While discrediting Fisher's article Coan also demonstrated the gravity with which the Maine veterans had come to view such attacks on their Gettysburg glory. "[I]f my pen does not endeavor to refute the statements that it contains," he wrote, "the very rocks of Round Top will cry out with indignation and our comrades in the National Cemetery at Gettysburg that fell under the colors of the 20th M[ain]e will rise from their graves and affirm the truth."[60]

Despite the efforts of the Mainers, Fisher's story gained some credibility. In 1887 Gen. Abner Doubleday published his account of the battles of Chancellorsville and Gettysburg, devoting only one sentence to the occupation of Big Round Top. Referring to the Pennsylvania Reserves, whom he had once commanded, Doubleday wrote that "The enemy retired before it, so that it was not engaged, and it then took possession of the main Round Top on the left of Little Round Top and fortified it." In many of their speeches and writings in years that followed, the Maine veterans sought to reclaim their credit for seizing and holding the bigger hill, frequently mentioning and refuting Fisher's statements.[61]

The controversy lingered as late as 1911, when Eugene Nash, the historian of the 44th New York, added his opinion. "It was understood at the time," he wrote, "that the failure of Col. Fisher to give adequate support in seizing and holding Big Round Top was not satisfactorily explained." When Nash wrote that "it was understood at that time" what he meant was that the men on the battle line that night were not satisfied with the explanation, if Fisher ever offered one, and that he should have been ashamed of himself for declining Rice's order.[62]

✠ ✠ ✠

One of the events that demonstrated the popularity of the regiment and the emotion that war memories stirred in them, occurred at the Grand Reunion of Maine Soldiers and Sailors in August 1881. One hundred thirty-seven veterans of the 20th Maine attended, and on the third evening of the Portland encampment they held their second reunion. The veterans had formed the 20th Maine Regimental Association five years earlier at the same event and their second reunion became the highlight of the weekend. Soldiers, sailors, and their guests began to arrive in the main tent long before the time set for the 20th's gathering, and when Holman Melcher formally opened the program more than two thousand people crowded in to witness the event.[63]

Joseph Tyler, the regimental bugler at Gettysburg, played the old brigade call to the cheers of the veterans while Andrew Tozier and Elisha Coan carried the remnants of their Little Round Top battle flag into the tent. As the cheers continued, the band struck up the chords of "Rally Round the Flag." Samuel Miller, the historian of the association, then read a history of the regiment, recalling in detail the famous fight on Vincent's Spur. When he closed, he introduced Joshua Chamberlain to great applause.[64]

When he reached the podium, the usually eloquent Chamberlain could find few words to express his feelings. He thanked Miller and recalled the praise that his old regiment had received from the likes of General Meade and even Jeff Davis for its work on Little Round Top. As he pondered it, he was astonished at how short a time he had actually been with the regiment, commanding it only a few months. "But I cannot speak," he said as he closed. "God bless the old flag and God bless you all."[65]

The next day, the local paper carried a story on the grand reunion, calling the 20th's meeting the "chief event," despite the fact that many other regimental associations had also met. In describing the 20th Maine it referred to "the gallant body of men which Chamberlain led to Little Round Top, and whose obstinate hold of that important position baffled

20th Maine veterans choose the site for their monument on the spur in October 1882. Left to right: Joe Land, Ellis Spear, Joshua Chamberlain, Elisha Coan (with flag), Holman Melcher (seated), Theodore Gerrish, and Albert Fernald.

the plans of Lee and made the battle of Gettysburg a Union victory." The war was only sixteen years in the past, but already the other battles and accomplishments of the regiment seemed to fall away, as if insignificant when held up against the legend of Little Round Top.[66]

In 1882 Ellis Spear and Howard Prince visited the old battlefield with a large group of officers from both sides and noticed that a number of units had placed monuments to mark where they had been involved in the battle. The Maine veterans had hoped to meet William Oates who had planned to attend, but the Alabama colonel, then in Congress, did not. After their trip, the two were anxious to talk with Oates about the battle so they traveled to the Capitol and paid a call on their old adversary. Their conversation was very pleasant—especially in relation to their previous meeting—leading Spear to remark that Oates was among the most admirable and courteous of the Confederate veterans he had met. Some time later, both Spear and Prince suggested that the 20th Maine regimental association ought to erect a monument or other memorial on Little Round Top.[67]

The association agreed, and in October 1882 a handful of them traveled to Gettysburg to choose a site. In addition they appointed Spear, Prince, Joe Land, Albert Fernald, and Theodore Gerrish as a committee to complete the task. Not long after, masons in Hallowell, Maine fashioned a block of granite, four feet square and five high, into a monument

Ellis Spear wrote on the back of this stereograph: "Position of battle flag at time of battle and the same flag used by the 20th Maine on Little Round Top." Taken in October 1882, the Oates boulder can be seen in the center background.

to the regiment and a memorial to the dead. They also created another marker of equal stature but different design for Big Round Top. Spear saw to their placement in 1886, and the association planned a formal dedication ceremony three years later.[68]

The placement of the left and right flank markers, supervised or at least approved by Joshua Chamberlain, contradicts the accounts of the regiment's action. If, as Chamberlain described, the regiment dwindled to just two hundred enlisted men in single rank, their regimental front would fill a space of at least four hundred feet, but the distance between the flank markers is less than 270. At the opening of the fight the regiment contained twice as many men, and yet the markers indicate that they held a position of 165 feet. Even elbow to elbow in two ranks, the regiment would have required at least three times this distance. Keeping in mind that the men of the 20th Maine spent little more than three hours on the spur, half of it engaged in battle and the other half in "a sleep-like swoon," it is no wonder their perception of the ground had faded by the time they placed the markers a quarter century afterward.[69]

Toward the latter part of the 1880s many of the veterans had written or spoken their version of the battle for the spur and, not surprisingly, the facts in these accounts varied. Bickering in the pages of the *National Tribune* and the *Lincoln County News* persisted as to who said what first actually happened, particularly in relation to the heart of the legend, the famous charge. So strong were the feelings over these minor skirmishes of facts that they spilled over into the ceremonies at the dedication of the monuments. On October 2, 1889, the regimental association held its annual reunion and the gathering of men whose postwar lives had scattered them around the country undoubtedly involved lengthy discussion sessions. The next day, the veterans held a dedication ceremony at the two monuments and at a smaller marker near Company B's position. Whatever the subject of the previous evening's deliberations, they raised the ire of Joshua Chamberlain enough that he used his speech at the dedication to quell some of the uprisings.

Departing from his usually liberal and general praise for everyone involved, Chamberlain had barely welcomed the guests before pointing out that the monument was in the wrong place adding, "I am not at all criticizing the judgement of our comrades who selected the great boulder for the base of the monument." This is a surprising statement in light of the fact that he was among those who chose the site in 1882. A few lines later, he again stated that he had not given the order which initiated the charge but asserted that he was with the colors during their lunge down the hill and that he and Andrew Tozier went with the men on the right wing. He then addressed two other controversies, including Gerrish's comment on hesitation and whether Spear or Nichols directed his attention to the flanking Alabamians. The fact that Chamberlain chose to openly discuss these issues at a ceremony hardly meant for such quibbling demonstrated the importance with which the veterans had grown to perceive every nuance of the battle. It was out of character for such a public event, but Chamberlain took advantage of the speech to stake his claim on the battle. "[Y]ou must permit me to add the remark," he said, "that I commanded my regiment that day." The dedication ceremony was not, however, the only time that placement of a monument on Vincent's Spur created controversy.[70]

In November 1902 the surviving veterans of the 15th Alabama—there were eighty-nine of them present—held a reunion in Montgomery and passed a resolution to place a monument on the spur. Colonel (now General) Oates adopted the project as his own and made plans to erect a relatively small shaft on the boulder where his regiment's assault peaked and his brother fell. When he first conceived the project, he set out with little apprehension that he would encounter difficulty. He had, after all, been among those in Congress who voted to establish and fund the battlefield as a national memorial, and Oates himself had recommended the Confederate representative on the official Battlefield Commission to his post.[71]

Reunion of the survivors of the 15th Alabama at the State Capitol in Montgomery, November 1902. At Oates' urging, the veterans voted to erect a monument to their dead at Gettysburg.

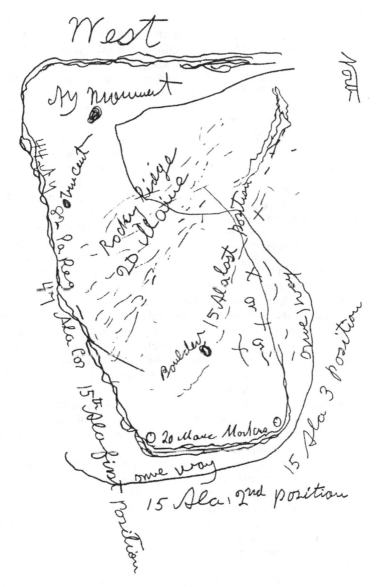

Oates' sketch to the Battlefield Commission in 1905. The "x" marks indicate the positions where he hoped to place the monument. The "Twentieth Maine Markers" indicate the monument and the left flank marker.

> *To the Memory of Lt. John A. Oates*
> *and his gallant Comrades*
> *who fell here July 2nd, 1863.*
>
> *The 15th Ala. Regt., over 400 strong,*
> *reached this spot, but for*
> *lack of support had to retire.*
>
> *Lt. Col. Feagin lost a leg*
> *Capts. Brainard and Ellison*
> *Lts. Oates and Cody and*
> *33 men were killed, 76 wounded*
> *and 84 captured.*
>
> *Erected 39th Anniversary of the battle*
>
> *by*
>
> *Gen. Wm. C. Oates*
> *who was colonel of the Regiment*

Oates' intended monument inscription

William Robbins, one of three commissioners, fought as a captain in the 4th Alabama at Gettysburg. He moved to North Carolina after the war and won election to the U.S. House of Representatives. When Oates was also in Congress, he recommended Robbins as the Confederate representative on the Gettysburg Battlefield Commission and he won the appointment. From the outset, the Alabama monument idea had its difficulties. Allowing veterans to erect any Confederate marker on the battle line would have set a dangerous precedent for the commissioners, since other groups would likely have overrun them with requests for more, and before long bronze and marble edifices would have completely obscured the battlefield. This, however, proved to be the least of the challenges facing Oates. He was a blunt man, and saw little point in the circuitous route to a point when a direct line was available. This may have served him well as a military commander, and helped make his memoirs among the most rich and informative first-hand histories of the war, but the monument issue was another matter. Trying to persuade three political appointees to support a precedent-setting act involving events as emotionally stirring as those that surround-ed Gettysburg required anything but bluntness. Getting the marker placed meant, above all else, that the location he chose for the marker had to be appropriate.[72]

The commissioners repeatedly informed him that they would welcome a memorial near the area along Confederate Avenue where the assault began. "I am not sufficiently interested in this," Oates replied, "as to expend $200 or more to have it put out as a memorial to that ave[nue]." Refusing the standard allowance for Confederate markers, Oates' plan was already doomed, but the controversy simmered for two years while Oates pushed his case to a commission looking for a way to get rid of the issue.[73]

One of the key differences between the two parties had to do with the the positions of the regiments around the spur and the complicated circumstances that got them there. Oates wanted the marker placed around the side of the spur, asserting that the 15th Alabama attacked the 20th Maine from the east while engaged in a one-on-one fight with them. The

142

position he chose also required an acceptance that Oates had turned the left of the 20th so far that he actually got behind Vincent's brigade. Robbins and the commission never accepted that Oates ascended Big Round Top or that the 15th and 47th Alabama became separated from the rest of the brigade. Robbin's 4th Alabama was the next regiment in line, and to say there was a gap might suggest that some of the blame for Oates' failure may lie with them. As a result, Robbins resisted the claim, telling the other commissioners, "He seems to think he was *far off to himself* in the fight there."[74]

In a letter to the secretary of war, Oates made an error that confused the issue beyond rectification, and one sentence in the letter scuttled whatever chance he may have had to get his monument. In justifying the location he had chosen, Oates asserted, "I turned the Union flank, and drove the right of the 20th Maine back on its left, and attacked the 83d Penna., and the 44th New York." Apparently, Oates typed the word "right" when he meant the left flank of the 20th, but the slight error, coupled with the exaggeration regarding the two other regiments of Vincent's Brigade, left him on untenable ground with the commission.[75]

Searching for a way to politely decline Oates' request—he did, after all, hold some political sway both in Washington and in the South—the commission sent the letter to Joshua Chamberlain, probably hoping he would offer some point upon which they could base a denial. Chamberlain was cordial in his response, saying that he had no objection to the monument, "but I should expect it to be placed on ground where [the 15th] actually stood at some time during the battle,—at the extreme point of its advance if desired,—so that it might not only represent the valor of a regiment but the truth of history." Chamberlain added that Oates' account was at odds with history, at least as legend had it. "The statements of Colonel Oates in his letter to the Secretary of War differ widely from the well established record of facts in the case."[76]

In truth, the distance between Oates' boulder and the left flank of the 20th Maine, as marked by Chamberlain, is little more than forty feet and, had the two former colonels ever visited the site together, they would probably have found only slight variation between their memories of the farthest point to which the Alabamians surged. But the legend of the 20th Maine's defense had become firmly entrenched in the record of the battle, and since winners of battles and wars get to write history the way they remember it, Oates never erected his monument.

✠ ✠ ✠

The two men who commanded the Maine troops during the fight wrote a sad but highly illuminating chapter of the story of Vincent's Spur. Ellis Spear and Joshua Chamberlain remained friendly but somewhat distant after the war, exchanging amicable letters and passing cordial hours during reunions. Their lives before the war had been near mirror images of one another. Both were the product of small Maine towns and Bowdoin College, and their postwar years held many similarities as well. The one major difference between the two men, played out in equally well-written speeches and correspondence, was the way each of them remembered the war.

"War!" Chamberlain wrote fifty years after he had lived through it. "Nothing but the final infinite good, for men and God, can accept and justify human work like that!" Across decades of contemplation the aging general sought to find some higher meaning for the war; some benefit which must have come out of the costly horror. As he did so, he looked back on a transformation that his own war experience had undergone only a few months after it began.[77]

Chamberlain's decision to enter the war was almost entirely a personal one. Having grown up within a family which did not strongly support abolition, he believed that bringing an end to slavery was not worth risking the Union. His entry into service was more the result of his need to break out beyond a sphere of life that he found highly restrictive. He longed to test his abilities and prove his manly qualities, at least as nineteenth-century society defined them for young men. Moreover, he longed to break free of his quiet professorial community and participate in some higher cause.

In September 1862 Abraham Lincoln's Emmancipation Proclamation elevated Chamberlain's personal war aims beyond his imagination. When Lincoln forced slavery to the center of the conflict, he transformed Chamberlain's view of the war dramatically. What had been an adventuresome release from his previously quiet life became a crusade to free the slaves, and Chamberlain saw himself taking an active role in an event on the level of the great campaigns of classical literature. No longer was this a personal struggle with his childhod insecurities. He was now engaged in a struggle to free a race of people, and his new view of the war formed the basis of his postwar memories.

"Fighting and destruction are terrible but are sometimes agencies of heavenly rather than hellish powers," he wrote in 1913. "War is for participants a test of character; it makes bad men worse and good men better." Rather than dwell on the horrors of war, Chamberlain chose to see the good that surfaces when people are challenged by great crises, depicting the war as an event which summoned the best traits in men.

War, to him, was glory, honor, sacrifice, duty; all of the romantic qualities embodied in the classical curriculum with which Bowdoin professors trained their students.[78]

Deeply scarred by the war, Ellis Spear found little good in it, feeling that whatever noble qualities it had elicited from soldiers were lost on Sam Keene, John West, and the others who did not come home. Nor could the benefit that society derived from the elevation of these qualities overcome the grief, pain, and hardships that the war visited upon those still living, some of whom had surrendered their loved ones to Spear with his promise to protect them as best he could. To Spear, the war was a horrific experience that he would rather have forgotten than immortalized. When he looked back on the war he remembered suffering, hunger, and most of all the dead, never shedding his remorse.

Their differing views represented a classic disparity between the way separate parts of society as a whole viewed war and still do. A large part of Chamberlain's motivation to serve in the war was rooted in a deep-seated youthful insecurity. Though his Bowdoin experience had helped him overcome much of these feelings, it did not rid him of a desire to prove himself in his romantic nineteenth-century idea of manhood. To succeed at war meant proving his courage and bravery in the manner of the ancients, perhaps finding a self-assuredness and confidence that had eluded him. As a young man in Brunswick he had no lack of tall timber to emulate. He was among a small group to whom Harriet Beecher Stowe read *Uncle Tom's Cabin* in her home before it was printed and he gave an oration at his Bowd-oin commencement while alumni such as Franklin Pierce, Nathaniel Hawthorne, and Henry Wadsworth Longfellow looked on. That oration also rekindled childhood insecurities that had done much to affect both his personality and ambition.[79]

As a young boy, Chamberlain struggled with a speech impediment, a stammer on hard consonants, and he grew up quiet, bashful, and somewhat insecure in a conservative Puritan family. The obstacle followed him to college where he remembered that "the sleepless anxiety on this score was a serious wear upon the nervous system." Through sheer force of will and dogged determination, he overcame the stammer well enough to master several languages and give numerous orations within the Bowdoin curriculum. At commencement, as he delivered an oration of honor in front of the assembled dignitaries, the affliction returned, and he left the ceremony humiliated, at least by his own measure.[80]

One of those who listened from the audience that day proved to be another drain on his feelings of security. Frances Caroline Adams, the local minister's adopted daughter, was the source of bittersweet feelings for the young professor-to-be. Chamberlain had admired the young woman from his seat in the choir at religious services on Sundays—including one during which Stowe received her inspiration for Uncle Tom and Simon Legree—and endured a long courtship and engagement, even by nineteenth-century standards. The two finally married in December 1855, and on the evening of the wedding, her father foretold the future when he wrote in his diary, "I feel sadly about poor Fanny, fearing greatly she will not make herself happy."[81]

Throughout the courtship and early years of their marriage, it seemed that the young professor was forever struggling to coax feelings from his wife that he repeatedly and eloquently expressed to her. He had little success. Once, somewhat overwhelmed by the forcefulness of his affection, she even went so far as to suggest that theirs should be a sexless, childless marriage. It is not beyond the realm of speculation that Chamberlain's decision to join the army in 1862 stemmed from a desire to prove his manly worth, not only to himself but also his hesitant wife. If outreaching his insecurities had been a goal when he entered the army, Chamberlain rode away from Gettysburg having never to doubt himself again. If insecurity about his abilities still lingered in his mind on July 1, 1863, he shed them on the Round Tops the following day, and firmly established a record which would constantly reaffirm his feelings of personal value.

The unrequited feelings of intense affection for his wife, however, were another matter entirely. Prior to Gettysburg, Chamberlain felt that Fannie had shrugged off his letters home and he started numbering them to be certain they had all reached her. On July 4, as he penned with swelling pride an account of the events in which he had played so crucial a role, he must have taken deep satisfaction in the fact that he could return to her a proven man, a war hero. After twelve days of glowing in the knowledge that his beloved should have received the letter and learned of his exploits, his heart sank when mail arrived from her headed New York, where his letter could not have reached her.

On July 17 the crestfallen colonel had to rewrite the letter to her, describing again the pivotal moments of his life fifteen days after they had passed. His disappointment permeated the letter. "But New York! I am sorry you are there," he wrote. "I wish you were at home. You should have been there before." Thanks to a letter from their sister, his brother Tom had known for two weeks that Fannie was in New York but had neglected, perhaps intentionally, to tell him. John was also aware of his sister-in-law's travels but he apparently also kept them from his older brother.[82]

Joshua L. Chamberlain, 1905
Major General, Maine State Militia

William C. Oates, 1898
Brigadier General, U.S. Army

Coming home at war's end a proven hero, albeit a somewhat disabled one, did not evoke the emotional response Chamberlain may have hoped from his wife. Nor did his election to governor, and in 1868 Fannie accused her husband of abuse and told him that she wanted a divorce. The couple eventually reconciled, at least the divorce never material- ized, and they struggled to find happiness together through many years. In the late 1890s Fannie began to loose her sight, and by the turn of the century she had become totally blind. This was not the only event that brought sadness into Chamberlain's life. In fact, the last quarter-century of his years were quite sad in general.[83]

His brother Tom, like Horace and John before him, died of tubercu- losis in 1896, after a long bout with alcoholism. In 1898 Joshua offered to serve again as a general in the war with Spain. The U. S. War Department declined his offer but granted commissions to Adelbert Ames and even William Oates, who both served as brigadier generals. His wife Fannie went blind in the late 1890s and died in 1905 while his business ventures proved unsuccessful as well. For complicated reasons, Chamberlain's political stock had slipped so badly that he could not even obtain a post as collector of customs in Portland which was traditionally reserved for former governors. Instead, he had to settle for the subordinate position of surveyor of port, a disappointment, if not an outright insult. Through all of this, the proud Mainer suffered greatly from the Petersburg wound, relying partly on a soldier's disability pension from the government.[84]

With all of this in mind, it is no wonder that Chamberlain frequently sought the comforting memory of his accomplishments at Gettysburg, and in speech after speech he contributed to the growth of the legend of Little Round Top. The one bright light that shone upon him in his later years was a package that arrived parcel post in 1893, containing a Medal of Honor. According to the citation, it was awarded for "daring heroism and great tenacity in holding his position on the Little Round Top against repeated assaults, and carrying the advance position on the Great Round Top." In 1902 the creation of a road around his regiment's position at Little Round Top must have cheered him as well, since the commission named it Chamberlain Avenue.[85]

It was from quite a different perspective that Ellis Spear looked back on what he called the "Great Tragedy" of the 1860s. Spear received much the same education as his commander, graduating from the same college just six years after him. Actually, Chamberlain was a professor of Spear's at Bowdoin and both their literary abilities reflect the classical training. Both of the men grew up on small Maine farms and their state's deeply Puritan foundation instilled in them a simplistic, somewhat cynical approach to life, even in their dry humor. If their backgrounds provided initially similar outlooks for each of them, their points of view diverged with the onset of the second year of the war.

In 1862 Ellis Spear set about recruiting men from around the small towns in the middle of Maine's coast. His friends Sam Keene, Joe Land, and Lysander Hill all did the same, and the governor commissioned each of them officers in Companies F, G, and H. Like many other bright young men, they did so out of a combination of patriotism and disgust. They felt that the American experiment of democracy must be preserved and continued, but that the administration of the army had been an abysmal failure. While they entertained no delusions that their service alone could turn the tide of war, they realized that it could not be won until intelligent men made sacrifices and offered their services to the government. Thus, they set about recruiting men in response to Lincoln's call for 300,000 more troops.[86]

The experience of recruiting the soldiers he later commanded in camp, on the march, and in battle set Spear's experience apart from that of Chamberlain. The Bowdoin professor earned his commission by virtue of his stature in society. College professors were not supposed to go to war in those days, their knowledge made them too valuable to the state as educators to waste on fields of battle. Commissioned a lieutenant colonel, Chamberlain joined the regiment to which the governor assigned him, not because of any connection he had to the men serving in it. Chamberlain had acquaintances in the original 20th Maine, a few had even been his students before the war but, excepting his brother Tom, no deep personal responsibility tied him to the well-being of his men, save that incumbent upon all army officers by definition. For Ellis Spear, however, it was quite different.

When the 20th Maine boarded a train heading south out of Portland in September 1862, Ellis Spear took with him a heart full of solemn promises to wives, mothers, and children that he would protect the men under his command, particularly those whom he had personally recruited. As he had paid recruiting calls on their sons a month or two previous, anxious mothers met Spear with tears, anger, or some combination of both, one even chasing him off the property with a pitchfork. But, whatever the reaction from family members, the recruiter turned captain inevitably felt a special responsibility to these people who, after all, were neighbors. This was especially important if he hoped to return to his hometown—and theirs—after the war.[87]

While recruiting in Wiscasset that summer, two young men came to him wanting to enlist. They were brothers, the oldest barely 21, and Spear learned that they were the only two sons of a widow in town. Feeling that the mother's sacrifice was too great, Spear sent the younger son home but enlisted the other. Less than a month into their service, the older son came to Spear's tent one day sick, and died shortly after. It was the first time that Spear had lost one of his recruits to the war, and he later recalled that "it made a deep impression upon my mind, and I thought often of that poor widow in her sorrow."[88]

Almost all of Spear's memory of the Gettysburg Campaign was dark and unhappy; and with good reason. Beginning in early June a malarial fever, coupled with chronic diarrhea and sore bowels, made the experience a miserable one for him. During the encounter with the enemy at Middleburg, Cpl. John West became the first of Spear's recruits to die after he had ordered him into a fight. Despite an exhaustive march and the nearly debilitating effects of his illness, Spear personally saw to the proper burial of West's body. After the war, when called upon by the members of the Washington, D.C., chapter of the Military Order of the Loyal Legion of the United States, Spear avoided seriously depicting war events or telling stories of heroism or bravery. Instead, he entertained the organization with anecdotal satires on army hard tack and Uncle Sam's recruiting methods. On Memorial Day 1888, he delivered a stern but emotional speech to the people of his hometown which reflected his concern over the memory of the war, particularly for young people. "For the generation now taking our places must not think that it was a holiday affair, either to those who were at home, or to those in the field." Later in his speech, Spear recalled the moment of the war that had its greatest impact on him.[89]

On June 22, 1864, he and his closest friend Sam Keene were in the trenches around Petersburg when a sniper's bullet hit Keene in the chest and he fell into Spear's arms. As he looked up at his friend, Keene said, "I am killed, write to my wife, It is all right, I die for the country." Twenty-four years later, Spear still remembered it clearly. "[T]hen his face turned white, blood gushed from his mouth, there was an instant slight movement of the muscles of his face, as if he would say more, and he was dead." These were Spear's memories of the war: not glory and honor, but death and misery.[90]

It was with this dark, sorrowful memory that Spear looked back upon the war, and as the nation grew more fond of what he called, "vaingloriousness" in the 1880s, he became disenchanted with veterans who took part in glorifying the war. Notable among these, was his old professor and commander Joshua Chamberlain. Through the last two decades of the century, they remained friendly and cordial. With the exception of Chamberlain's address at the dedication, they only occasionally took exception with each other's account of the battle.

In a letter to John Bachelder, the official historian of the battle, Spear related an account of the fight on the left wing of the regiment which differed from his commander's account of the right. As he closed the letter, he was careful not to take issue with Chamberlain or accept any of the credit for himself. "This is the story, but I believe it is not wholly in accordance with the fact as related by Gen. Chamberlain, and of course what Gen. Chamberlain says must be taken as history...As for myself, I charged with the line and helped gather prisoners. That was all."[91]

Shortly before the fiftieth anniversary of the battle, an article appeared in the *National Tribune* giving him much of the credit for Little Round Top, to which he responded with genuine embarrassment. "I am sorry to see that some kind, but indiscreet, comrade has 'slobbered' over me and the battle of Gettysburg...The battle at that point (Little Round Top) was fought by the sturdy men who carried the guns." He went on to shift all of the credit for the victory to Colonel Vincent who, of his own responsibility, moved the brigade there in the first place. "He lost his life in that gallant defense, and I can conceive nothing meaner than to take anything of the credit that belongs to him. He died there, and others have lived who have not been careful enough to preserve his memory and give him the credit due. Please print this and let me out, for I feel much disturbed by the undeserved praise." Half a century after the battle, Spear still struggled with the tinge of guilt and responsibility that he felt for those who had given the ultimate sacrifice, whether as his recruit, his friend, or his commander.[92]

The fiftieth anniversary of Gettysburg sparked a wave of renewed interest in the battle and in Civil War stories in general. Around this time, two writings of Chamberlain's appeared in print. An article in the January 1913 issue of *Cosmopolitan* magazine called "My Story of Fredericksburg," and "Through Blood and Fire at Gettysburg," which followed six months later in *Hearsts* magazine. Chamberlain wrote both of these partly to inform and partly to entertain his audience. Both were published in magazines owned by William Randolph Hearst, well known as one of the kings of sensationalism and yellow journalism, and they were heavily edited to suit the Hearst style of hyperbole and exaggeration. They need not have been. Even at the age of 82, the old professor and theologian never lost his mastery of the nineteenth-century literary style. He wrote eloquently, and while he took many of the liberties to which writers of the period were entitled, even expected to use, he captured the events more vividly than almost any other veteran.[93]

The changes that Hearst editors made in the articles, particularly the Gettysburg account, greatly irritated him. In June 1913 he wrote to a friend that the article "is much curtailed and changed by the insertion of 'connective tissue' by the editor," and he refused to keep his own copy of "Through Blood and Fire at Gettysburg," or send one to friends who requested it.[94]

With the Hearst twist applied, the articles enraged Ellis Spear, who prepared but never published his own article, "Two Stories of Fredericksburg," in which he refuted Chamberlain's account of that battle literally point by point. When Chamberlain wrote an account of the surrender at Appomattox, equally laced with "vain gloriousness," Spear responded with his own more practical description, saying that "the men at Appomattox were too hungry and too tired to care for theatrical spectacle. Nobody indulged in any heroics, even though they appreciated the magnitude of the occasion. Fatigue and hunger are great suppressors of shown sentimentalism." This was the only time Spear ever publicly contradicted his former professor and commander, and even then it was without a mention, or even hint, of Chamberlain's name.[95]

In a sense there need not have been a controversy between Spear and Chamberlain, and it is unfortunate that their relationship decayed as it did, largely over literary styles. They simply saw things differently. Spear was a practical man, Chamberlain a romantic. The two men experienced different battles at Gettysburg, owing to their different locations

Rallying 'round the colors. At the dedication of their monument on the spur in October 1889, Elisha Coan held the colors of the 20th Maine on the site they stood in the battle, while the rest of the veterans gathered around. Among those present in this photo are (by company): (A) Sylvester, True; (C) Bean, Heald, Latham; (D) Coan, Swett, French, Safford; (E) J.Q. Fernald, S.L. Miller; (F) DeWitt, Melcher; (G) Kennedy; (H) Bickford, Rogers, Gerrish; (I) Ruel Thomas (orderly), Wescott; (K) Keating, J. Tyler (bugler), I. Tyler; Joshua Chamberlain.

on the spur, and the manner in which they viewed the war from different perspectives—their similarities in background and education notwithstanding—is simply illustrative of the paradox of war. War is horrible, gruesome, and tragic on an enormous scale, but this tragedy also calls up a level of virtue in people that is otherwise seldom witnessed in society. While the death of so many soldiers, and the suffering of their families and friends cast war in a somber light, the same events bring something higher from people like Elisha Coan, William Livermore, and Sam Keene. As the disparate feelings of Spear and Chamberlain illustrate, war, despite its unjustifiable tragedy and horror, elicits a measure of courage, endurance, and self-sacrifice that is irresistibly admirable. Both the good and the bad create a sense of wonder in their witnesses. As Robert E. Lee said at Fredericksburg, pondering the courage of Federal troops marching in lines to their slaughter, "It is well that war is so terrible—we should grow too fond of it."[96]

6 American Legend, American Shrine

You were making history. The world has recorded for you more than you have written. The centuries to come will share and recognize the victory won here, with growing gratitude.[1]

Joshua Chamberlain, 1889

As Joshua Chamberlain looked out upon the surviving veterans of the regiment that he had commanded to an unlikely victory on Vincent's Spur thirty-five years earlier, he struggled to put into words the meaning of the event that had so greatly transformed his life, and the lives of many of his men. His foresight was remarkable. The world has continued to record the events on the spur to an extent beyond what the veterans themselves wrote and, as he foretold, the centuries have recognized the events with growing gratitude and importance. Such is the place that the Civil War, and Gettysburg in particular, has grown to occupy in the American psyche.

Carefully examined, the spur is a worthless piece of land. Two hundred feet in diameter, it is little more than a pile of loose rocks and large boulders of no monetary or agricultural value whatsoever. Neither cows nor sheep could or would graze on the stony slopes, trees do not grow straight, tall, or plentifully in its shallow soil, and it yields neither water nor minerals. Yet despite its uselessness, it has become a national shrine, attracting as many as a million visitors each year.

153

In spite of its apparent uselessness, it has become the object of a pilgrimage for thousands of people for many reasons. The romantic nature of the legend, the military significance of the maneuvering and, in no small measure, the eloquence of Joshua Chamberlain, have attracted Americans and travelers from abroad for more than a century. It is the meaning of the place, interpreted differently by nearly every visitor, that brings them; meaning that commanders of both armies attributed to the hill in 1863, and veterans and historians have confirmed ever since. By many of these, the events that took place on Little Round Top have come to represent the hinge upon which the Civil War swung.

It is not surprising that veterans of the fight above the Valley of Death viewed their part of the battle with higher significance than any other. What is surprising is that the significance spread to others, and with the possible exception of Pickett's Charge on the third day, no other portion of the battle—perhaps the entire war—has attained such extraordinary significance. Beginning with the resurgence of Civil War reminiscence in the 1880s, veterans of all ranks began to publish their interpretation of what the Confederate assault and Federal defense of Little Round Top represented.

Somewhat unusual among these recollections was the candidness with which many Confederate commanders discussed their failure on Gettysburg's second day. Evander Law, commander of the Alabama brigade, described the opening moments of his brigade's approach toward Little Round Top saying, "Just here the battle of Gettysburg was lost to Confederate arms." James Longstreet, Law's corps commander, viewed with regret many different parts of the battle and chief among them was his failure to seize the hill on the far left of the Union line. "I was ten minutes late in occupying Little Round Top." Even Jefferson Davis attached great significance to the hill, saying that the men on Little Round Top foiled his plans.[2]

As veterans placed such high significance on Little Round Top, it seems that a disproportionate share of this fell to the 20th Maine's position on the spur. To a large extent, this is the result of a lack of testimony about the fight on the right of Vincent's Brigade. Virtually everyone on the summit of Little Round Top who might have filed a report testifying to the desperation there either died or left their command in the area. Most notably, the commanders of two brigades, Weed and Vincent, fell mortally wounded, as did the battery commander, Hazlett.

Following the regiments from right to left around the hill, the absence of surviving witnesses reveals much. Colonel O'Rourke, who led his 140th New York into the breech at the height of the crisis, also fell

154

dead. Colonel Vincent's bugler, returning from an errand, found the commander of the 16th Michigan with half his regiment in a road some three hundred yards in rear of the hill just as the fight closed. Colonel Rice of the 44th New York took Vincent's place and was undoubtedly distracted from his own regiment by the needs of the whole brigade. Orpheus Woodward, a captain, commanded the 83rd Pennsylvania which was bent around somewhat out of view from the right of the brigade. With the exception of Chamberlain, not one commander above the rank of captain remained unharmed and at his regular post through the fight. At least partly as a result, details of the fight for the spur gained greater clarity and thus greater importance.

Another reason for the unbalanced importance of the spur has to do with the requirements of the struggle there. Unlike the other regiments of the brigade, the 20th Maine had to shift, maneuver, and protect a flank during the fight, and nothing scared Civil War soldiers more than the threat of being flanked. They accomplished this under the guidance of the newest colonel in the Fifth Corps, who performed his duties remarkably well, given his inexperience.[3]

Herein lies the key to what really made Joshua Chamberlain a hero at Gettysburg. His country awarded him the Medal of Honor for "daring heroism and great tenacity in holding his position on the Little Round Top against repeated assaults, and carrying the advance position on the Great Round Top." Neither the citation nor Chamberlain himself ever tried to depict him gloriously leading a desperate bayonet charge down the hill waving his sword over his head. That Joshua Chamberlain could stand up on the spur, given his health in the weeks prior to the battle, is itself a remarkable accomplishment. He learned from Ames the importance of instilling confidence in his men by demonstrating personal bravery and coolness in the fight and this quality did more for his victory on the spur than the legend ever recorded. In perceiving Oates' movement and bending back his left, Chamberlain placed his men so that they delivered to the Alabamians the most destructive fire they ever saw, and as the fight continued he stoically demonstrated his own confidence, walking calmly among his men. Chamberlain did all of this despite the desperate nature of the fight and while hobbled by a wound in each leg.[4]

Where this confidence came from is difficult to determine. He was sick and weak. One brother was close behind. He ordered another, even nearer at hand, into a desperate place, doubting he would return unharmed. Chamberlain commanded a regiment worn from the march, inexperienced, and with half its normal officers. Neither he nor the regiment, save sixty-eight men of the 2nd Maine, had ever been in a stand-up fight before and certainly not one on a hill in the woods nearly cut off from their brigade. With all of this playing on his mind, Chamberlain surpressed youthful insecurities and doubts about his own abilities and commanded his men to legendary glory.

The modern image of courageous, cool-headed Maine men sweeping the field with a parade ground tactical maneuver is romantic, but belies the chaotic nature of the event. While many imagine the legendary right wheel of the 20th Maine's left wing, the men who are said to have carried it out remembered something far more confused, with men running in every direction but the rear. The charge was less tactics and more instinct; adrenaline-driven rather than the result of practiced maneuvering. No parade ground, where men practiced drill until their legs ached from the effort, ever had the slope of the spur, the boulders, trees, or gaps in the line that 30 percent casualties created in the 20th Maine that day.

The real significance of the charge from a military standpoint was not that it drove the Alabamians away from Little Round Top, they were ready to leave, charge or not. The rush down the sides of the spur brought into the hands of the Mainers at least ninety more captives who would otherwise have continued to fight for the Confederacy, and war is, after all, about diminishing the enemy's strength. In addition, the scattering effect of the charge on Oates and his men prevented them from holding Big Round Top as he had hoped. Though unlikely, establishing a position on the larger hill in the night might have made Little Round Top untenable for the Federals. With seven hours of darkness and proper reinforcements, there is at least a slight possibility that Oates may have had his Gibraltar after all and, in preventing this, the charge of the 20th Maine may have indirectly saved Little Round Top.

✠ ✠ ✠

No one in either army perceived the fight for the spur with greater significance than the man whose regiment was unable to seize it. William Oates spent the rest of his life pondering one July evening in 1863, trying to understand how and why he failed. In his 1905 book he listed twelve reasons for the Confederate failure at Gettysburg. He agreed with Law, saying that if the 48th Alabama had not moved to the left, it would have been able to chase the sharpshooters away from Big Round Top, leaving the 15th and 47th Alabama a clear and direct path to the smaller hill. He further argued that had he gotten support for his position on Big Round Top and reinforced it with artillery, he could have forced the troops on the hill below to withdraw. Lastly, he stated that the loss of Colonel Bulger at a key moment caused his companies to retreat, an event that he said prevented his taking the spur "in ten minutes."[5]

The only person Oates seems to not have held accountable for the Confederate failure to take Little Round Top was himself. Had he strictly followed orders, he would have taken, as General Law desired, the clear and direct route to Little Round Top, arrived there with the rest of the brigade, and probably inflicted more damage than he did after arriving later. Moreover, his decision to detach Company A in order to accomplish a task completely outside the intent of Law's order, or the mission of the assault, cost him the use of forty or more riflemen who could have meant the difference on the spur.

No one in authority ever blamed Oates for the failure of the assault, partly because so few people knew of his side trip up Big Round Top, excepting his friend Law, and partly because of an attitude regarding orders that permeated the Confederate army. From General Lee on down, Southern commanders had developed a habit of making orders in a general way and those who received these orders were allowed to interpret them in light of the situations that presented themselves. In this sense, Oates' decisions to veer right just when Law told him left, and to detach Company A to capture wagons that were useless to the assault, were among the kinds of judgements expected of field officers. For this reason, Oates was never taken to task for his poor decisions. In his book, however, he took care to address his reasons for making them, even passing some of the blame on to Captain Schaaff of Company A for his delay in returning from Oates' ill-conceived side-mission.[6]

What Oates never knew, or at least never accepted, was the fact that his fight with the 20th Maine never imperiled Little Round Top as gravely as he perceived. Had he been able to force the Mainers from the rocky spur, he would then have had to face the 83rd Pennsylvania which had sustained relatively few casualties in the fight, and then move on up toward the crest as the 140th New York arrived, then the rest of Weed's Brigade and Crawford's Division close at hand. It is highly doubtful that his parched, exhausted, and unsupported group of less than three hundred men, after a thirty-mile march and the fight on the spur, could have taken *and held* Little Round Top. And had his men held the summit, Oates would have better understood the limits of his prize as an artillery position and perhaps reconsidered the importance of the hill. Though Law, Longstreet, Meade, Jeff Davis and others all favored Little Round Top as a *point d'appui* in the battle, an artillery site from which the Union army along Cemetery Ridge could be pummelled into submission, none of them ever took the time to walk the summit or northern slope saying, "I would have placed a gun here, here, and here." Had any of them done so, they would quickly have encountered terrain on which only eight guns, at best, could have been brought to bear against the line that Meade's army held on July 3. Carefully studied, the boulder–strewn "round top" of the hill simply does not provide the flat open ground needed to operate more than a pair of batteries firing northward to strike the Union line. Even in this ideal sense at least two pair of guns would have had to fire over the heads of the others, a dangerous practice even on the best ground, and this only with ammunition run up from farther below. In advance of the huge Confederate assault on July 3, twenty times this number of cannon fired at a small span of the Union line at much closer range for two hours and were unable to break it. No eight cannons on Little Round Top, under fire from dozens of Federal batteries in response, could have destroyed any significant portion of the Union army that day.[7]

Oates never studied the hilltop either. Instead, he chose to view his part in the greatest battle of the war as the key to it, and his inability to overcome numerous setbacks the difference, perhaps, in the entire war. "It is remarkable how small an occurrence or omission," he wrote, "trivial in itself, often turns the tide of battle, and changes governments and the maps of nations…No battle in the world's history ever had greater consequences dependent upon it, nor so many mishaps, or lost op-portunities—especially on the side of the Confederates—as that of Gettysburg."[8]

To Oates, only the combination of these two regiments, the 20th Maine and the 15th Alabama, could have ended with the same result. No other Southern unit could have come so close and no other Union regiment could have stopped him. Explaining the first and worst defeat his men ever experienced, he said, "There was no better regiment in the Confederate Army…if it failed to carry any point against which it was thrown no other single regiment need try it…The other regiments of the brigade did their duty, but the Fifteenth struck the hardest knot." That knot was Chamberlain and his Mainers, and upon them he heaped great praise. "There never were harder fighters than the Twentieth Maine men and their gallant Colonel. His skill and persistency and the great bravery of his men saved Little Round Top and the Army of the Potomac from defeat. Great events sometimes turn on comparatively small affairs." [9]

✠ ✠ ✠

The real result of Gettysburg, and its primary importance as a military event, was the destruction of men and materiel that the Confederacy could not replace. This was Lee's risk when he launched the invasion into Pennsylvania and he lost the gambit. To this end, Gettysburg was a tremendous turning point. In that fundamental sense, the 20th Maine did its share, the charge contributing great significance to its role. The charge added nearly one hundred men to the Confederate loss. Men who might have escaped in an orderly Alabamian retreat. Overall, the Mainers inflicted one-and-a-half casualties for each one of their own against an Alabama force half again as large, depleting all three regiments by more than a third. But, back in Maine, three more regiments were headed out of Portland that month, while Alabama, like most of its Southern counterparts, had but few more replacements.[10]

Looking at the larger picture of Longstreet's entire assault on the Union left, the contribution of the Maine men on the spur was very important. Federal troops on that part of the field significantly outnumbered Confederates and fought on ground of their choosing, a substantial military advantage. Yet, despite the unbalanced odds, the fight as a whole was only closely decided. Had every Federal regiment opposing Longstreet's Corps that day been as fundamentally successful as the 20th Maine, there may have been no third day, no Pickett's Charge. But not all of Longstreet's regiments marched more than thirty miles, lost their canteens, and crested Big Round Top, and not all of the Federal regiments on the left had the benefit of the spur's boulders and height. As a military element, the battle for Vincent's Spur can hardly be proven *the* decisive point of the Civil War, or even the Battle of Gettysburg. Despite Oates' feelings on the matter, events this large simply do not turn on such small affairs. It did, however, greatly affect the lives of many among the more than one thousand combatants, some more dramatically than others.

For many people, Gettysburg was the central event of the mid-nineteenth century, and veterans of the war saw it as a measure of how significant one's war experience had been. For many Mainers, and certainly the 1,621 men who at one time or another appeared on the 20th Regiment's rolls, to have been on Little Round Top was to have participated in the most significant event of the war. It was the one great Union victory of the war's eastern theater, and the greatest of all in the minds of most veterans.[11]

In this great event, the 20th Maine bore no small part, but its contribution has been unusually swelled, though only in recent years, by the popularity of Michael Shaara's Pulitzer Prize-winning novel *Killer Angels* and the subsequent movie *Gettysburg*, based upon it. Like no other piece of literature, this romanticized version of the 20th Maine's work at Gettysburg has spawned cult-like interest in the regiment and especially its colonel, making him the largest commercial subject in the Civil War community. Sculptures, paintings, T-shirts, even credit cards and commemorative plates; anything bearing the image of Chamberlain surpasses, in marketability, all other items. In most, if not all cases, they perpetuate the legendary novelized description of events. This, despite Shaara's own admission that his was a novel and not to be taken as accurate history and that the Pulitzer Prize committee recognized it as a winner in the category of fiction, not history.

It was not always so. Most serious scholarship of the battle dating back to the 1880s makes only brief mention, at best, of the Maine regiment on the left wing of the Union army. Until Shaara's work was published, General Warren was almost universally considered the hero of Little Round Top. While the history of the Fifth Corps, written in 1895, understandably places one of its own regiments as the savior of the Battle of Gettysburg, few other works even mention the 20th Maine except in passing. Jacob Hoke's 1887 work *The Great Invasion of 1863,* for example, mentions both Chamberlain and his regiment but with no greater significance than many other units.[12]

In the 1950s and '60s, scholars produced a wave of volumes on the Battle of Gettysburg, including Edward Stackpole's *They Met at Gettysburg* in 1956 and Glenn Tucker's *High Tide at Gettysburg* in 1958. Stackpole made no mention of the Mainers' work at all, while Tucker addressed the action more from a Confederate perspective, calling William Oates, "The gallant commander whose spirit had been the dominating factor of the attack on Little Round Top." In addition to these, perhaps the most widely respected scholarly work on the Battle of Gettysburg is Coddington's *The Gettysburg Campaign: A Study In Command*, published in 1968. In it the author examines the battle for Vincent's Spur as a significant part of the larger battle for Little Round Top, but makes no mention of it as the central or decisive factor in the overall battle at Gettysburg.[13]

Though absent from much of the scholarly work, the 20th Maine's story and the legend of Vincent's Spur has not been without its benefactors. Just twenty-five years after Joshua Chamberlain's death, Kenneth Roberts, a noted Maine writer of historically based fiction, mused on how wonderful it would have been if he had written the story, as fiction, of the Maine men on Little Round Top. Quoting a newspaper reporter of the time, he wrote, "As an example to inspire patriotism it would rank with Leonidas and his three hundred Spartans. America is secure against the world as long as she has such sons to spring to her defence in the hour of darkness and danger."[14]

In 1952 popular Civil War writer Bruce Catton used the account of the absent Theodore Gerrish in his book *Glory Road*, calling the 20th

Maine's fight one of many crises that day. Five years after Catton, John Pullen set a course as yet unequalled when he redefined the art of writing Civil War regimental histories with his *The Twentieth Maine: A Volunteer Regiment in the Civil War*. Pullen's work appropriately depicted the fight on the spur as the most significant event in the history of the regiment but never leaped so far as to attribute to it the salvation of the country. Still, his work, though unwittingly, had great impact on the legend as it piqued the interest of Shaara who made a novelized experience of the 20th Maine one of the central themes of his book.[15]

Two elements of the fight on the spur are key to Shaara's story and have become the most misconstrued elements of the legend. The first is the concept, as Shaara depicted it, of an organized parade ground maneuver through which the 20th Maine swept the Rebels away in a great right wheel. Joshua Chamberlain wrote of a wheeling movement in three of his major writings. The first was in his revised official report of the battle, the second in his speech at the dedication of the monument, and the third in his 1913 article "Through Blood and Fire at Gettysburg," which he decried for its sensationalized editing. In the revised official report Chamberlain condensed his description of the charge from his first version saying "holding fast by our right, and swinging forward our left, we made an extended 'right wheel.' " Clearly, Chamberlain never reported that he conceived of and then ordered a textbook maneuver and he placed the phrase right wheel in quotes indicating that what had occured did not exactly meet the military definition of the phrase. In reality, what the left wing of the 20th Maine did during its rather confused charge was to chase the Confederates back the way they had come—toward the Maine right. Viewed from any direction this was, in rough form, a right wheel but it was not executed by design and Chamberlain never claimed to have ordered it.

The second element of the legend that has become an integral part of the modern story is one that Chamberlain himself spent most of his postwar life trying to remedy. In nineteenth-century warfare commanders of military units received all of the credit and blame for the actions of their men. Understanding that, it is not surprising that veterans of the war gave Chamberlain credit for having ordered the charge, even though he denied having done so. The only mention Chamberlain made in his major writings of giving an order to charge was in his first official report which he revised later the same day. In the revised report, he wrote that he had ordered only "bayonet" and that "the word was enough." Fifty years after the battle, in his final reflective account, he wrote "It were vain to order 'forward.' No mortal could have heard it in the mighty hosanna that was winging the sky." Later in that same article he described the charge as a self-starting event saying, "There are still things of the first creation 'whose seed is in itself.' "16

Perhaps the two most telling pieces of evidence on the issue lie in the letters that Chamberlain wrote to his wife and the words expressed at the monument dedication in front of the survivors on the actual ground. In neither of the two letters that he wrote to his wife, one and ten days after the battle, did he tell her that he had ordered a charge—something he most certainly would have included had it occured. In addition, when the survivors met in 1889 to dedicate the monuments on both of the Round Tops—a meeting where exaggeration and invention on delicate points had no place—two statements rang clear. The first was by Howard Prince, the historian of the regiment, who allowed that "The lines were in motion before the word of command was completed, and Colonel Chamberlain does not know whether he ever finished that order." Later in the ceremony, Chamberlain tried again to settle the issue by saying "In fact, to tell the truth, the order was never given, or but imperfectly."17

That he would not accept credit for ordering the charge, when the norms of that time allowed commanders this privilege, reflects positively on Chamberlain. It would have been perfectly fitting and proper in the style of the period for him to have taken full responsibility for ordering the charge. Few, if any, would have objected to this, especially since he did conceive of the charge and was in the process of informing his men. Given another thirty seconds he would have ordered the charge that instead occured on its own. That he continually denied himself the honor of having ordered the charge and instead tried to pass it on to his men, sets him apart from countless other commanders who gave themselves far more credit than they ever earned.

If Chamberlain marveled in his time at the human urge to construct great heroes, he would stand in awe today at the legend-building power of one best-selling book and a subsequent motion picture. Shaara's novel and its depiction by Hollywood have so swelled the legend that it brings hundreds of visitors to the 20th Maine monument every day, and it has become the most visited Civil War site in the country each year. Ten years ago the monument was difficult for even knowledgeable visitors to locate, but through recent years it could hardly be missed by more than a million people who have made the pilgrimage down the paved pathway that brings onlookers into the midst of the 20th Maine's line of battle.

Were he alive today, Shaara would undoubtedly be pleased with what his work has accomplished. When a British acquaintence criticized America for having no heroes of the stature of the European legends such as Napolean or Alexander the Great, he set out to write *Killer Angels* in an effort to prove him wrong. Given the overwhelming folk-hero status that Chamberlain has now achieved, it would appear that Shaara has given his country a legendary hero all its own, and while Joshua Chamberlain's historical stature is still not considered on par with the classical giants of Europe, the surging fascination with his story is indeed remarkable. Shaara's novel undoubtedly tapped into a need in American society to admire such heroes even if they are at least partially a creation of literature and film.

✠ ✠ ✠

In the final analysis, the 20th Maine's work at the Battle of Gettysburg was indeed a remarkable feat that had important implications in the larger scope of the battle. But it is *despite* the legend of Vincent's Spur that they should be praised for their contribution. The legend has greatly romanticized and distorted what really happened on the spur, but not in such a way that leaves it completely devoid of great value. The soldiers in that fight overcame remarkable hardships and made a record for themselves that exceeds most of the other regiments who fought on those three days. They simply did not save the Union or doom the Confederacy in their ninety minutes of combat. In the same vein, praising Joshua Chamberlain for his work in the battle—as it would be foolhardy not to since few deserve greater praise—should not, however, diminish the endurance, tenacity, and courage of the rest of the men, Mainers and Alabamians alike, who did what they believed was their duty, whether out of commitment to home, God, country, or comrades. On the Union side, few examples exist where soldiers with so little experience in such confused and dire circumstances performed as well as the 20th Maine. Equally significant is the Confederate side. One would be hard pressed to scour the pages of military history and find an instance when soldiers endured more and then came closer to victory against greater odds than the 15th Alabama at Gettysburg.

Pondering this, those who visit the spur today encounter a very different piece of land than the one the Maine troops occupied in 1863. On the far right of the 20th's line Sykes Avenue, built in the late 1890s, has raised the small valley between the 20th Maine and 83rd Pennsylvania positions by as much as eight feet, belying the once separate nature of the spur and transforming it into more of a sloping outgrowth of Little Round Top itself. In 1902 heavy steam-powered equipment, dynamite, and rock crushers forever destroyed the slope down which the men of the left wing charged into the surprised Alabamians. In June of that year, workers completed Chamberlain Avenue, built to enable aging veterans

During and after construction of Sykes Avenue and a retaining wall in 1897. Notice the rebuilt four-foot-high wall in the background to which Chamberlain objected. The 20th Maine's right flank originally rested where the wall ends (top left) and the 83rd Pennsylvania's left flank rested at center left. Many of the rocks and boulders in these views are no longer there.

Top: Looking down Sykes Avenue in 1897. The 83rd Pennsylvania was on the right, the 20th Maine on the left, and the Alabamians at the bottom of the hill. Bottom: Looking down newly completed Chamberlain Avenue in 1902. The Alabamians attacked the 20th Maine's left flank from left to right, and the main portion of the retreat moved toward the back of this view.

165

to move closer to the area in vehicles, rather than on aching limbs. Construction of the road dramatically altered the landscape over which the most severe fighting took place. It also created a road that was named, not for the martyred Strong Vincent, but for a regimental commander who served under him and survived. In the 1930s, when the aging veterans had passed and the road had outlived its usefulness, workers removed the surface of the road, altering the area even further. In building the avenue, engineers lay several feet of crushed granite as road bed. But instead of hauling the rock from another location they simply destroyed several boulders which had provided protection for men of both sides. Even the boulders upon which the 20th Maine monument now stands were badly damaged by dynamite and black powder, though apparently by workers in 1886 trying to sculpt a proper site for the memorial rather than construct a road.[18]

Stone walls now trace some unknown purpose across the right wing of the 20th's position. Some drew the ire of Joshua Chamberlain on a visit to the spur in the late 1890s. In 1897 park workers rebuilt some of the walls that soldiers had built on the third day of the battle. When he first saw the wall, now raised to nearly four feet, Chamberlain felt it gave the false impression that the Maine men had the advantage of protection during their fight on July 2. He later addressed the issue by saying that his men "threw up on the more exposed places in our line what could scarcely be called 'breastworks,' being nowhere more than eighteen inches high, but serving to cover a little man lying down." Such was Chamberlain's influence at the time that the Gettysburg Battlefield Commission placed what is still the only marker on the battlefield that corrects a misconception. On the far right of the 20th Maine's position along what is now Sykes Avenue it reads, "This wall was built for defense July 3rd PM, 1863."[19]

Oblivious to these alterations, each of the visitors who stands at the crest of the spur looking down into the vale from which the Alabamians came has a different view. Children, some of them amazingly fluent in the details of the fight even at 8 years old, stand with a gift-shop sword or musket, imagining themselves gallantly defending the rocks with the Mainers. Many seem drawn to the romantic image of Chamberlain, a romantic himself, while visitors from the U.S. Army War College twenty miles northward see the tactics in it. Even today, the popularized story of Chamberlain's actions on the spur form the introduction to the U.S. Army Leadership Training Manual, ironically ignoring an even greater lesson in leadership underneath the legend. Much could be learned comparing and contrasting the actions of Chamberlain and Oates. What

Chamberlain really did—calmly commanding and overcoming his inexperience and ill health—is a much better lesson in leadership than that of abandoning higher ground in an impromptu bayonet charge upon an unknown enemy.[20]

Southerners come to the spur as well, content to stand in the valley below admiring the valor of the exhausted Alabamians who, against all odds, nearly accomplished the improbable. Almost all of the people who visit the spur ponder the closeness of the fight, wondering how things might be different had there been one more company of Alabamians, if the canteens had returned, or if Vincent had chosen different ground. Some wonder whether ours would be two nations today if the spur had been lost, or whether any but Chamberlain and his Mainers could have defended it so well.

There is no harm in this pondering. Indeed, we should admire the commitment and self-sacrifice with which so many men on both sides risked all for what they deeply believed—a good lesson in putting a larger cause above personal desires. But, it is not a complete experience, this pilgrimage, unless we understand that the measure of the 20th Maine's success is that they killed more than they lost, all for a piece of ground that the army abandoned three days later.

The unavoidable lesson of Gettysburg is taught also by the memory of widows, orphans, mothers, and fathers whose loved ones lie in the National Cemetery or in the anonymous graves at Richmond's Hollywood. Theirs was a great sacrifice to which there are no monuments at Gettysburg, and many of them endured their loss having never consented to risk it. The slaves became free, the Union remained whole, but the price of the victory and the defeat is beyond measure. When we think of the tragedy of Little Round Top and look for reasons or explanations which justify the suffering and the death, it is no wonder we feel the need for legends.

✠ ✠ ✠

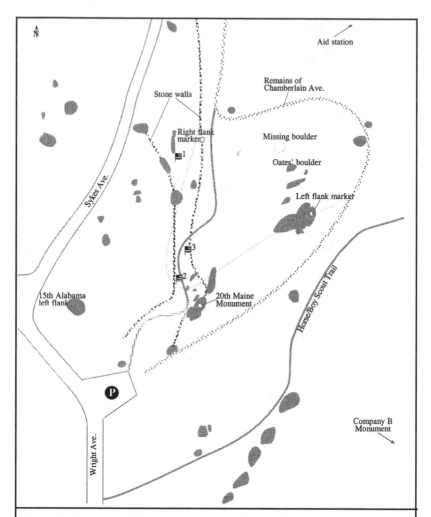

Vincent's Spur today. Changes to the area make it difficult to visualize the battle. Construction of stone walls, roads, and the destruction of several boulders (all more than ninety years in the past) have altered the ground significantly. There is now easy access to the area by vehicle, on horseback, or on foot.

168

ROSTER OF 20TH MAINE SOLDIERS AT GETTYSBURG

The following data was assembled from a number of sources, including the *Annual Reports of the Adjutant General of Maine, 1861–65*, *Maine at Gettysburg*, the *Descriptive Rolls* of the 2nd and 20th Maine Regiments, and from the personal correspondence and papers of the veterans. This information usually applies to the date that the soldier was mustered in. For the 20th Regiment, this is September 1862, and for the 2nd Regiment, July 1861.

The "S" in company indicates Staff. Residence is where the soldier was staying when he enlisted, m/s represents married or single, and Ht = height which is listed in inches. St = status, or how the soldier came out of the fight: killed, wounded, mortally wounded, or captured.

All of the information is slightly questionable as it was often taken from the replies of soldiers rather than any recorded material or certificate. For example, soldiers who claimed to be 18 years old were very often over-estimating their age. Likewise, since 45 was the maximum age, some of the older soldiers may have understated theirs.

Name	Rnk	Co.	Residence	Age	m/s	Occupation	Ht	St
Adams, Aaron	pvt	H	Linneus	27	s	farmer	72	k
Allen, Alonzo P.	mus	D	Gray	18	s	drummer	68	
Allen, Charles	sgt	K	Brunswick	32	s	lumberman	66	
Allen, Elliot C.	pvt	C	Wilton	21	s	farmer	68.5	
Ames, Addison M.	pvt	D	Cornville	23	m	farmer	69	w
Ames, John H.	pvt	K	Rockland	18	s	farmer	71	
Anderson, James	pvt	D	Bangor	30	s	laborer	68.5	
Andrews, Aaron M.	pvt	I	Camden	21	s	farmer	69	
Andrews, Obediah	pvt	I	St. George	20	s	farmer	66	
Augustine, Peter	pvt	D	Dexter (Italy)	23	s	laborer	65	
Averill, Edward	pvt	G	Jefferson	18	s	farmer	67	
Avery, Charles E.	cpl	A	Sidney	28	s	shoemkr	65	w
Ayer, Charles N.	pvt	G	Brewer	22	s			
Bailey, David A.	pvt	G	Woolwich	24	s	student	69	
Bailey, George T.	pvt	D	Dexter	18	s	wool sorter	66	
Bailey, Harlan P.	pvt	G	Woolwich	18	s	farmer	70	

169

Name	Rnk	Co.	Residence	Age	m/s	Occupation	Ht	St
Bailey, Samuel G.	cpl	G	Woolwich	22	s	student	69	
Baker, Daniel S.	pvt	K	Winterport	18	s	farmer	70.5	
Baker, Granville	hs	S	Standish	28	s	student	68	
Baker, James H.	pvt	G	Woolwich	18	s	farmer	63	
Baker, Josiah H.	pvt	G	Edgecomb	18	m	farmer	63	
Baker, Sylvester P.	pvt	D	Solon	19	s	farmer	64	
Barker, Eugene A.	pvt	C	Rumford	18	s	farmer	72	
Barker, Isaac C.	pvt	D	Exeter	21	m	farmer	70	
Barnes, Moody D.	pvt	G	Nobleboro	32	s	farmer	70	w
Barron, George W.	pvt	I	Warren	18	s	farmer	71.5	
Bartlett, Charles H.	pvt	A	Sidney	21	s	farmer	68	
Bates, Calvin	pvt	E	Waldoboro	28	s	cooper	67.75	
Beadle, Charles M	pvt	C	Buckfield	30	m	farmer	70	m
Bean, Arthur M.	pvt	C	Bethel	18	s	farmer	67	
Bean, Edgar F.	pvt	C	Bethel	18	s	farmer	67	
Benner, George G.	pvt	E	Waldoboro	33	m	farmer	68	
Benson, Thomas S.	pvt	A	Sidney	19	s	farmer	65	
Besse, Elisha Jr.	lt	I	Oakfield Pl.	38	m	farmer	67.75	
Bickford, William K.	lt	H	Thomaston	25	s	hotel clerk	68.5	
Bickmore, Charles E.	pvt	E	Waldoboro	22	s	farmer	70	
Bickmore, Eli	pvt	I	Friendship	29	m	seaman	70	
Billings, Charles W.	cpt	C	Clinton	37	m	lumberman	69	m
Blackington, Rufus R.	pvt	I	Hope	27	m	farmer	67	
Boothby, Adney D.	pvt	F	Athens	19	s	farmer	68.5	
Borneman, Luther C.	pvt	G	Jefferson	32	s	farmer	69.5	w
Bosworth, Michael	pvt	F	Solon	18	s	farmer	68.5	
Bowden, Levi O.	pvt	K	Winterport	27	m	farmer	69	
Bowman, George W.	cpl	G	Jefferson	20	s	cooper	67	
Brackett, Chandler	pvt	E	Union	28	s	cooper	69	
Bradford, I. John L.	pvt	I	Cushing	20	s	farmer	69.5	
Bradford, William B.	pvt	I	Cushing	18	s	farmer	65	
Bray, Walter S.	cpl	B	Dover	27	m	farmer	66	
Breen, John H.	pvt	A	Augusta	17	s	laborer	67	
Bresnahan, Timothy	pvt	I	Ellsworth	18	s	farmer	67	
Briggs, William J.	pvt	I	Union	19	s	farmer	69	
Brock, Lowell	pvt	E	Waldoboro	19	s	carpenter	69.5	
Brown, Albion	cpl	F	Harmony	30	m	farmer	71	w
Brown, Charles C.	pvt	E	East Benton	26	s			
Brown, Elisha A.	pvt	F	Solon	29	m	farmer	64	w
Brown, Timothy F.	cpl	E	Bristol	26	s	mstr mariner	70	
Brown, William A.	pvt	B	Sebec	20	s	farmer	68	
Bryant, Ellbridge R.	pvt	E	Bristol	21	s	farmer	70	
Bryant, Varano G.	pvt	C	Bethel	22	s	farmer	68	
Buck, Charles T.	pvt	C	Sumner	23	s	farmer	70.25	
Buck, George W.	p/s	H	Linneus	20	s	farmer	66.5	k

Name	Rnk	Co.	Residence	Age	m/s	Occupation	Ht	St
Buck, Thomas H.	cpl	I	Biddeford	27	s	laborer	71.25	
Buker, James J.	pvt	K	Ellsworth					
Buker, William G.	pvt	G	Brunswick	21	s	farmer	72	
Burding, George W.	pvt	I	S. Thomaston	34	m	mechanic	66	
Burr, Frank	pvt	G	Brewer	24	m	machinist	65	
Burrill, Newell E.	pvt	B	Dover	24	s	farmer	70	
Bussell, Oshea	pvt	F	Wellington	23	s	farmer	70	
Butler, Alvin	pvt	G	Mt. Vernon	21	s	farmer	69	
Buxton, Willard W.	pvt	K	N. Yarmouth	18	s	farmer	68	m
Card, George W.	sgt	D	Dexter	37	m	carpenter	67	w
Carpenter, Henry A.	pvt	C	Charleston	20	s			
Carpenter, Sanford A.	cpl	D	Portland	28	m	mason	68	
Carr, Almon P.	pvt	G	Mt. Vernon	18	s	farmer	70	
Carr, Elijah	pvt	F	Bangor	26	s			
Carter, Lewis D.	pvt	G	Woolwich	18	s	farmer	67	
Caswell, George B.	pvt	E	Bristol	21	s	mariner	69	
Chamberlain, J.L.	col	S	Brunswick	33	m	professor	68	
Chamberlain, T.D.	lt	S	Bangor	21	s	clerk	68	
Chapman, Edward K.	pvt	E	Waldoboro	20	s	caulker	67.5	
Chase, Benjamin F.	pvt	C	Sumner	32	m	farmer	66.75	
Chase, Charles M.	cpl	K	Freeport	19	s	farmer	72	
Chase, Stephen G.	pvt	K	Winterport	20	s	farmer	66.5	k
Chesley, Hiram H.	pvt	H	Patten	19	s	farmer	70	w
Church, Chandler K.	pvt	A	Burnham	30	m			
Clark, Albert M.	sgt	A	Waterville	21	s	mechanic	71	
Clark, Atherton W.	cpt	S	Waldoboro	36	m	farmer	71.5	
Clark, Horace B.	pvt	F	Cornville	19	s	farmer	69	
Clark, Nathan S.	cpl	H	Masardis	24	m	farmer	68	
Clark, Seth W.	pvt	F	Solon	38	s	farmer	69	k
Cleaves, Daniel	pvt	I	Biddeford	38	m	machinist	69	
Clifford, Benjamin F.	pvt	H	Linneus	20	s	farmer	68	w
Clifford, John F.	pvt	F	Bangor	18	s	farmer	68.5	
Coan, Elisha S.	pvt	D	Garland	19	s	farmer	66	
Cobb, George W.	pvt	K	Brunswick	19	s	farmer	70.75	
Collins, Elias S.	pvt	F	Harmony	19	s	farmer	70	
Colson, Theophilus	pvt	K	Winterport	29	s	farmer	70	
Conway, John	pvt	E	Bangor	23	s			
Coombs, Augustus F.	pvt	F	Parkman	18	s	farmer	74	
Coombs, Thomas A.	pvt	D	Brunswick	18	s	farmer	68	
Copeland, Charles A.	pvt	I	Warren	25	s	sailor	64.5	
Cotton, Richard G.	pvt	B	Williamsburg	35	m	farmer	69.5	
Courson, David H.	pvt	K	Harpswell	19	s	mechanic	69	
Crane, Daniel	pvt	H	Linneus	36	s	farmer	66	
Creighton, Emerson	cpl	I	Warren	21	s	farmer	69	
Crocker, George	sgt	F	St. Albans	28	m	farmer	68	

Name	Rnk	Co.	Residence	Age	m/s	Occupation	Ht	St
Crocker, George A.	pvt	D	Dexter	18	s	farmer	68	w
Crocker, Samuel G.	sgt	B	Brownville	37	m	farmer	73.5	
Cross, Eli W.	pvt	B	Dover	18	s	harness mkr	67	
Cross, Frederick H.	pvt	K	Rockland	18	s	farmer	65	
Cudworth, Levi	pvt	E	Bristol	20	s	farmer	72	
Cummings, Leonard N.	pvt	B	Albany	18	s	farmer	71	
Cummings, Wesley	pvt	B	Albany	25	s	student	68	
Cunningham, Albert	pvt	G	Edgecomb	32	m	brickmkr	68	w
Curtis, Frank B.	pvt	F	Wellington	23	s	farmer	67	k
Curtis, Merrill G.	pvt	D	Dexter	18	s	farmer	68	w
Cushman, Llewellyn	pvt	G	Woolwich	21	s	farmer	71	w
Cushman, Wales H.	pvt	G	Woolwich	26	s	carpenter	73	
Cutler, Alvin	pvt	E	Bristol	21	s	mariner	69	
Daggett, Isaac T.	pvt	F	Bingham	27	m	farmer	69	
Daniels, George G.	pvt	F	Harmony	44	m	farmer	67	
Davis, Fred T.	pvt	H	Freeport	19	s	carpenter	69	
Davis, Gilman	pvt	F	Wellington	19	s	farmer	70	
Davis, Milton H.	pvt	I	Friendship	20	s	fisherman	68	
Davis, Moses	pvt	C	Caribou	24	s	farmer	68	m
Davis, William H.	pvt	F	Cambridge	21	s	farmer	68	
Davis, William L.	pvt	E	Union					
Dawes, Calvin	pvt	A	Cumberland	21	s	farmer	68	
Day, Melville C.	cpl	G	Jefferson	21	s	farmer	66	k
Decker, Royal B.	sgt	B	Lagrange	25	s	farmer	72	
Deering, Andrew C.	cpl	C	Foxcroft	31	m	blacksmith	69.5	
DeWitt, Joseph E.	pvt	F	Ripley	19	s	farmer	69	
Dinsmore, Eben F.	pvt	F	Hartland	27	m	farmer	67	
Drake, Elisha O.	pvt	C	Livermore	41	m	farmer	68	
Dunbar, Harlow	pvt	G	Nobleboro	18	s	farmer	69	
Dunham, Dawson J.	pvt	F	Cornville	38	m	farmer	70	
Dunlap, Horace	pvt	F	Ripley	27	s	farmer	67	
Durgin, Cyrus C.	cpl	B	Sebec	24	m	blacksmith	71	
Edes, Augustus	pvt	B	Abbot	19	s	farmer	70.5	
Ellis, Augustus	pvt	D	Dexter	18	s	farmer	66	
Elwell, Freeman	pvt	I	St. George	18	s	farmer	65	
Elwell, Ira G.	pvt	I	St. George	20	s	stone cutter	65	
Erskine, James H.	pvt	G	Bristol	34	m	brickmkr	72	w
Estabrook, George F.	cpl	H	Amity	21	s	farmer	68.5	
Estabrooke, Glazier	pvt	H	Amity	45	m	farmer	66	
Estes, Isaac W.	sgt	C	Bethel	23	m	farmer	70.5	m
Estes, Nathaniel S.	cpl	C	Bethel	23	s	farmer	68	
Farrand, Austin	pvt	I	Thomaston	27	s	farmer	66.5	
Faunce, Edward	pvt	C	Rumford	23	m	farmer	66	
Fenderson, Lewis	pvt	K	Winterport	20	s	farmer	69	
Fernald, Albert E.	sgt	K	Winterport	24	s	tailor	65	w

Name	Rnk	Co.	Residence	Age	m/s	Occupation	Ht	St
Fernald, John Q.A.	pvt	E	Waldoboro	23	m	tanner	71	
Fickett, Amasa W.	pvt	K	Brewer	18	s	farmer	64.5	
Field, Benjamin R.	pvt	B	Foxcroft	34	m	sailor	70	
Field, Ira M.	pvt	K	Freeport	21	s	miller	73.5	
Fish, Benjamin N.	pvt	I	Union	20	s	farmer	69	w
Fitch, Joseph B.	cpt	D	Bristol	34	m	merchant	70	w
Fogg, Elliott L.	pvt	C	Sumner	20	s	farmer	67	k
Fogler, Prentiss M.	cpt	I	Hope	23	m	merchant	67	
Foss, Elfin J.	pvt	F	Embden	32	s	farmer	67.5	k
Foss, John	cpl	F	Athens	27	s	yeoman	69	k
Foss, Washington	pvt	A	Cornville	18	s	farmer	66	
Fowles, Gowen W.	pvt	H	Medway	24	s	farmer	70	
Fox, Samuel A.	pvt	F	Cornville	20	s	farmer	68	w
Foy, Edwin B.	cpl	K	Brunswick	19	s	laborer	65	
Frederick, Edward	pvt	H	Bangor	21	s			
Freeman, Samuel	pvt	B	Medford	19	s	farmer	69	
Frees, William L.	pvt	B	Maxfield	30	m	farmer	69	
Freethy, John G.	pvt	K	Brooklin	24	s	cook	69.5	
French, Benjamin F.	pvt	H	Linneus	21	s	farmer	72	w
French, Edward B.	pvt	F	Athens	24	s	farmer	68	w
French, Oliver	cpl	D	Solon	25	m	farmer	68	w
Frost, Albert	pvt	F	St. Albans	18	s	farmer	66	
Fuller, Emulus S.	pvt	A	Eustis	29	m	farmer	67	
Fuller, Joseph II	lt	K	Brunswick	26	m	mechanic	66	
Getchell, Henry W.	sgt	A	Winslow	40	m	farmer	71	
Geyer, Francis	pvt	I	Friendship	17	s	seaman	71	
Given, John T.	pvt	G	Brewer	25	m	clerk	69.5	
Goff, Edmund	pvt	H	Patten	21	s	farmer	67	
Gordon, Edmund	pvt	F	Bangor	19	s	farmer	67.5	
Gordon, Frank	pvt	F	St. Albans	18	s	farmer	67	
Gordon, Isaiah L.	pvt	F	St. Albans	20	s	farmer	72	
Gould, William F.	mus	B	Eastport					
Grant, Benjamin W.	pvt	F	Cornville	20	s	farmer	73	k
Grant, Enoch T.	pvt	K	Freeport	18	s	farmer	64.5	
Grant, George N.	pvt	I	S. Thomaston	18	s	quarryman	64	
Gray, Samuel F.	pvt	K	Ellsworth	35	m	lumberman	69.75	
Greeley, Cyrus S.	pvt	D	Dexter	29	m	farmer	70	
Greenwood, Wm. B.	sgt	G	Wiscasset	32	m	blacksmith	65.5	
Griffin, Benjamin N.	pvt	I	Stockton	18	s	farmer	68.5	
Griffin, William	sgt	B	Stockton	22	s	joiner	68.5	
Grindle, Joseph	pvt	A	Bangor	42	m	laborer	73.5	w
Hall, Charles F.	pvt	F	Bangor	19	s			k
Hall, Isaac C.	pvt	A	Freedom	35	m	farmer	71	
Hall, Leonidas	pvt	F	Portland					
Hall, Lewis	pvt	I	Warren	21	s	farmer	68	

173

Name	Rnk	Co.	Residence	Age	m/s	Occupation	Ht	St
Ham, Mansfield	pvt	H	Hodgdon	19	s	farmer	66	w
Harrington, James H.	sgt	A	Burnham	28	m	farmer	68	w
Harris, Myron W.	cpl	H	Littleton	24	s	farmer	67	
Hasey, William H.H.	sgt	E	Bangor	21	s	farmer	68	
Haynes, Charles H.	sgt	E	Ellsworth	26	m	seaman	69	
Heald, Benjamin F.	pvt	C	Sumner	19	s	farmer	71	w
Heald, Llewellyn B.	pvt	C	Sumner	19	s	farmer	70	w
Herrin, Benjamin F.	pvt	D	Skowhegan	36	s	teamster	70	
Herscomb, Andrew	pvt	G	Edgecomb	22	s	farmer	65	w
Higgins, David S.	pvt	B	Sebec	28	s	farmer	69	
Hill, William E.	pvt	A	Burnham	18	s	farmer	66	w
Hilt, Byron	pvt	H	Presque Isle	19	s	farmer	66.5	w
Hilton, Daniel	pvt	F	Cornville	27	m	farmer	70	
Hiscock, Abner S.	sgt	G	Damariscotta	27	m	mechanic	71.5	w
Hitchborn, George W.	pvt	B	Medford	28	s	farmer	70	
Hock, George A.	cpl	E	Waldoboro					
Hodgdon, George D.	mus	G	Richmond	24	s	machinist	67.5	
Hodgdon, Josiah S.	pvt	C	Peru	40	m	farmer	73	w
Hodgdon, Thomas F.	cpl	B	Milo	21	s	farmer	72	
Hodgdon, William S.	cpl	F	Embden	18	s	farmer	68	k
Hodgman, Osgood A.	pvt	C	Rumford	18	s	farmer	68.5	
Hoffses, Raymond W.	cpl	E	Waldoboro	27	s	caulker	72	
Hogue, Thomas R.	lt	E	Waldoboro	33	m	mason	70.5	
Horton, James A.	sgt	H	Haynesville	19	s	shoemkr	67	
Howes, Oliver	pvt	I	Washington	37	m	farmer	71	
Huff, Gilman P.	pvt	G	Edgecomb	18	s	mariner	71	
Hughes, Richard	cpl	B	Brownville	33	m	quarryman	66	
Humphrey, Albert E.	pvt	E	Waldoboro	18	s	farmer	68	
Hunnewell, Franklin S.	pvt	D	Portland	19	s	clerk	70	
Hussey, Wright W.	pvt	I	Biddeford	32	m	machinist	65	
Hutchins, Alvah L.	pvt	A	Freedom	19	s	farmer	67	
Hyler, Sylvanus	pvt	I	Cushing	27	m	farmer	71	
Ingalls, Joshua	pvt	I	Bridgton	29	m	farmer	65	
Ireland, Goodwin S.	pvt	H	Presque Isle	18	s	farmer	65	k
Ireland, John F.	pvt	H	Presque Isle	23	s	farmer	69	
Jackson, Eugene R.	sgt	G	Jefferson	22	s	farmer	71	
Jameson, John H.	pvt	I	Cushing	24	s	farmer	72.5	
Johnson, John	pvt	B	Solon	18	s	farmer	67	
Johnson, Jonathan G.	sgt	D	Garland	24	m	farmer	67	
Johnson, Sullivan	pvt	F	St. Albans	20	s	farmer	70	
Jones, Charles A.	pvt	I	Hope	19	s	farmer	64.25	
Jones, Danville F.	pvt	D	Cornville	18	s			
Jordan, William S.	sgt	G	Bangor	21	s	scholar	72.5	k
Kalloch, Elmas M.	cs	S	Warren	22	m	farmer	69	
Keating, Edwin	pvt	K	Appleton	24	s	carriage mkr	67	

Name	Rnk	Co.	Residence	Age	m/s	Occupation	Ht	St
Keene, Daniel W.	cpl	I	Bremen	19	s	farmer	67	
Keene, Samuel T.	cpt	F	Rockland	29	m	attorney	67.5	w
Keene, Weston H.	lt	D	Bremen	24	s	student	72	
Kelleran, Eugene B.	pvt	I	Cushing	24	m	farmer	69	
Kendall, Warren L.	lt	G	Belfast	24	s	carver	71	k
Kennedy, John M.	pvt	G	Jefferson	24	s	teacher	69	w
Knapp, Charles A.	sgt	C	Rumford	19	s			w
Knight, James A.	pvt	G	Edgecomb	18	s	joiner	68	k
Knowlan, Freeman H.	pvt	H	Masardis	30	s	farmer	68	
Knox, Sumner	pvt	D	Garland	25	m	farmer	68	
Lamson, Iredell	pvt	H	Presque Isle	19	s	farmer	68.5	k
Lamson, Wm. P. Jr.	pvt	B	Sebec	18	s	farmer	66.5	
Land, Joseph F.	cpt	H	Edgecomb	24	s	merchant	65.5	
Lane, Clement W.	pvt	K	Winterport	28	m	farmer	67.5	
Lane, Frederic W.	lt	B	Milo	24	s	teacher	71	
Langley, Samuel	pvt	A	Sidney	41	s	farmer	68	
Latham, Arthur B.	cpl	C	Buckfield	19	s	farmer	70.5	
Lathrop, Isaac N.	sgt	H	Bangor	24	s	farmer	72	m
Leach, George W.	pvt	B	New B'swick	25	s	millman	66.5	c/d
Leach, John D.	sgt	I	Camden	23	m	millman	69	
Leighton, Adriel	pvt	H	Augusta	22	s			
Lenfest, John	pvt	E	Union	40	m	farmer	67	
Leonard, Abial E.	pvt	B	Milo	18	s	miller	70.5	
Lester, Alexander E.	pvt	I	St. John, NB	18	s	millman	68.5	k
Levensaler, Elijah S.	pvt	E	Waldoboro	18	s	farmer	67	
Lewis, Addison W.	lt	A	Waterville	31	m	merchant	69	
Lewis, David J.	cpl	A	Waterville	26	s	farmer	69	w
Libby, Benjamin D.	pvt	F	Athens	41	m	farmer	61.5	w
Libby, Findley B.	pvt	I	Camden	18	s	farmer	65	
Libby, John M.	cpl	H	Biddeford					w
Libby, Leander M.	pvt	D	Corinna	18	s	farmer	66	
Libby, Samuel B.	pvt	K	Durham	22	m	butcher	69	
Libby, Seth H.	pvt	B	Lagrange	18	s	farmer	68	
Light, Alva	pvt	G	Edgecomb	18	s	farmer	69.75	
Light, Edward	pvt	I	Washington	18	s	farmer	71	
Lincoln, Oliver W.	pvt	I	Washington	19	s	farmer	60	
Linnekin, John F.	pvt	K	Appleton	18	s	farmer	67	
Linscott, Arad H.	lt	I	Jefferson	18	s	farmer	70	m
Little, Thomas C.	pvt	E	Bristol	42	m	farmer	65	w
Livermore, Wm. T.	cpl	B	Milo	22	s	farmer	69.5	
Long, Hezekiah	sgt	F	Thomaston	37	m	prison guard	69	
Lore, Charles	pvt	A	Waterville	18	s	farmer	68	w
Lowell, Samuel T.	pvt	G	Alna	33	m	clerk	68	
Lyford, Danville B.	pvt	B	Sebec	28	m	farmer	71	
Lyford, John	pvt	B	Sebec	44	m	farmer	74	

Name	Rnk	Co.	Residence	Age	m/s	Occupation	Ht	St
Lynes, John Jr.	pvt	D	Bangor	19	s	lumberman	68.25	
Mabury, Andrew D.	cpl	D	Windham	33	m	farmer	69	k
Maddox, Aaron W.	pvt	E	Union	30	s	cooper	66.5	
Mank, Leander M.	pvt	E	Waldoboro	24	s	blacksmith	66.75	
Mann, Fred H.	cpl	A	Sidney	19	s	farmer	66	
Mann, Patrick	pvt	E	Bristol	32	m	farmer	75	
Marden, Ezra B.	pvt	A	Bangor	20	s	joiner	68.5	
Martin, James R.	sgt	F	Parkman	33	m	blacksmith	70	w
McGuire, Seth	pvt	H	Linneus	31	m	farmer	68.5	
McIntyre, John J.	pvt	E	Bristol	25	s	mariner	63.5	
McIntyre, Joseph	pvt	E	Bristol	28	s	mariner	70	
McKim, William D.	pvt	E	Bristol	34	m	carpenter	63	
McLain, Jacob	pvt	K	Damariscotta	34	s	shoemkr	68	
McLain, Thomas B.	cpl	K	Brunswick	32	s	laborer	63.5	
McPhee, Michael J.	pvt	D	Bangor	30	m	lumberman	66.75	
Melcher, Holman S.	lt	F	Topsham	21	s	teacher	72	
Melcher, Samuel G.	pvt	C	Brunswick	34	s			
Mero, Charles H.	pvt	E	Waldoboro	19	s	farmer	71	
Merriam, Lewis Jr.	sgt	H	Houlton	19	s	millman	68	
Merrill, James R.	pvt	K	Auburn	16	s	farmer	68	k
Merrill, William F.	pvt	K	Freeport	21	s	machinist	72	k
Meserve, Elisha	cpl	G	Wiscasset	38	s	farmer	66.5	
Messer, Thomas G.	pvt	K	Damariscotta	28	m	harness mkr	71	
Miller, George	pvt	H	Bangor	20				
Miller, Samuel	pvt	E	Waldoboro	18	s	clerk	68	
Mills, George V.	pvt	C	Brooksville	18	s	farmer	66	
Mink, Orchard F.	pvt	E	Waldoboro	27	s	farmer	65.5	w
Monk, Decatur	pvt	C	Buckfield	30	m	farmer	66	w
Monroe, Horace	pvt	I	Thomaston	23	s	student	65.5	
Moody, Albert A.	pvt	G	Waldoboro	25	s	farmer	71.5	
Moon, Moses	pvt	D	Ellsworth	34	m	seaman	69	
Moore, Henry H.	pvt	C	Canaan	25	s	cooper	65.5	
Morin, John W.	cpl	F	Embden	22	s	farmer	72	w
Morrell, William W.	lt	H	Brunswick	26	s	lawyer	68	
Morrill, Edwin	pvt	B	Sebec	18	s	farmer	69.5	w
Morrill, Walter G.	cpt	B	Williamsburg	21	s	quarryman		
Morrison, Edmund	pvt	H	Linneus	21	s	farmer	72	w
Morse, Hiram	sgt	I	Warren	35	m	farmer	70	
Morse, John D.	cpl	I	Thomaston	23	m	millman	69	
Morse, Winfield S.	pvt	K	N. Yarmouth	18	s	farmer	66	
Morton, Daniel W.	pvt	C	Windsor	21	s			
Morton, Randall B.	sgt	D	Windham	33	m	teacher	69	
Moulton, George H.	cpl	B	Lagrange	25	s	farmer	71	
Murdock, Sylvester E.	pvt	C	Buckfield	34	m	painter	67.5	
Murphy, Jeremiah	pvt	G	Bangor	44	m			

Name	Rnk	Co.	Residence	Age	m/s	Occupation	Ht	St
Nash, James A.	pvt	G	Nobleboro	23	s	farmer	69	
Neal, George D.	pvt	C	Livermore	22	s	farmer	72	
Newell, Enoch F.	pvt	K	Brunswick	19	s	farmer	70	w
Newton, William F.	pvt	K	Freeport	22	s	fisherman	68	
Nichols, James H.	lt	K	Brunswick	33	m	tailor	69	
Norton, Hiram	pvt	A	Solon	24	s	farmer	68	w
Noyes, George S.	sgt	K	Pownal	27	f		69	k
O'Connell, John	pvt	C	Waterford	21	s			w
Oakes, Hudson S.	pvt	B	Foxcroft	34	m	farmer	67.5	
Odlin, Waldo P.	pvt	C	Bangor	21	s	farmer	72	
Osborn, Cyrus	cpl	G	Alna	31	m	caulker	69	w
Owen, William H.	cpl	B	Milo	19	s	farmer	68	
Page, David F.	pvt	B	Atkinson	18	s	farmer	69.25	
Palmer, George	pvt	E	Bristol	19	s	mariner	69	
Palmer, Luther L.	pvt	F	Cornville	21	s	farmer	71	
Parkman, Franklin B.	pvt	B	Guilford	30	m	millman	71	
Patten, David	pvt	F	Cornville	40	m	farmer	71	w
Peabody, Jason T.	pvt	I	Union	28	m	farmer	65.5	w
Pennell, William B.	pvt	K	Harpswell	25	m	fisherman	68	
Pennington, Chris.	pvt	D	Garland	43	m	farmer	69	
Pero, Henry	pvt	G	Wiscasset	19	s	seaman	67	
Pinhorn, Vincent W.	cpl	C	Orrington	25	s	mariner	67	w
Pinkham, Willard	cpl	D	Charleston	41	s	farmer	69	k
Plummer, Rufus B.	lt	G	Linneus	34	m	carpenter	68	
Poland, Samuel	pvt	F	Athens	43	m	farmer	71	
Powers, Charles P.	pvt	C	Newry	18	s	farmer	67.5	w
Preble, George	pvt	G	Edgecomb	23	s	brickmkr	69.5	
Preble, Henry C.	pvt	G	Woolwich	19	s	farmer	67	
Prescott, Eli L.	pvt	D	Dexter	44	m	farmer	69	
Prescott, Stephen A.	pvt	D	Dexter	39	m	farmer	68	k
Proctor, Charles W.	sgt	H	Oxbow Pl.	18	s	shoemkr	70	
Quimby, Michael	mus	F	Bangor	18	s	drummer	67.5	
Ramsdell, Benj. F.	pvt	D	Gray	27	s	farmer	65	
Ramsdell, George A.	cpl	K	Brunswick	24	s	farmer	70	w
Ramsdell, John N.	pvt	D	Exeter	18	s	farmer	66	w
Rankin, William	pvt	G	Newcastle	18	s	farmer	68.5	
Rankins, William	pvt	A	Waterville	18	s	farmer	68.5	w
Redmond, George K.	pvt	F	Embden	19	s	farmer	69	
Reed, Charles H.	cpl	A	Freedom	23	s	harness mkr	69	w
Reed, Herbert M.	pvt	K	Pownal	21	s	mariner	69	w
Reed, John Jr.	cpl	A	Eustis	25	s	farmer	70	k
Reynolds, George W.	sgt	A	Sidney	21	s	farmer	72	w
Rhodes, Charles	pvt	K	Rockland	32	m	machinist	72	w
Rich, George R.	pvt	D	Charleston	22	s	farmer	66	
Richards, Sylvester S.	cpl	K	Knox	21	m	farmer	71	w

Name	Rnk	Co.	Residence	Age	m/s	Occupation	Ht	St
Richardson, George H.	pvt	B	Denmark	29	m	millman	68.5	
Rideout, Luther M.	cpl	D	Garland	22	s	farmer	69.5	
Ring, Benjamin T.	pvt	K	N. Yarmouth	24	s	farmer	66.5	w
Ring, William D.	pvt	H	Freeport	18	s	farmer	68	
Roberts, Albert	pvt	C	Livermore	18	s	farmer	70	
Roberts, Andrew J.	sgt	C	Sumner	33	m	shoemkr	68.5	
Robinson, Hance	pvt	I	Cushing	23	s	farmer	71.5	
Rogers, Frank M.	pvt	H	Appleton	18	s	farmer	64	
Roosen, Theodore	pvt	I	Thomaston	18	s	farmer	66	
Royal, David H.	pvt	C	Bangor	18	s	farmer	64.25	
Royal, George H.	cpl	K	Topsham	25	s	sailor	65	
Rundlett, James C.	sgt	G	East Pittston	24	s	teacher	71	
Safford, John M.	cpl	D	Corinna	18	s	farmer	71	
Sanborn, Edmund R.	pvt	B	Lagrange	18	s	student	67.5	
Sanborn, Mattson C.	lt	D	S. Berwick	19	s	student	69.5	
Sanborn, William S.	pvt	B	Lagrange	21	s	farmer	70	
Sanders, Henry C.	pvt	B	Brownville	19	s	farmer	69	w
Schwartz, Gardiner	sgt	E	Waldoboro	18	s	clerk	67	
Shaw, Resolvo	pvt	A	Waterville	21	s	millman	66	
Shay, Michael	pvt	D	Bangor	22	s	laborer	66	
Sherman, John M.	cpl	E	Waldoboro					
Sherwood, John M.	sgt	E	Bangor					
Shorey, Charles R.	sgt	A	Waterville	22	s	carpenter	70.5	
Sidelinger, Henry F.	lt	E	Union	19	s	farmer	69	
Simpson, Joseph D.	cpl	A	Waterville	25	m	laborer	72	k
Skillings, Charles A.	pvt	B	Guilford	19	s	farmer	66	
Skillings, Sumner L.	pvt	D	Garland	20	s	farmer	68	
Small, Alva B.	pvt	C	Caribou	23	s	farmer	70	m
Smith, Ammi M.	sgt	F	Parkman	18	s	shoemkr	71.5	
Smith, Andrew H.	pvt	K	Denmark	32	m	farmer	74	
Smith, James H.	pvt	G	Wellington					
Smith, John T.	pvt	G	Edgecomb	40	m	farmer	70.5	c
Southard, Joel	pvt	K	Harpswell	25	m	fisherman	69	
Spaulding, Randall H.	pvt	B	Foxcroft	36	m	farmer	71	
Spear, Ellis	cpt	S	Wiscasset	27	s	teacher	69.75	
Spooner, William E.	pvt	H	Hodgdon	18	s	farmer	65	
Stanwood, James H.	lt	C	Waldoboro	37	m	potter	68.5	w
Steele, Charles W.	sgt	H	Oakfield Pl.	34	s	farmer	66.5	k
Sterling, George	pvt	I	Thomaston	27	s	rock digger	68	
Stevens, Colver	pvt	I	Biddeford	28	s	laborer	68.75	
Stevens, Daniel	pvt	D	Wellington	18	s	farmer	70	
Stevens, Jeremiah C.	pvt	A	Sidney	42	s	farmer	71	
Stevens, Oliver L.	pvt	C	Livermore	19	s	farmer	71	m
Stevens, William H.	pvt	I	Bucksport	27	s	painter	68.25	
Stinson, Merritt	pvt	A	Clinton	19	s	farmer	69.5	

Name	Rnk	Co.	Residence	Age	m/s	Occupation	Ht	St
Stone, George W.	pvt	B	Richmond	18	s	farmer	67.5	
Stone, Jesse M.	pvt	F	Ripley	18	s	farmer	67	
Stover, Andrew W.	sgt	I	S. Thomaston	21	m	painter	72	w
Surry, Joseph L.	pvt	A	Castine	18	s	laborer	64.5	w
Swanton, Albert J.	cpl	D	Dexter	21	s	farmer	71	
Sweeney, Eugene	pvt	G	Newcastle	18	s	farmer	68	c
Swett, Henry A.	pvt	D	Garland	21	s	farmer	69.5	w
Swett, Jason H.	pvt	H	T8 R5	33	m	farmer	70	
Swett, Nathaniel L.	pvt	G	Orrington	21	s	teamster	72	
Sylvester, Ira R.	pvt	A	Freedom	19	s	farmer	68	w
Tarbell, Erastus	pvt	A	Clinton	18	s	farmer	69	
Tarbell, Joseph E.	pvt	H	Merrill Pl.	25	s	farmer	71	
Taylor, Alfred	pvt	A	Eustis	21	s	farmer	70	w
Thomas, James	pvt	C	Rumford	44	m	farmer	72.5	
Thomas, Moses S.	pvt	C	Woodland	22	s	farmer	69	w
Thomas, Oscar	pvt	I	Lee	21	s	farmer	70	
Thomas, Reuel	sgt	S	Thomaston	23	s	mason	70.5	w
Thompson, Arad	sgt	C	Livermore	21	s	farmer	68	
Thorn, John F.	pvt	K	Brunswick	24	s	laborer	69	w
Thorndike, Hosea B.	pvt	I	Camden	24	m	farmer	69	
Tibbetts, Caleb B.	pvt	H	Haynesville	21	s	lumberman	69	
Tibbetts, Jotham D.	pvt	G	Woolwich	19	s	farmer	64	c
Titus, Albert E.	cpl	E	Union	18	s	farmer		
Tobin, John	pvt	C	Caribou	33	m	farmer	65.5	w
Toothaker, George A.	pvt	K	Brunswick	32	m	painter	67	
Torrey, Charles L.	pvt	I	Bangor	22	s	seaman	66	
Town, Alfred M.	pvt	K	Brunswick	29	s	painter	67	
Townsend, Thomas	pvt	E	Houlton					
Tozer, Henry M.	cpl	A	Waterville	19	s	lythomaker	67	
Tozier, Andrew	sgt	S	Plymouth	27	s	sailor		
Tripp, Paschal M.	cpl	F	Ripley	32	m	farmer	69	k
True, Franklin	pvt	A	Clinton	18	s	farmer	69	w
True, Laforrest P.	cpl	A	Clinton	18	s	farmer	69	w
Trundy, Hiram W.	pvt	E	Union	34	m	carriage mkr	67	
Turner, Barden	pvt	E	Waldoboro	21	s	farmer	72	
Turner, Winslow	pvt	C	Buckfield	37	m	shoemkr	69	
Twomey, Thomas	pvt	E	Bangor	20	s			
Tyler, Irving	pvt	K	Durham	19	s	carriage mkr	70	
Veazie, Samuel W.	pvt	G	Bangor	18	s	lumberman	67.5	
Verrill, Moses F.	pvt	C	Buckfield	24	m	farmer	68	
Vinal, John	pvt	G	Jefferson	38	m	farmer	67	
Walker, Gustavus F.	pvt	H	Hodgdon	19	s	farmer	70	w
Walker, Joseph Jr.	sgt	D	Atkinson	36	s	millman	71.5	
Walker, Orrin	pvt	K	Stoneham	37	m	carpenter	67	m
Wall, Vinal E.	cpl	K	Rockland	18	s	clerk	66	

179

Name	Rnk	Co.	Residence	Age	m/s	Occupation	Ht	St
Ward, Franklin B.	cpl	F	Brighton	20	s	farmer	72	w
Ward, William H. Jr.	pvt	K	Orono	19	s	seaman	69.5	
Wardwell, David S.	pvt	A	Clinton	31	m	farmer	68	
Warner, Sumner L.	pvt	B	Dover	18	s	millman	69.5	
Weaver, Leander S.	pvt	F	Parkman	20	s	farmer	67	
Weed, John E.	pvt	I	S. Thomaston	21	s	quarryman	69	
Welch, Thomas	pvt	H	Houlton	37	s	farmer	69	
Wentworth, Sanford	pvt	F	Athens	24	s	farmer	66	k
Wentworth, Wm. A.	pvt	K	Hope	21	s	farmer	70	w
Wentworth, Wm. H.	pvt	E	Bangor	20	s	seaman	66	
Wescott, James B.	pvt	I	Biddeford	21	s	saw repairer	66.5	
West, Joseph	pvt	H	Carmel	40	m	farmer	69	w
Wheeler, Henry L.	pvt	G	Grnfield, MA	19	s	farmer	69.25	
White, Sylvanus R.	pvt	F	St. Albans	26	m	farmer	68	w
Whitman, Ezekiel	pvt	F	Brighton	22	s	farmer	72	w
Whitney, Charles A.	pvt	E	Etna	24	s	laborer	70	
Whitney, William H.	pvt	K	Brunswick	18	s	farmer	68.25	
Whitten, Isaiah	pvt	A	Alfred	20	s	farmer	67	
Whitten, Melvin W.	pvt	H	Dexter	18	s	farmer	66	
Whittier, Charles G.	pvt	C	Caribou	21	s	farmer	70	
Willey, William E.	pvt	A	Belgrade	26	m	mechanic	68	w
Winslow, Joseph	pvt	H	Oxbow Pl.	19	s	farmer	67.5	
Witham, Charles J.	pvt	I	Washington	24	s	farmer	69	w
Witherell, Edwin S.	pvt	E	Augusta					
Witherell, Robert A.	pvt	F	Bangor					
Wood, George H.	sgt	C	Hartford	22	s	farmer	68	
Worthing, William A.	pvt	K	Harpswell	28	m	fisherman	69	
Wright, Fred R.	pvt	G	Wiscasset	18	s	farmer	66	
Wright, John	pvt	C	Veazie	35	s	laborer	68	
Wyer, Oscar	pvt	F	Bangor	18	s			k
Wyman, Spencer M.	sgt	K	Freeport	26	m	farmer	60.5	
Wyman, Thomas C.	pvt	H	Phippsburg	18	s			
York, Andrew J.	cpl	H	Pownal					
York, George H.	pvt	C	Woodstock	28	s	farmer	71	w
Young, Ervin S.	pvt	A	Solon	21	s	farmer	72	

Numbers of Combatants

Numerical strengths of the three regiments

20th Maine

Company	E	I	K	D	F	A	H	C	G	B	St	Total
Officers	2	3	2	3	2	1	3	2	2	2	4	26
Enlisted	45	52	53	43	55	41	43	48	52	42	3	477
Total Strength	47	55	55	46	57	42	46	50	54	44	9	503

The number of 20th Maine combatants–soldiers present with the regiment during the Battle of Gettysburg–was determined using the list of "Participants" in *Maine at Gettysburg*. Non-combatant personnel such as musicians and those listed sick or on detached duty were excluded from these numbers. The companies are listed in the order they appeared in line on the spur; E on the regiment's right and G on the left. "St" represents staff.

The total strength figure (503) exceeds considerably the strength of the regiment as listed on the Vincent's Spur monument (396) which comes from the official reports. The origin of the official report figures is unclear but it was a common and accepted practice at that time for a commander to underestimate his own stregnth, and overestimate his enemy's, thus raising the odds upon which a regiment's honor in battle was judged. The discrepancy may also be the result of several other factors.

First, it is not clear whether the numbers on the monument include the forty-two enlisted men of Company B who did not fight with the rest of the regiment on the spur. With or without these, the difference of more than one hundred men may be accounted for when several factors are considered. The last official roll call of the regiment before the battle was taken on June 30, in order to complete the June monthly reports. At this time, approximately sixty hours before the action on the spur opened, the company rolls indicate that 511 men were present in the regiment.

During the eighteen hours between that roll call and the fight, the regiment marched only three miles, leaving a window of opportunity for men who may have straggled to catch up to their unit. Footnote (b) of *Maine at Gettysburg* (p. 254) states that men who had been listed as absent sick "came up and took their places," as did the pioneers, provost guard, and all but three of the remaining men of the 2nd Maine still under guard. The *Maine at Gettysburg* list includes four musicians who likely were combatants. In his official report, made four days after the fight, Joshua Chamberlain wrote that "Every pioneer and musician who could carry a musket went into the ranks."

In a letter written shortly before the fiftieth anniversary of the battle, Joshua Chamberlain explained that it was difficult to determine how many men were actually involved in the fight because, "several of these men [stragglers], I should say, most of them, did come up on the morning of July 2nd, at Gettysburg, and took their places in the ranks, and did their best."[1]

The list of "Participants" was created for the Maine at Gettysburg Executive Committee for the purposes of publishing the record in its report in 1898. This was accomplished through a long period of correspondence during which veterans stated their case to the committee as to why they should be listed in the report. The correspondence, supervised by Joshua Chamberlain, followed the publication of a draft of the list in the *Lincoln County News* which was owned by Samuel Miller, a veteran of the regiment and the battle.[2]

The list was open to criticism by anyone who could provide information, and Chamberlain apparently sought the input of former company commanders and regimental record-keepers as well. Records indicate that at least some who claimed in later years to have been present on the spur were consciously left off the list of participants. However, at least two who were not there, are on the list: Private Theodore Gerrish of Company F and Quartermaster Sergeant Howard Prince. Also, the number of officers (26) is different from the official figures (28) in that Prince and Quartermaster Alden Litchfield were not present on the field but were listed in the reports.[3]

Since the regiment was separated from its baggage for a period of weeks before and after the battle, no written records were kept. Company records indicate that clerks did not record morning rolls after June 10, and the regiment's regular morning roll call book shows no entry from June 25 through July 28, suggesting that the papers were separated from the unit on the approach march and record-keeping diminished. In a letter written within a week after the battle Chamberlain explained to the

Adjutant General of Maine why the regiment's paperwork was overdue.[4]

"Our Corps has been so cut off from the main army for two months back," he wrote, "that we have been sometimes three weeks without mail, and our baggage and papers have not been up with us for nearly a *month*." He added, "I am aware that many reports are due your office which shall be sent as soon as we can get our papers." The letter, Chamberlain said, was written on a piece of paper that he had "accidentally found."[5]

On the Confederate side, the numbers are more difficult to examine in such a detailed manner. Colonel Oates, however, gave some insight in his history of the war. "The absence of Company A from the assault on Little Round Top," he wrote, "the capture of the water detail, and the number overcome by heat who had fallen out on scaling the rugged mountain [Big Round Top], reduced my regiment to less than four hundred officers and men who made the assault." Oates explained that his original estimate of 644 men was in error, saying that he took it from the last muster before his regiment began the march to Pennsylvania.

His later estimate seems credible given that the Alabamians marched thirty-two miles to reach the fight July 2. It is more than likely that straggling had an even greater effect on their strength than it did on their Federal adversaries from Maine. According to one private's recollection, Company B of the 15th had 42 men in line on the Emmittsburg Road when Hood began his assault and Waddell reported 45 men in Company A. If these were average company's strengths at that time, then Oates' figures appear accurate.

Also, Oates remembered that the first roll call taken after the fight for the spur, recorded early morning of July 3, indicated that 242 men were still in line with the 15th. When this figure is added to the regiment's loss on the field (see Apendix Four) of 142, it indicates a figure of 384, much nearer his estimate of 400 than 650. In addition, Oates lited his regiment's strength at "over 400 strong" on an inscription he intended to place on a monument at Gettysburg.[6]

When all of the data is considered, the strengths of the two regiments probably included between 400 and 450 men each. For a substantial portion of the early stages of the fight, seven companies of the 47th Alabama were also involved, boosting the Confederate numbers by about 150 men. Only about half of these faced the 20th directly, however, and they were affected by fire from the 83rd Pennsylvania as well.

The numbers for the 47th Alabama may appear low, even for seventy percent of the unit. However, records indicate that it had a consistently low level of strength, mostly due to sickness. Major Campbell, in the regiment's official report after Gettysburg (OR 27(2): 395) indicated that "one third of the whole number of men were killed and wounded," and since the regiment suffered 64 casualties, this would indicate a total strength (in all ten companies) of around 200. Also, the Regimental Muster Rolls seem to confirm Oates' estimate of 154.[7]

During the early phase of the fight, the Alabamians held something like a 600- to 450-man advantage over the 20th Maine. But at the hottest moments, after the 47th retreated, the odds were more likely close to even. This estimate does not include the enlisted men of the 20th's Company B or the squad of sharpshooters that joined them behind the stone wall just east of the main fight. Although these men were not directly engaged on the spur, they sent sporadic fire into the rear of the 15th Alabama throughout the battle.[8]

It must also be noted that some wounded men on both sides remained on duty while other soldiers, who were not hurt, helped carry the wounded to the rear and engaged in various other activities that temporarily took them off the firing line. In this, the 20th also had great advantage since its field hospital was just a few hundred feet behind the battle line.

Appendix Two

Recollections of the Participants

First-hand accounts of the fight on Vincent's Spur

Chapter Two: The Death-Strewn Slope is based on the accounts in the following list of recollections of the fighting on Vincent's Spur between the 20th Maine and the 15th and 47th Alabama. Each of these is an account by a member of one of these regiments who was present at the battle, except the Gerrish and Prince accounts which are second-hand as told to them by veterans, and only those accounts that provided substantial and useful information are listed. Unless otherwise noted, the individuals were 20th Maine members.

The numbers in parentheses indicate the Alabama regiment to which the other soldiers belonged and the initials in parentheses indicate where the item may be found (see *List of Abbreviations Used*).

Clark, Nathan S. Personal diary entries, June/July 1863. (MSA)
Fernald, Albert E. Personal diary entries, June/July 1863. (PHS)
Keene, Samuel J. Personal diary entries, June/July 1863. (AMS)
Livermore, William. Personal diary entries, June/July 1863. (UMO, AMS)
Spear, Ellis. Personal diary entries, June/July 1863. (MSA)
Lamson, William, to "Father" July 1–6, 1863. (Engert, *Maine....*)
Keene, Samuel J., to Sarah (wife), July 3–5, 1863. (AMS)
Chamberlain to Fannie (wife), July 4, 1863. (LC)
Boothby, Adney, to "Folks at home," Gettysburg, July 4, 1863. (NOR)
Chamberlain, J.L., to "Lieut.," July 6, 1863. (MSA)
Chamberlain, J.L. "Official Report," July 6, 1863. (MSA, OR)
Livermore, William T., to Charles (brother), July 6–9, 1863. (AMS)
"Soldier" (47th) to Montgomery Daily Mail, July 7, 1863.
Morrill, Walter G. (Company B). Report to Chamberlain, July 8, 1863.
   (NHS,
Chamberlain, J.L., to Gen. John L. Hodsdon (Maine Adj. Gen.), July 11,
   1863. (MSA)

Chamberlain, J.L., to Gen. John L. Hodsdon, July 13, 1863. (MSA)
Chamberlain to Fannie (wife), July 17, 1863. (LC)
Chamberlain, J.L., to Gov. Abner Coburn, July 21, 1863. (MSA)
Kennedy, John M., to Governor Coburn, July 25, 1863. (MSA)
Spear, Ellis. "The 20th Maine at Gettysburg," *Portland Press*, July 1863.
Sidelinger, Henry F. (Company E), Battle Report, July 30, 1863. (LC)
Stanwood, James H. (Company C), Battle Report, July 30, 1863. (LC)
Coan, Elisha to "My Dear Brother," August 5, 1863. (BCL)
Campbell, J.M. (47th). "Official Report," August 7, 1863. (OR)
Oates, William C. (15th). "Official Report," August 8, 1863. (OR)
Chamberlain, J.L., to Gen. Barnes, September 3, 1863. (NYH)
Spear, Ellis, to Adjutant General, December 1, 1863. (MSA)
Chamberlain, J.L. "The Maine 20th at Gettysburg,"*The Maine Farmer*, December 28, 1865.
Morin, John, letter in Pension Record, April 4, 1872. (NA)
Oates, William C. (15th), to John Bachelder, March 29, 1876. (NHS)
Miller, S.L. "The Maine 20th at Gettysburg" *Lincoln County News* (*LCN*), January 18, 1877.
Oates, William C. "Gettysburg—The Battle On the Right," *Southern Historical Society Papers*, 1878.
Miller, Samuel L. "Address at the Second Reunion of the Twentieth Maine Regiment Association," August 1881. (BPL)
Unknown, "The Twentieth: Sketch of the Regiment that Held Little Round Top," August 1881. (MHS)
Gerrish, Theodore. Article in *Portland Advertiser*, March 13, 1882.
Gerrish, Theodore. *Army Life*, 1882 (same as above).
Nichols, James H. Letter in *Lincoln County News* (*LCN*), April 1882.
Spear, Ellis. "A Visit To Gettysburg" (*LCN*), June 9, 1882.
Gerrish, Theodore. "Battle of Gettysburg," *National Tribune*, November 23, 1882.
Unknown. "Rear Rank," (*LCN*) April 1883.
"C" (Elisha Coan). "Reply to Rear Rank," (*LCN*) May 1883.
Melcher, Holman S. "Still Another," (*LCN*) 7 May 1883.
Prince, Howard L. "A Probable Theory," (*LCN*) May 22, 1883.
Chamberlain, J.L., to John Bachelder, January 25, 1884. (NHS)
Chamberlain, J.L., to John Bachelder, March 10, 1884. (NHS)
Melcher, Holman S. "The Twentieth Maine at Little Round Top," *Battles and Leaders*, 1884-9.
Melcher, Holman S. "The Twentieth Maine at Gettysburg," (*LCN*) March 13, 1885.
Coan, Elisha. "Round Top," article in *National Tribune*, June 4, 1885.

Spear, Ellis. "Memorial Day Address" (in Spear *Memoirs*) 1888. (AMS)

Oates, William (15th), to Homer Stoughton, November 22, 1888. (UOA)

Prince, Howard L. "Address at the Dedication of the Twentieth Maine Monuments at Gettysburg," October 3, 1889. (UMO)

Chamberlain, J.L. "Address at the Dedication of the Twentieth Maine Monuments at Gettysburg," October 3, 1889. (UMO)

Miller, Samuel. "Address at the Dedication of the Twentieth Maine Monuments at Gettysburg," October 3, 1889. (UMO)

Coan, Elisha. Untitled description of the Battle of Gettysburg circa. 1890. (BCL)

Spear, Ellis, to John Bachelder, November 15, 1892. (NHS)

Miller, S.L., to J.L. Chamberlain, May 15, 1895. (LC)

Spear, Ellis, to Chamberlain, May 22, 1895. (LC)

Wescott, J.B., to J.L. Chamberlain, February 1896. (LC)

Spear, Ellis, to J.L. Chamberlain, November 25, 1896. (AMS)

Chamberlain, J.L., to Ellis Spear, November 27, 1896. (AMS)

Chamberlain, J.L., to William C. Oates, February 27, 1897. (BCL)

Oates, William C., to J.L. Chamberlain, March 8, 1897. (UMi)

Miller, S.L., and J.L. Chamberlain. "Twentieth Maine Engaged," in *Maine at Gettysburg*, 1898.

Spear, Ellis. "Twentieth Regiment Historical Sketch," in *Maine at Gettysburg*, 1898.

Bulger, Michael J. (47th). Interview in *New Orleans Picayune*, September 18, 1898.

Livermore, William T., to Gen. J.L. Chamberlain, May 22, 1899. (AMS)

O'Connell, John. Civil War Memoirs, October 1900. (MHI)

Oates, William C., to Elihu Root, June 2, 1903. (GNP)

Chamberlain, J.L., to William Nicholson, August 14, 1903. (GNP)

Oates, William C., to J.L. Chamberlain, April 14, 1905. (GNP)

Oates, William C., to William Nicholson, March 1, 1905. (GNP)

Chamberlain, J.L. to William C. Oates, May 18, 1905. (GNP)

Oates, William C. (15th). *The War Between the Union and the Confederacy*, 1905.

Oates, William C. (15th). Sketch of the positions of regiments during Battle of Little Round Top, March 1, 1905. (GNP)

Botsford, T.F. and J.Q. Burton (47th). *Sketch of the Forty-Seventh Alabama Regiment of Volunteers, C.S.A.*, 1909. (ADH)

Jordan, William C. (15th). *Events and Incidents During the Civil War*, 1909.

Spear, Ellis. Unpublished essay on military surprise, circa 1910. (AMS)

Spear, Ellis, to Mildred (grandaughter), March 14, 1910. (AMS)

Chamberlain, Joshua L. "How General Chamberlain With the 20th Maine Held Little Round Top," *Lewiston Journal*, May 25, 1912.
Chamberlain, J.L., to General Elliott, April 25, 1913. (MSA)
Chamberlain, J.L. "Through Blood and Fire At Gettysburg," *Hearsts Magazine*, June 1913.
Spear, Ellis. "The Left at Gettysburg," *National Tribune*, June 12, 1913.
Spear, Ellis. Personal memoirs, circa. 1914–1916. (AMS)
Edwards, Wm. A. (15th), to W.R. Painter, November 11, 1915. (ADH)
Lindsey, H.C. (47th) *History of the Forty-Seventh Alabama*, undated and unpublished manuscript. (ADH)
Chamberlain, J.L. Unpublished, undated manuscript on the Battle of Gettysburg. (BCL)
Burton, J.Q. *Forty-Seventh Regiment Alabama Volunteers C.S.A*, n.d. (ADAH)

APPENDIX THREE

20th Maine Casualties

Killed, wounded, or captured July 2 and 3

Company	E	I	K	D	F	CG	A	H	C	G	B	St	Total
Killed	0	1	4	2	7	1	2	2	0	0	0	0	19
Wounded	2	5	11	9	16	1	16	13	18	12	2	1	106
[Mortally]	0	1	2	1	3	0	1	4	6	3	0	0	21
Captured	0	0	0	0	0	0	0	0	0	3	1	0	4
Total Loss	2	6	15	11	23	2	18	15	18	15	3	1	129

Notes: Companies are listed in the order that they appeared on the spur (right to left).

CG = color guard, St = staff

The data in the following list are drawn from *Maine at Gettysburg*, the *Revised Report of the Select Committee Relative to the Soldiers National Cemetery* (often referred to as the "Book of the Dead"), J.G. Frey's book of burials at GNMP, John Busey's *The Last Full Measure*, and from Gregory Coco's, *A Vast Sea of Misery*. Some information is gleaned from soldiers' recollections and from hospital returns of nurses, including Isabella Fogg. "The Book of the Dead" was a record of the bodies that were disinterred around Gettysburg and reinterred at the National Cemetery. Items found on bodies during this process are listed.

Unless otherwise noted, the date of wound or death is July 2. Also, a number of men received slight wounds that were not recorded, including Chamberlain who was twice hit. In a letter to the adjutant general of Maine eleven days after the battle he wrote, "Some who were very slightly struck are not reported here. Hardly anyone in the Regt. escaped without some mark in his clothing at least. All who are at all *hurt* are reported here."

When the fighting on Little Round Top ended, wounded of both sides were moved from the temporary aid station in the "sheltered nook" to the Fifth Corps field hospital that had been set up at the Jacob Weikert farm, just east of Little Round Top. It was Weikert's stone wall that Company

189

B lay behind. On the morning of July 3, members of the Ambulance Corps transferred the wounded to more permanent hospitals designated by corps and division.

Those listed as killed are those who died instantly or within a few minutes of the end of the fight. The mortally wounded are those who lived at least long enough to be transported to the Jacob Weikert farm, though some of these are listed in official figures as killed.

The Michael Fiscel, Henry Beitler, and John Trostle farms, and the Third Corps hospital mentioned, are all on the White Church Road approximately one mile southeast of Big Round Top. These are all fairly close to one another and the hospital tents and burial plots were all in fields around the farms. As a result, the exact location of a hospital or burial is often confused in the records.

A handful of soldiers was well enough to be transferred to more permanent army hospitals around Washington or Philadelphia. Except for these, the burial sites indicated are original sites near the battlefield, from which bodies were eventually moved to the Gettysburg National Cemetery. The symbol **[GNC- #]** indicates that the soldier is buried in the Maine plot of the cemetery in the row indicated.

This list represents figures for the entire battle, not just the fight on Little Round Top.

Name	Rank	Co.	Status
Adams, Aaron	private	H	killed, shot in breast died instantly.
Ames, Addison	private	D	wounded in wrist and arm.
Avery, Charles	corporal	A	wounded in arm.
Barnes, Moody	private	G	wounded in arm.
Beadle, Charles	private	C	wounded mortally, died August 6 at Satterlee Hospital in Philadelphia and buried there.
Billings, Charles	captain	C	wounded mortally, shot in left knee, died July 15 in Fifth Corps hospital (Fiscel farm). Body returned to Maine by his wife and buried in River View Cemetery, Clinton, Maine (Section A, Lot #23).
Borneman, Luther	private	G	wounded in face.
Brown, Albion	corporal	F	wounded slightly in hand.
Brown, Elisha	private	F	wounded severely in head.
Buck, George	pvt./sgt.	H	wounded mortally, shot in right shoulder, died July 4. Restored to rank of sergeant on the field by Colonel Chamberlain.

190

Name	Rank	Co.	Status
Buxton, Willard	private	K	wounded mortally, shot in left arm, died July 10, buried at First Division, Third Corps hospital.
Card, George	sergeant	D	wounded slightly in face.
Chase, Stephen	private	K	killed.
Chesley, Hiram	private	H	wounded severely in neck.
Clark, Seth	private	F	killed.
Clifford, Benjamin	private	H	wounded in face, lost eye.
Crocker, George	private	D	wounded slightly in shoulder.
Cunningham, Albert	private	G	wounded in arm.
Curtis, Frank	private	F	wounded mortally, shot in left arm, died July 11, buried east of Fiscel house. **[GNC- C]**
Curtis, Merrill	private	D	wounded in shoulder.
Cushman, Llewellyn	private	G	wounded in arm.
Davis, Moses	private	C	wounded mortally, died July 3, buried near Beitler house. Thanksgiving book found on body. **[GNC-F]**
Day, Melville	corporal	CG	killed, buried behind Weikert house. **[GNC- E]**
Estes, Isaac	sergeant	C	wounded mortally, shot in both breasts, died July 16. Buried on Fiscel farm, east of house.
Erskine, James	private	G	wounded in side.
Fernald, Albert	sergeant	K	wounded in hip.
Fish, Benjamin	private	I	wounded in head.
Fitch, Joseph	captain	D	wounded in thigh.
Fox, Samuel	private	F	wounded slightly in head.
Fogg, Elliott	private	A	killed.
Foss, Elfin	private	F	wounded mortally, buried on Fiscel farm, east of house. **[GNC- C]**
Foss, John	corporal	F	killed, buried behind Weikert house. Letter and fish hook found on body.
French, Benjamin	private	H	wounded, left leg amputated below the knee.
French, Edward	private	F	wounded severely in side.
French, Oliver	corporal	D	wounded.
Grant, Benjamin	private	F	wounded mortally, shot in abdomen, died July 5, buried on Fiscel farm. **[GNC- D]**
Grindle, Jo seph	private	A	wounded in hand.
Hall, Charles	private	F	killed.
Ham, Mansfield	private	H	wounded severely in side, thumb shot off.

Name	Rank	Co.	Status
Harrington, James	sergeant	A	wounded in face.
Heald, Benjamin	private	C	wounded severely in hand.
Heald, Llewellyn	private	C	wounded severely in leg.
Herscomb, Andrew	private	G	wounded in neck.
Hill, William	private	A	wounded in arm.
Hilt, Byron	private	H	wounded severely in left shoulder.
Hiscock, Abner	sergeant	G	wounded, arm amputated.
Hodgdon, Josiah	private	C	wounded severely in arm.
Hodgdon, William	corporal	F	killed. Stone at GNC reads "W.S. Hodgden." [GNC- E]
Ireland, Goodwin	private	H	killed, shot in neck, died instantly. A testament, purse, glass, and letters were found on the body. [GNC- E]
Jordan, William	sergeant	G	wounded mortally, shot in left lung, died July 24, buried at Sixth Corps hospital cemetery east of Fiscel house. [GNC- C]
Keene, Samuel	captain	F	wounded, shot in sword belt, badly bruised.
Kendall, Warren	lieutenant	G	wounded mortally, shot in throat and vertebrae, died July 5. Buried east of Fiscel house. [GNC- C]
Kennedy, John	private	G	wounded in thigh (groin).
Knapp, Charles	sergeant	C	wounded severely in arm.
Knight, James	private	G	wounded mortally, died in Fifth Corps hospital, buried on Trostle farm (near Fiscel farm).
Lamson, Iredell	private	H	wounded mortally, shot in right leg, died July 3, buried near First Division, Third Corps hospital.
Lathrop, Isaac	sergeant	H	wounded mortally, shot in abdomen (bowels), died July 5, buried on Fiscel farm. [GNC- D]
Leach, George	private	B	wounded, captured, died in prison December 1, 1863, in Richmond.
Lester, Alexander	private	I	killed.
Lewis, David	corporal	A	wounded in head.
Libby, Benjamin	private	F	wounded severely in hand.
Libby, John	corporal	H	wounded in right hand, lost two fingers.
Linscott, Arad	lieutenant	I	wounded mortally, shot in thigh on skirmish line on Big Round Top, evening of July 2. Died July 27 after being furloughed home. Buried in Village Cemetery, Jefferson, Maine (lot #23).

Name	Rank	Co.	Status
Little, Thomas	private	E	wounded severely in head.
Lore, Charles	private	A	wounded in arm.
Mabury, Andrew	corporal	D	wounded mortally, died July 3, buried near First Division, Third Corps hospital.
Martin, James	sergeant	F	wounded severely, shot under right eye, ball permanently lodged inside.
Merrill, James	private	K	killed, buried behind Weikert house. Family headstone in Durham (Maine) cemetery says he died at age 16 yrs, 3 mos., 29 days.
Merrill, William	private	K	killed, buried behind Weickert house.
Mink, Orchard	private	E	wounded severely in leg.
Monk, Decatur	private	C	wounded, arm broken.
Morin, John	corporal	F	wounded slightly in thigh.
Morrill, Edwin	private	B	wounded through calf.
Morrison, Edmund	private	H	wounded slightly in side.
Newell, Enoch	private	K	wounded in hand.
Norton, Hiram	private	A	wounded in head.
Noyes, George	sergeant	K	killed. **[GNC- F]**
O'Connell, John	private	C	wounded slightly in head.
Osborn, Cyrus	corporal	G	wounded in arm
Patten, David	private	F	wounded in arm and side.
Peabody, Jason	private	I	wounded in finger.
Pinhorn, Vincent	corporal	C	wounded severely in hip.
Pinkham, Willard	corporal	D	killed. Stone at GNC reads "W.K." **[GNC- F]**
Powers, Charles	private	C	wounded slightly in side.
Prescott, Stephen	private	D	killed.
Ramsdell, George	corporal	K	wounded in breast.
Ramsdell, John	private	D	wounded slightly in face.
Rankins, William	private	A	wounded in arm.
Reed, Charles	corporal	CG	wounded in wrist.
Reed, Herbert	private	K	wounded in thigh.
Reed, John, Jr.	corporal	A	killed.
Reynolds, George	sergeant	A	wounded in thigh, side, arm.
Rhodes, Charles	private	K	wounded in neck.
Richards, Sylvester	corporal	K	wounded in face.
Ring, Benjamin	private	K	wounded in head.
Sanders, Henry	private	B	wounded severely in hand.
Simpson, Joseph	corporal	A	wounded mortally, shot in the neck, died July 3, buried near Beitler house. A gold ring was found on his body. **[GNC- F]**

Name	Rank	Co.	Status
Small, Alva	private	C	wounded mortally, died August 28 at Satterlee Hospital in Philadelphia and buried there.
Smith, John	private	G	captured.
Stanwood, James	lieutenant	C	wounded slightly in leg.
Steele, Charles	sergeant	H	wounded mortally, shot in breast, buried behind Weickert house. [GNC- E]
Stevens, Oliver	private	C	wounded mortally, shot in left thigh and right hip, died July 6.
Stover, Andrew	sergeant	I	wounded in leg.
Surry, Joseph	private	A	wounded in leg.
Sweeney, Eugene	private	G	captured.
Swett, Henry	private	D	wounded slightly in shoulder.
Sylvester, Ira	private	A	wounded in side.
Taylor, Alfred	private	A	wounded in hand.
Thomas, Moses	private	C	wounded severely in leg.
Thomas, Reuel	sergeant	St	wounded in shoulder.
Thorn, John	private	K	wounded in leg.
Tibbetts, Jotham	private	G	captured.
Tobin, John	private	C	wounded, arm broken.
Tripp, Paschal	corporal	F	killed.
True, Franklin	private	A	wounded in arm.
True, Laforrest	corporal	A	wounded in arms.
Walker, Gustavus	private	H	wounded, knee bruised.
Walker, Orrin	private	K	wounded mortally, shot in thigh, buried behind Weikert house. [GNC- E]
Ward, Franklin	corporal	F	wounded, leg amputated.
Wentworth, Sanford	private	F	killed.
Wentworth, William	private	K	wounded in leg.
West, Joseph	private	H	wounded, arm bruised.
White, Sylvanus	private	F	wounded severely in hand.
Whitman, Ezekiel	private	F	wounded slightly in shoulder.
Willey, William	private	A	wounded in head.
Witham, Charles	private	I	wounded in finger.
Wyer, Oscar	private	F	killed.
York, George	private	C	wounded, transferred to Veteran Reserve Corps.
Young, Thomas	private	F	wounded in arm slightly.

APPENDIX FOUR

15th Alabama Casualties

Killed, wounded, or captured July 2 and 3

Company	A	B	C	D	E	F	G	H	I	K	L	Total
Killed	1	6	3	0	2	1	4	0	1	2	1	21
Wounded	4	9	4	4	3	2	10	5	3	4	3	57
[then captured]	1	4	4	2	1	0	2	3	2	0	2	22
[mortally]	0	2	0	1	1	0	4	1	0	1	0	10
Captured (not wounded)	0	8	2	6	15	5	13	11	6	12	9	89
Total Loss	5	23	9	10	20	9	27	21	10	18	13	167

Notes: Company A was not engaged on the spur. Lit. Colonel Feagin and Assistant Surgeon Rives are included not in any company but in the totals. Though not listed as such, most of the mortally wounded were also captured. The bottom captured row indicates those captured but not listed as wounded, though some may have been.

The information listed here was taken from recollections of the participants, data in the Alabama State Archives, prison and hospital records, and the files of the library at the Gettysburg National Military Park. Much of the information on the 15th Alabama comes from the Regimental Muster Rolls at the Alabama Department of Archives and History, and from Oates, *War Between the Union and Confederacy*, particularly the regimental roster in his Appendix A. Information on Hollywood Cemetery burials comes from Mary Mitchell, *Hollywood Cemetery: The History of a Southern Shrine*, Virginia State Library, 1985 (Appendix 2), and from "Hollywood Cemetery, Richmond, Va." list in folder 7-20, in the park library at Gettysburg. In addition, the author is deeply indebted to Edward G.J. Richter, who provided valuable data based on his years of research on Confederate casualties at Gettysburg.

As with the 20th Maine casualties in Appendix Three, this list represents figures for the entire battle, not just the fight on Little Round Top. Some of the captured were wounded soldiers left at the division hospital on the Slyder Farm. Point Lookout and Fort Delaware were Federal prisons. The General Hospital was a tent hospital established at

195

Gettysburg about a month after the battle and named "Camp Letterman" for Jonathan K. Letterman, the medical director of the Army of the Potomac.

This list appears to be fairly complete since Oates, in a letter written August 8, estimated his losses at "17 killed, 54 wounded and brought off the field, and 90 missing," a total loss of 161 men. In 1902, William Oates wrote an inscription for a monument to his regiment which he never placed at Gettysburg. Having had thirty-nine years to collect the information he listed 33 killed, 76 wounded and 84 captured out of "over 400" engaged.

Name	Rank	Co.	Status
Albritton, Thomas J.	private	K	captured, died at Point Lookout.
Alexander, William C.	private	G	captured, died February 8, 1864, at Fort Delaware.
Anderson, Manly	private	K	captured, died at Fort Delaware.
Atkinson, Cornelius	private	E	captured, not exchanged.
Austin, Albert	private	E	captured.
Bagwell, James A. J.	private	G	killed.
Balkom, Larkin	private	G	captured.
Beasley, J. C.	private	B	captured, died at Fort Delaware.
Bell, Olin	private	B	captured, died at Fort Delaware.
Bethune, William J.	captain	K	wounded severely in the face.
Bibby, Bailey L.	sergeant	C	killed.
Bigby, Benjamin F.	private	E	captured, died at Point Lookout.
Bledsoe, J. T.	private	B	captured, not exchanged.
Bonner, D.D.	private	L	wounded.
Brainard, Henry C.	captain	G	killed leading his company over a ledge of rock. He exclaimed, "O God, that I could see my mother!" and died.
Breare, Joseph R.	private	E	captured, exchanged fall of 1863.
Broughton, William	sergeant	A	wounded.
Brown, James M.	private	K	killed.
Byrd, Major Ed	private	G	killed.
Bynum, William T.	private	K	wounded.
Calloway, J. D.	private	B	wounded, captured, exchanged October 30, 1864.
Carpenter, Coleman N.	private	I	captured, not exchanged.

Name	Rank	Co.	Status
Champion, Frank D.	private	I	captured, escaped May 20, 1864, from Point Lookout.
Cody, Barnett H.	lieut.	G	wounded mortally, died July 23. Cared for with John Oates at the Fifth Corps hospital and buried near the Fiscel farm. Reinterred in Hollywood Cemetery, Richmond.
Coleman, Thomas J.	sergeant	B	captured, died in 1864 at Fort Delaware.
Cowart, Jonathan W.	private	H	captured, later exchanged.
Craft, Reuben J.	private	K	captured, not exchanged.
Crawford, James	private	H	captured.
Cureton, Jasper	private	E	killed.
Denham, Alfred	private	B	captured.
Dooley, William	corporal	E	captured, died at Fort Delaware.
Dudley, George	private	K	captured.
Duke, George L.	private	G	captured, died in September 1864 at Fort Delaware.
Eason, George J.	private	A	"Jeff" was wounded severely, captured, exchanged in 1864.
Edwards, Ambrose N.	sergeant	E	captured, not exchanged.
Eidson, J. R.	private	D	wounded, captured, not exchanged.
Eidson, J. W.	private	D	captured, died October 3, 1863, at Fort Delaware.
Ellison, James H.	captain	C	killed, shot in the head while ordering his men forward.
Enfinger, William	private	G	captured.
Faust, William H.	private	E	captured, not exchanged.
Feagin, Isaac	lt. col.	-	wounded by sharpshooter volley on the approach, leg amputated, left to Yankees who captured him July 5. Had second amputation in prison and was exchanged.
Fleming, Wm. C. D.	private	E	captured, not exchanged.
Galloway, Ransome J.	private	G	captured, died August 15, 1864, at Fort Delaware.
Gardner, Samuel H.	corporal	I	killed.
Garrett, George W.	private	L	captured while sick in field hospital, July 5, escaped August 17, 1863.
Gray, Thomas B.	private	H	wounded.
Gresham, Ferdinand	private	B	killed.

Name	Rank	Co.	Status
Hall, William H.	private	K	captured, not exchanged.
Harrell, William Holl	private	K	captured, not exchanged.
Hartzog, Daniel	private	D	wounded mortally, died on the field or in the hands of the enemy.
Henderson, George R.	private	L	wounded, captured, exchanged May 1, 1864.
Henderson, Joseph	corporal	L	captured, died June 4, 1864, at Fort Delaware.
Henly, J. D. L.	corporal	H	captured, not exchanged.
Hitchcock, James G.	sergeant	B	wounded.
Holloway, William R.	private	G	killed, shot in left temple while next to Colonel Oates on top of a boulder.
Holmes, Abner	private	H	captured, died at Point Lookout.
Holmes, Augustus	private	H	captured, sent to Fort Delaware, not exchanged.
Horn, James C.	private	A	wounded.
Hurt, William H.	sergeant	C	captured, not exchanged.
Hutchinson, James B.	private	F	captured, not exchanged.
Ingram, John	private	K	wounded mortally, died August 13 at General Hospital, buried there and then reinterred in Hollywood Cemetery, Richmond.
Jackson, C. J.	private	D	captured, later exchanged.
Jenkins, George	private	G	captured, not exchanged.
Johns, William N.	sergeant	B	wounded severely in hip and thigh, left on the field for twenty-four hours before being discovered, captured, and taken to a Union field hospital. He was exchanged as soon as he could be moved.
Johnson, Felder	sergeant	D	captured.
Jones, W. F.	private	E	wounded mortally, died July 16 in enemy hands.
Jordan, John C.	private	G	wounded mortally, died at Fifth Corps hospital, body reinterred at Hollywood Cemetery, Richmond.
Keels, John	private	H	wounded mortally in throat during retreat, died in field hospital.
Kelly, David A.	private	K	captured, not exchanged.
Kelly, Samuel O.	private	G	captured, exchanged in December 1864.
Kendrick, Benj. E.	private	B	killed trying to get behind the large rock

Name	Rank	Co.	Status
			on the 15th's left.
Kendrick, Robert S.	private	B	"Sam" was wounded in the foot trying to get behind the large rock on the 15th's left. He was captured and never exchanged.
Kennedy, A.	private	B	killed by sharpshooters on the approach.
Kirkland, Aaron S.	private	G	wounded severely, captured, exchanged in September 1864.
Landingham, John	private	E	captured, died at Fort Delaware.
Lane, Elisha	private	B	wounded in the thigh near large rock on the 15th's left during the retreat. He was sent to a hospital in Richmond where he died March 6, 1864, of smallpox.
Latimer, James	private	E	wounded severely.
Lecroy, G. B.	private	F	captured, died at Fort Delaware.
Lindsey, William	private	F	killed.
Loveless, Judge	private	H	captured.
Lynch, Pat	private	K	captured.
Madden, Cicero	private	K	captured, died at Fort Delaware.
Mallet, C. N.	private	I	wounded seriously.
Mansel, Amos	private	C	killed.
Mansel, William II.	private	C	wounded severely, captured, sent to David's Island, paroled in August 1863, never exchanged.
Martin, Thomas	private	I	wounded, captured, later exchanged.
McCormick, John C.	private	I	wounded severely, captured, lost right arm.
McDonald, Jack	private	B	wounded.
McDonald, Richard M.	private	C	wounded, captured with the wagon train July 4 while trying to escape back to Virginia. Never exchanged.
McEntire, James A.	private	H	captured, not exchanged.
McGilvery, A.	private	D	captured, later exchanged.
McGuire, Michael	corporal	H	captured, not exchanged.
McKlevane, Burrell	private	K	captured, died at Fort Delaware.
McLeod, John T.	sergeant	H	captured, not exchanged, killed Pvt. Ned Swinny in a prison fight.
McLeod, Neil	private	H	wounded severely.
McMillan, A. P.	private	B	"Sandy" was killed trying to get behind the large rock on the 15th's left.
McMorris, Phillip	private	L	captured, died August 13, 1863, in

Name	Rank	Co.	Status
			prison.
McNeil, N. E.	private	H	captured, died December 2, 1863, at Point Lookout.
Melvin, John	private	G	wounded.
Melvin, McKinny	private	H	wounded.
Meredith, M. E.	private	F	wounded.
Merrill, Jordan	private	E	captured, not exchanged.
Metts, Francis	orivate	F	captured.
Miles, Dennis	private	F	wounded.
Mills, Thomas S.	private	E	wounded severely.
Mizzell, C.L.	private	E	captured.
Moore, J. F.	private	L	captured, exchanged November 1, 1864.
Moore, James P.	private	F	captured, not exchanged.
Mullin, John	private	E	captured.
Murdock, James H.	private	K	captured, not exchanged.
Nelson, John	private	K	killed.
Newman, Charles	private	B	captured.
Newton, J. L.	private	L	wounded, captured, exchanged October 1, 1863.
Norris, Hardy R.	private	B	wounded mortally, buried at General Hospital, reinterred in Hollywood Cemetery, Richmond.
Oates, John A.	lieut.	G	wounded mortally, died July 25. Cared for with B. H. Cody at the Fifth Corps hospital and buried near the Fiscel farm. Reinterred in Hollywood Cemetery, Richmond.
Ogletree, Absalom J.	private	I	captured, not exchanged.
Owens, George J.	private	B	wounded, captured, not exchanged.
Painter, Wm. Rufus	private	E	captured, not exchanged.
Parker, C. A.	sergeant	B	wounded mortally, died July 21.
Parker, Robert	private	G	wounded, captured, exchanged the following winter.
Peters, Benton W.	private	H	wounded.
Peters, Noah J.	private	I	captured, not exchanged.
Pope, Calvin	private	H	wounded severely, captured next day, sent to David's Island.
Pope, George	private	B	captured.
Pound, James W.	sergeant	G	captured, later exchanged.
Pugh, Whitson	private	B	killed.
Purdue, James M.	private	A	missing, believed killed (or captured).

200

Name	Rank	Co.	Status
Raleigh, Charles W.	private	G	captured, not exchanged.
Reeves, George B.	private	F	captured, not exchanged.
Rice, Frank M.	private	H	wounded.
Riley, Daniel	private	G	wounded severely.
Rives, Alexander	assistant surgeon		left to care for wounded at division field hospital, captured.
Roney, Alfred	private	G	wounded severely, captured the day after, sent to David's Island, later exchanged.
Roundtree, A. R.	private	E	captured, not exchanged.
Rudd, William E.	private	F	captured, not exchanged.
Rutledge, James	private	K	wounded.
Seegars, J. A.	private	D	captured, exchanged in September 1864.
Sellars, E. A.	private	L	captured, not exchanged.
Sellars, W.P.	private	L	captured, died at Fort Delaware.
Shepherd, James N.	private	G	"Nick" was wounded mortally, died August 26, and was buried at General Hospital and then reinterred in Hollywood Cemetery, Richmond.
Sholar, Allen	private	G	missing.
Short, Richard	private	G	captured, died November 7, 1863, at Fort Delaware.
Slaton, James A.	private	C	wounded, captured, not exchanged.
Smedley, Capel S.	private	I	captured, exchanged December 13, 1863.
Smith, John D. L.	private	H	wounded, captured, sent to David's Island, exchanged in August 1863.
Smith, Pink H.	private	A	wounded.
Spence, Lewis	sergeant	D	wounded, captured (or died of wounds).
Spencer, G. E.	private	D	severely wounded by sharpshooter on the approach, sent to David's Island.
Stewart, D. A.	private	D	captured, died at Fort Delaware.
Stewart, J. F.	private	L	captured, not exchanged.
Stewart, Sidney A.	corporal	I	captured, died at Fort Delaware.
Stone, Christopher C.	private	G	captured, not exchanged.
Stone, Henry D.	private	B	killed, left on the field.
Stough, Jacob H.	private	L	captured, not exchanged.
Sugar, John E.	sergeant	C	wounded and captured, not exchanged.
Swinny, Edward B.	private	B	"Ned" was captured. When he was at Fort Delaware, killed by J.T. McLeod of Company H, who hit him in the head

Name	Rank	Co.	Status
			with a piece of iron during a fight.
Tate, James F.	private	K	captured, died at Fort Delaware.
Trimner, William	private	G	killed by sharpshooters on the approach.
Vinson, Leven	sergeant	L	killed.
Welch, James M.	private	E	captured, not exchanged.
Weston, W. W. B.	private	H	captured, died at Fort Delaware.
Wicker, Julius A.	private	C	captured, not exchanged.
Wicker, Robert H.	lieut.	L	captured by J.L. Chamberlain after firing at him and missing. Released from Fort Deleware in June 1865.
Wood, William	lieut.	H	wounded slightly.
Woodham, James R.	private	G	wounded severely.
Woodham, John R.	private	H	"Bob" was wounded severely, captured, exchanged in August 1864.
Woodham, Samuel E.	private	G	captured, not exchanged.

APPENDIX FIVE

47th Alabama Casualties

Killed, wounded, or missing July 2 and 3

Company	A	B	C	D	E	F	G	H	I	K	St	Total
Killed	0	5	1	0	0	0	0	0	0	1	0	6
Wounded	0	12	7	0	12	0	6	2	2	4	1	46
[mortally]	0	0	1	0	4	0	0	1	1	0	0	7
Missing/Captured	1	4	1	0	3	0	1	1	0	0	1	12
Total Loss	1	21	9	0	15	0	7	3	2	5	1	64

The information listed here was taken from recollections of the participants, data in the Alabama State Archives, prison and hospital records, the files of the library at the Gettysburg National Military Park, the Regimental Muster Rolls at the Alabama Department of Archives and History, and from an article printed in the *Montgomery Daily Mail*, July 26, 1863, written from the camp of the 47th near Hagerstown, and signed, "Soldier." Information on Hollywood Cemetery burials from Mary Mitchell, *Hollywood Cemetery: The History of a Southern Shrine*, Virginia State Library, 1985 (Appendix 2), and from "Hollywood Cemetery, Richmond, Va." list in folder 7-20, in the park library at Gettysburg.

Edward G.J. Richter provided data for this list as well. As with the casualty lists in Appendices Three and Four, this list represents figures for the entire battle, not just the fight on Little Round Top. Some of the captured were wounded soldiers left at the division hospital on the Slyder Farm.

Name	Rank	Co.	Status
Acker, William	sergeant	E	wounded severely.
Adrian, John G.	lieut.	E	killed July 3.
Baker, Andrew J.	private	B	missing.
Barnes, Isaac A.	private	B	wounded slightly.
Bentley, Martin	private	B	wounded slightly.
Blackmore, Henry J.	private	E	wounded, captured July 4. Sent to Ft.

Name	Rank	Co.	Status
Brooks, Isaac M.	private	B	Delaware, then to Chester, PA Gen. Hospital September 10. wounded mortally, buried at Camp Letterman General Hospital, reinterred in Hollywood Cemetery, Richmond.
Browning, William W.	corporal	G	wounded, captured.
Bulger, Michael. J.	lt. col.	St	wounded in shoulder, captured.
Burson, Isaac J.	private	B	wounded slightly.
Carpenter, Elisha	private	I	wounded slightly.
Chandler, William	private	E	wounded slightly.
Duke, Richard H.	private	G	wounded slightly.
Flurry, Augustin	private	I	captured, died at Fort Delaware.
Geer, Jasper A.	corporal	E	wounded dangerously.
Gilbert, Lindsay B.	private	H	missing.
Gilder, John	private	A	missing.
Golden, Joseph	private	B	wounded slightly.
Golden, William	corporal	B	wounded slightly.
Gray, William	private	B	wounded slightly.
Green, Henry	private	K	killed.
Hammond, John G.	sergeant	G	wounded slightly.
Harr, Pleasant H.	private	E	wounded, left at division field hospital, captured.
Hight, William	private	B	killed.
Hollis, George	private	H	wounded mortally, died July 17 at Gettysburg.
Hood, Joseph H.	lieut.	E	wounded slightly.
Howell, Jasper	private	B	killed.
Hughes, M.	private	E	missing.
Jack, Patrick	private	E	wounded severely.
Johnston, George	private	K	wounded slightly.
Johnston, Joseph, Jr.	captain	B	wounded mortally, died July 19 at Gettysburg.
Jordan, Baron D.	private	B	killed.
Law, James	corporal	B	captured.
McCurley, Daniel	private	E	wounded mortally, died September 8, 1863, at Davids Island.
McDonald, Taylor	private	B	missing.
McDonald, Thomas S.	sergeant	B	wounded slightly.
Martin, Benjamin	private	H	wounded severely.
Morgan, Henry A.	private	G	missing.
Motes, John	sergeant	B	missing.

Name	Rank	Co.	Status
Motes, James W.	private	B	captured.
Naugher, Robert	corporal	E	missing.
Owens, Columbus W.	private	K	wounded severely.
Pannell, Thomas	private	G	wounded slightly.
Patterson, Benjamin F.	private	C	wounded severely.
Penny, William	private	E	wounded mortally, died July 8 at Gettysburg.
Peters, Lewis C.	private	C	wounded severely.
Pitman, Stephen E.	private	B	wounded slightly.
Rains, H.	private	E	wounded severely.
Ray, Andrew	lieut.	E	wounded mortally, died July 22.
Ray, R.	private	E	wounded slightly.
Rich, T. A.	private	E	wounded slightly.
Russell, B. F. C.	sergeant	C	wounded slightly (ensign sergeant).
Simmons, Allen D.	private	B	captured, died at Fort Delaware.
Simmons, Henry D.	lieut.	B	killed by a sharpshooter July 3.
Smith, Samuel M.	private	K	wounded slightly.
Solley, Seabron G.	private	C	wounded mortally, died in Union hospital at Gettysburg, body reinterred in Hollywood Cemetery, Richmond.
Stacks, M. D.	private	C	wounded slightly.
Tatum, H. J. D.	private	C	captured.
Towns, B. D.	private	C	wounded slightly.
Waldrup, James	private	B	wounded slightly.
Webb, A. J.	corporal	G	wounded severely.
Whitaker, James	captain	G	wounded severely, captured, later exchanged.
Wilson, Andross J.	private	I	wounded slightly.
Wise, James W.	private	K	wounded severely.

NOTES

Chapter 1. NORTH FROM THE RAPPAHANNOCK

1. Hezekiah Long to Sarah (wife), June 23, 1863 (SVM).

2. Sam Keene diary, copy in possession of Abbott Spear, Warren Maine, entry for June 26 (AMS).

3. Description of Keene from Records of the Adjutant General of Maine (MSA), and from prewar correspondence between several members of the regiment including Ellis Spear and Lysander Hill (AMS).

4. Ibid.

5. Melcher to "Dear Brother," June 27, 1863, reprinted in Styple, *With a Flash of His Sword*, p. 35. Melcher spent a year enrolled at what is now called Bates College in Lewiston, Maine. Melcher's rise through the ranks from Records of the Adjutant General of Maine (MSA), and from descriptions of Fredericksburg by Joshua Chamberlain and Ellis Spear (AMS).

6. *Annual Report of the Adjutant General of Maine, 1862*; Records of the Adjutant General of Maine Descriptive Rolls, (MSA).

7. Chamberlain in *The Maine Farmer*, December 28, 1865. By the summer of 1862, the departure of troops from their rendezvous camps in Portland, Augusta, and Bangor, had become old hat to the local citizens. By then, saying farewell to the regiments and presenting flags as they left was "all played out" as the soldiers used to say.

8. See *Bowdoin in the War*; also see appendix: "Roster of 20th Maine Soldiers at Gettysburg." According to the occupations listed by the soldiers upon mustering in, 64 percent of the men were farmers, 6 percent worked in ocean-related trades, and 5 percent in timber-related work. There were less than a half dozen sailors or fishermen.

9. Tom Chamberlain to John, October 30, 1862 (UMO).

10. Diary of William Livermore, copy in Fogler Library Special Collections, Orono, Maine, entry for October 5, 1862. The 20th rendezvoused at Camp Mason in Cape Elizabeth, just across the Fore River from Portland. Their official mustering was on September 1, 1862. The area is now in South Portland very near the airport runway between I-295 and Forest City Cemetery. The circumstances surrounding Ames' commission and the troops' dislike for his methods can be found in the 20th Maine Correspondence (MSA). Leeds, Maine, a town of just over one thousand in 1860, provided two generals to the war: Howard, and Confederate Gen. Danville Leadbetter (West Point, 1836). For more on Ames, see the biography written by his

granddaughter, Blanche A. Ames, titled *Adelbert Ames: General, Senator, Governor, 1835–1933* (New York, 1964).

11. Chamberlain, "My Story of Fredericksburg," *Cosmopolitan*, January 1913; Spear, "Two Stories of Fredericksburg," original typescript in possession of Abbott Spear, Warren, Maine. A controversy regarding the soldiers' opinions of Ames' fitness to command can be found in the 20th Maine Correspondence, (MSA). After learning more about the true circumstances, partly from a nurse from Maine named Isabella Fogg, a number of officers wrote to the governor recanting their previous complaints. Apparently Ames rid the unit of nearly all of the officers that he felt were incompetent. At Fredericksburg, the 20th lost a half dozen killed and three dozen wounded.

12. Powell, *Fifth Army Corps*, pp. 404–09; Livermore diary (UMO); Ellis Spear memoirs, original TMs in possession of Abbott Spear, Warren, Maine; Gerrish, *Army Life*. According to state agents and nurses traveling with the army who reported back to the governor and adjutant general, the condition of the 20th was worse than that of most Maine units in the field at that time. See correspondence of Isabella Fogg, Harriet Eaton, and C. C. Hayes (Relief Records—MSA). In particular, Hayes was explicit about the incompetence of the 20th's surgeon, Nahum Monroe.

13. Details of the story at Chancellorsville from Livermore diary (UMO), June 30, 1863.

14. Carter, "Reminiscences of the Campaign and Battle of Gettysburg." *War Papers*, vol. 2, pp. 152–53.

15. Albert Fernald diary, typed copy in Pejepscot Historical Society, Brunswick, Maine, entries of June 17–18; Nathan Clark diary, original and microfilm copy at Maine State Archives, entry of June 20. Despite the fact that he had tendered his resignation, "in apprehension of the consequences...," Lewis was held in arrest. See Chamberlain to Third Brigade adjutant, July 30, 1863, Chamberlain Service Record (LC); Clark diary, June 21 (MSA).

16. Statistics from "Roster of 20th Maine Soldiers at Gettysburg," see Appendix. The "average" soldier in the regiment at that time was five feet, eight inches tall, single, a farmer, and 24 years old.

17. The Italian natives were Peter Augustine of Company D and Michael Bosworth of Company F. Theodore Roosen, of Company I, listed his birthplace as Denmark (service records, MSA). Down East quote from Livermore diary, October 5, 1862. The term "Down East" usually applies to the eastern two-thirds of the coastal portion of Maine.

18. Chamberlain to Fannie (wife), October 26, 1862 (Chamberlain papers, LC).

19. Livermore diary (UMO), October 5, 1862. In 1860 Chamberlain, though a younger professor, was respected enough by the college that he

received the same salary as the older professors, $1,600 per year. Soldiers' opinion from John Chamberlain's journal, original and typed copy in Pejepscot Historical Society, Brunswick, Maine.

20. Before the war, Gilmore was sheriff of Penobscot County which included Bangor, home of the adjutant general of Maine at that time. More of the nature of Gilmore's political connections is made evident by the letters in the 20th Maine Correspondence (MSA).

21. Chamberlain to Gov. Abner Coburn, August 25, 1863 (20th Maine Corr., MSA); Spear memoirs (AMS). Details of Spear's life from his grandson, Abbott Spear of Warren, Maine, and Ellis's collection of writings and photographs in Abbott's possession.

22. Clark diary (MSA), June 21; Livermore diary (UMO), June 21.

23. Keene diary (AMS), June 20; Livermore diary (UMO), June 21.

24. Description of the battle from entries in Clark, Livermore, Fernald, and Spear diaries, June 21. A casualty list in the *Bangor Whig & Courier*, July 4, 1863, and records from the *Report of the Adjutant General for 1863*, include the following: Cpl. John P. West (Company G)—killed; Sgt. James H. Miller (Company K)—wounded in the breast; Pvt. Asbury Dickinson (Company G)—wounded seriously. Pvt. Albert Robinson (Company G) of Jefferson died of his wounds on July 31. Privates William Runkins (Company F), Samuel Gray (Company K), and Edwin Keating (Company K), and Lt. Holman Melcher (Company F) were slightly wounded. Gray was one of the 2nd Maine transfers. List in the *Whig* is from a letter to the editor from Lt. Col. Charles Gilmore dated at Aldie, June 23, 1863.

25. Hezekiah Long to Sarah (wife), June 23, 1863, Long letters, Shore Village Museum, Rockland Maine.

26. Livermore diary (UMO), June 21. Captain Morrill incident from Clark diary (MSA), June 21.

27. Capt. Phineas M. Jeffards and Lt. James Lyford of Company B resigned on November 29, 1862 (Service Records, MSA). Morrill reported for duty on October 8, 1862.

28. John Lenfest to "wife," June 25, 1863, Lenfest Letters, Pejepscot Historical Society.

29. Keene and Livermore diaries (AMS), June 22.

30. Spear diary, June 21; Spear, "Memorial Day Address, Warren, Maine 1888." Original TMS in possession of Abbott Spear, Warren, Maine.

31. Burial of Corporal West from Spear memoirs (AMS). Details of march from Keene and Livermore diaries, June 22.

32. Keene diary (AMS), June 22; Livermore diary (UMO), June 22; John Chamberlain's journal (PHS). Joshua's requesting of John's aid from "Through Blood and Fire…"

33. John Chamberlain's journal (PHS); Judson, *History of the 83rd…*, pp. 64–65.

34. Another brother, Horace, also attended Bowdoin but died of tuberculosis before the war.
35. Composite of Tom Chamberlain from Chamberlain family correspondence (UMO, BCL, and PHS). McClellan's description of 83rd Pennsylvania from Norton, *Attack and Defense*, p. 284.
36. Nash, *History of the 44th...*, p. 137.
37. Numbers and dates of 2nd Maine transfers from the 20th's *Consolidated Morning Reports* (MSA), and from Military Service Cards in the Records of the Adjutant General of Maine (MSA). A great many of the men transferred on paper were absent sick or on detached duty so that, while their names were transferred to the rolls of the 20th, they were not physically present.
38. Ibid.
39. Keene diary (AMS), June 23. Livermore diary (UMO).
40. Livermore diary (UMO).
41. Fernald, Clark, Livermore, and Keene diaries, June 23. Cherry story from Livermore diary (UMO).
42. Livermore diary (UMO), June 23. Lyford listed himself as 44 years old when he mustered in, conveniently one year shy of the 45-year maximum. He may have been older.
43. Clark, Keene, and Fernald diaries, June 24; Lamson to "Dear Aunt," June 24, 1863, in Engert, *Maine to the Wilderness*, p. 68.
44. Keene diary (AMS), June 25. Major Fairfax later carried the order to attack the Union left from Longstreet to Hood on July 2 at Gettysburg. He resembled and was often mistaken for Longstreet (Pfanz, *Gettysburg: Second Day*, p. 164).
45. *Consolidated Morning Reports* (MSA), June 25. The other man still in arrest was Lt. Addison Lewis of Company A.
46. Spear diary (AMS), June 26. John Chamberlain's journal (PHS).
47. John Chamberlain's journal (PHS). Southern justice was served a month later in Washington, D.C., when the flag got John held in arrest overnight under suspicion that he was a Rebel spy.
48. Ibid.
49. Livermore, Fernald, Keene, Clark, and Spear diaries, June 26; Spear memoirs (AMS); Nash, *History of the 44th*.
50. Livermore diary (UMO), June 26.
51. Ibid.; John Chamberlain's journal (PHS).
52. Ibid.
53. Keene and Livermore diaries, June 26; John Chamberlain's journal (PHS).
54. Clark and Livermore diaries, June 26; John Chamberlain's journal (PHS). The estate that they passed was the home of a Widow Cower.
55. Clark, Keene, Livermore, and Spear diaries, June 27.

56. Livermore diary (UMO), October 5, 1862. The 20th was between surgeons at this time. Nahum Monroe had resigned and Abner Shaw, his eventual replacement, did not arrive until late July.

57. Long to Sarah, June 28, 1863 (Long Letters, SVM).

58. Keene diary (AMS), June 28. In ten months of service, the 20th had been on campaign six months and in winter quarters the other four.

59. Spear diary (AMS), June 28.

60. Livermore diary (UMO), June 28.

61. John Chamberlain's journal (PHS); Livermore and Keene diaries, June 29.

62. Spear memoirs (AMS). Shortly after it was organized in September 1862, the regiment was hurried to the battle of Antietam and passed through Frederick on the march.

63. Clark and Livermore diaries, June 29. By "broke," he meant reduced to a private.

64. Andrew Tozier Pension File (Department of Veterans Affairs); Ezra Tozier Pension File (NA). Tozier was captured at Gaines Mill and spent time in both Belle Isle and Libby prisons.

65. Nash, *History of the 44th...*, p. 140; Meade's order in the *Official Records*, vol. 27, pt. 3, p. 416.

66. Carter, "Reminiscences...," p. 158.

67. Clark, Fernald, Keene, and Spear diaries, June 30.

68. Livermore and Spear diaries, June 30.

69. Ibid.

70. Smart, *A Radical View*, vol. 2, pp. 12–15.

71. Spear memoirs (AMS).

72. Keene diary (AMS), July 1; Nash, *History of the 44th...*, p. 141. The term "skirmishers" was usually reserved for battle. The term "flank guard" was probably more appropriate in official military language when describing the march, but the soldiers were more familiar with the former and frequently used it out of its normal context.

73. Service Record Cards (MSA). The three deserters were Benjamin West, Samuel Morrison, and James Kelley. West had been in the army nine months, Kelley eleven, and Morrison just over two years.

74. Keene diary (AMS), July 1; John Chamberlain's journal (PHS); Nash, *History of the 44th...*, p. 141; Chamberlain, "Through Blood and Fire at Gettysburg." Gen. Oliver O. Howard was from Leeds, Maine, a very small farming community between Lewiston and Augusta.

75. Chamberlain, "Through Blood and Fire at Gettysburg"; Keene diary (AMS), July 1.

76. Spear memoirs (AMS); Livermore diary (UMO), July 1; Judson, *History of the 83rd...*, p. 66.

77. Livermore diary (UMO), July 1.

78. Howard Prince, in *Dedication of the 20th Maine Monuments*, (UMO, AMS); Livermore diary, October 5, 1862. Katahdin, the state's highest peak, is a moutain in north central Maine.

79. Keene and Livermore diaries, July 1; Spear memoirs, p. 39; John Chamberlain's journal (PHS).

80. John Chamberlain's journal (PHS).

81. Newcomb, "A Soldier's Story..." *The Maine Bugle*, III (Jan. 1896) pp. 100–102.

82. Chamberlain, "Through Blood and Fire at Gettysburg."

83. Clark, Keene, Livermore and Spear diaries, July 1; Nash, *History of the 44th...*, p. 141. Bonnaughtown is now called Bonneauville.

84. John Morin Pension Records (NA). Morin reached the regiment in the Bucher peach orchard as they were being issued extra ammunition.

85. Howard Prince, in *Dedication of the 20th Maine Monuments* (UMO, AMS); Clark and Keene diaries, July 2; Chamberlain, "Through Blood and Fire at Gettysburg"; Nash, *History of the 44th...*, pp. 141–2; Spear memoirs (AMS); Coan, unpublished manuscript on Gettysburg, Coan Papers, Hawthorne–Longfellow Library, Special Collections, Bowdoin College, Brunswick, Maine. Positions and approach of First Division, Fifth Corps from diaries and from the John Bachelder maps. The 20th halted on the left of Williams' Division of the Twelfth Corps at Wolf's Hill. They later moved to the Bucher peach orchard on the south end of the intersection of the Granite Schoolhouse Road and Baltimore Pike. This area is just south of Powers Hill.

86. Livermore diary (UMO), entry on back page for July 2. The testament ran out of pages and he began a new book with an entry for July 1.

Chapter 2. THE DEATH-STREWN SLOPE

1. Joshua Chamberlain, "How General Chamberlain...," *Lewiston Journal*, May 25, 1912.

2. Chamberlain, "Through Blood and Fire at Gettysburg."

3. Livermore diary (UMO), July 2; ibid.

4. Ibid.

5. Chamberlain, "Through Blood and Fire at Gettysburg."

6. Chamberlain's Official Report (OR).

7. Elisha Coan, unpublished manuscript (Coan papers, BCL); 20th Maine Correspondence (MSA). For more on the 17th Maine, see George W. Verrill, "The Seventeenth Maine at Gettysburg and in the Wilderness," in *War Papers, Vol. I*, Maine Commandery (MOLLUS), and *Maine at Gettysburg*.

8. Chamberlain, "Through Blood and Fire at Gettysburg."

9. Ibid. A lot has been made of one account by Warren in which he claims to have ordered a portion of Smith's Battery to fire a round over the wooded area beyond Devil's Den and that the movement of Confederate troops avoiding the shell caused reflections of sunlight off their metallic accoutrements.

This is difficult to imagine since the men of Law's and Robertson's brigades were at that time double-quicking (jogging) across the area under fire from artillery at Devil's Den and the Peach Orchard. One more shell would hardly have altered their movements. Also, the area from Devil's Den to the step-off point of the Confederate assault, though wooded now, was an open field in 1863.

    10. Norton, *Attack and Defense...* , pp. 264–65; Chamberlain's Official Report (OR); Elisha Coan, unpublished manuscript (Coan papers, BCL); Chamberlain, "Through Blood and Fire at Gettysburg."

    11. John Chamberlain's journal (PHS); Chamberlain, "Through Blood and Fire at Gettysburg."

    12. Chamberlain, "Through Blood and Fire at Gettysburg." S.L. Miller remembered that the horse belonged to an adjutant named Jacklin.

    13. Elisha Coan, unpublished manuscript (Coan papers, BCL).

    14. Chamberlain's Official Report (OR); Chamberlain, "Through Blood and Fire at Gettysburg." The three holdouts were Charles Brown (E), Henry Moore (C), and William Wentworth (E).

    15. Oates, *The War Between the Union and the Confederacy and its Lost Opportunities.* New York: Neale Publishing Co., 1905, pp. 569–772. For more on regimental strengths, see Appendix One. In Appendix A of his book, Oates gives a full roster of the regiment, with brief descriptions of each man.

    16. Information on Oates from Lafantasie, "The Other Man," *Quarterly Journal of Military History*, 5 (Summer 1993), and from the introduction to Oates, *The War...*, Morningside Bookshop edition (Dayton, 1973).

    17. Oates, *The War...*, p. 674.

    18. Botsford and Burton, *A Sketch of the Forty-Seventh Alabama Infantry Regiment, Volunteers, C.S.A.* Montgomery: Paragon Press, 1909. At Cedar Run the regiment lost ninety eight men killed and wounded and this was nearly a third of the unit at that time.

    19. Reynolds, "The Reluctant Rebel," in *History of Tallapoosa County; Memorial Record of Alabama*, p. 998. As a young man, Bulger made a comfortable living selling goods to Creek Indians until 1836, when he sold his business to invest in stock, slaves, and farming implements. Bulger's attempt at thwarting secession was so well known in the South that Gen. Braxton Bragg of Louisiana once referred to Tallapoosa as "that abolitionist county— Bulger's county." Many recalled that Bulger was more than 60 years old at Gettysburg, but he once stated that he was born February 13, 1806.

    20. Oates, *The War...*, pp. 207–8 (n); Letter from the camp of the 47th printed in *Montgomery Daily Mail*, July 26, 1863. Companies A, D, and F, of the 47th were detached as skirmishers under Capt. H. C. Lindsey.

    21. Final positions of regiments from Bachelder map, *Second Day's Battle*, and from Rice, "The Role of Colonel Strong Vincent...," *Journal of Erie Studies*. There is some differing recollection as to where the 16th Michigan

was originally placed. There is ample evidence to support any one of three theories but the accounts written by the men of the 16th Michigan and the 20th Maine indicate that the 16th Michigan was first placed on the extreme left, then moved to the extreme right of the brigade. Elisha Coan of the 20th Maine wrote an account that reflected the view of many of his comrades when he wrote: "The 20 M[ain]e on that day was second from the left. The 16th Michigan being upon our extreme left, the 44 N.Y. + 83 Penn[sylvania] on our right. These are the 4 reg[imen]ts that comprise Vincent's command. Immediately upon the line being formed the 16th Mich[igan] was moved past our own rear to the right of the brigade. This left the 20th Me on the left of the brigade and the extreme left of the army" (Elisha Coan, unpublished manuscript, Coan Papers, BCL). Ellis Spear, Walter Morrill, Holman Melcher, and others agreed with Coan's recollection. B.F. Partridge of the 16th Michigan remembered that "Vincent's Brigade, halted and reformed having the 16th Mich. in the ravine nearly where the 20th Maine [later] charged, but immediately changed position" (Col. B.F. Partridge to Bachelder, March 31, 1866, Bachelder Papers, GNP, NHS). Col. Norval Welch of the 16th made a similar statement in his Official Report (OR, Series I, Vol. 29, p. 628).

22. Chamberlain's Official Report (OR); Chamberlain, "Through Blood and Fire at Gettysburg."

23. Howard Prince, in Dedication of the Twentieth Maine Monuments, (UMO, AMS); Morrill to Chamberlain, July 8 (Bachelder Papers, NHS).

24. Morrill to Chamberlain July 8 (Bachelder Papers, NHS).

25. Oates, The War..., p. 210.

26. Oates' Official Report (OR); Oates to Stoughton, November 22, 1888 (UOA); Oates to J.L. Chamberlain, March 8, 1897 (UMi); Oates, The War..., pp. 210, 687. In addition to Feagin's wound, privates A. Kennedy (Company B) and Wm. Trimner (Company G) were killed by the sharpshooters' volley. Pvt. G.E. Spencer (Company D) was severely wounded. Feagin lost the leg but survived and retired to Alabama.

27. Oates to Stoughton, November 22, 1888 (UOA); Oates, The War..., p. 211.

28. Oates, The War..., pp. 211–12. Oates remembered that the pump was "about one hundred yards in our rear," which would make it the Kern (or Currens) farm.

29. Oates to Stoughton, November 22, 1888 (UOA); Oates to J.L. Chamberlain, March 8, 1897 (UMi); Longstreet, From Manassas to Appomattox, p. 365.

30. Oates, The War..., p. 213.

31. Ibid., pp. 212–13.

32. Ibid. Dispatching these forty-five men, about one-tenth of his force, to capture wagons that had nothing to do with his objective or orders, depleted his force significantly and, years later, he listed the absence of the company as key to his loss of the fight (Oates, The War..., p. 222).

33. Elisha Coan, unpublished manuscript (Coan papers, BCL); Chamberlain's Official Report (OR); Nash, *History of the 44th...*, p. 144; Chamberlain, "Through Blood and Fire at Gettysburg."

34. Howard Prince, in *Dedication of the Twentieth Maine Monuments* (UMO, AMS). Prince wrote, "But for the men of the 20th this was their first real stand up fight," and went on to explain this in light of the regiment's previous battle experience. Henry Sidelinger, of Union, commanded Company E. Chamberlain placed Clark and Spear on the wings to act as field officers but he placed them near their own companies so that they could help their replacements if circumstances required it.

35. Chamberlain, "Through Blood and Fire at Gettysburg."

36. Ibid.

37. Ibid. Lt. Nathaniel Robbins, Bowdoin class of 1857, was captured in the Den.

38. Chamberlain, "Through Blood and Fire at Gettysburg."

39. Ibid.

40. Elisha Coan, unpublished manuscript (Coan papers, BCL); Spear memoirs (AMS); Hays, *Under the Red Patch*, pp. 240-41; Howard Prince, in *Dedication of the Twentieth Maine Monuments* (UMO, AMS).

41. Chamberlain's Official Report (OR).

42. Chamberlain to Bachelder, March 10, 1884 (NHS).

43. Chamberlain's Official Report (OR); Chamberlain, "Through Blood and Fire at Gettysburg"; Elisha Coan, unpublished manuscript (Coan papers, BCL); S.L. Miller to Chamberlain, May 21, 1895 (Chamberlain Papers, LC); John Chamberlain's journal (PHS).

44. Elisha Coan, unpublished manuscript (Coan papers, BCL).

45. Livermore diary (UMO, AMS), July 2. A rod is 16.5 feet.

46. Ibid.

47. Chamberlain's Official Report (OR); Chamberlain, "Through Blood and Fire at Gettysburg"; Morrill to Chamberlain, July 8 (Bachelder Papers, NHS).

48. Morrill to Chamberlain, July 8 (Bachelder Papers, NHS). Sharps breech-loading rifles were known to fire at a rate three times faster than muzzleloading rifles.

49. Chamberlain, "Through Blood and Fire at Gettysburg."

50. Ibid.; Chamberlain's Official Report (OR); Chamberlain to Bachelder, March 10, 1884, Bachelder Papers (NHS); Chamberlain, "The Maine 20th..." in *The Maine Farmer*, December 28, 1865; *Maine at Gettysburg*, p. 261.

51. Chamberlain, "Through Blood and Fire at Gettysburg"; Chamberlain's Official Report (OR).

52. Oates, *The War...*, pp. 213, 674; Oates' Official Report (OR).

53. Livermore diary (UMO, AMS), July 2.

54. Jordan, *Incidents During the Civil War*, p. 43. Sandy McMillan and Ben Kendrick were killed and Sam Kendrick was wounded in the foot.

55. Oates' Official Report (OR); Chamberlain's Official Report (OR).

56. Oates' Official Report (OR).

57. Spear memoirs (AMS); Spear, "The Left at Gettysburg," *National Tribune*, June 12, 1913.

58. Spear memoirs (AMS); Elisha Coan, unpublished manuscript (Coan papers, BCL).

59. O'Connell Memoirs (MHI).

60. Oates, *The War...*, p. 216; Rice, "The Role of Col. Strong Vincent...," *Journal of Erie Studies*. Colonel Robbins of the 4th Alabama later denied that a gap existed between the 4th and 47th Alabama (see Robbins to Nicholson, February 26, 1903, Oates Corr., GNP). This is not surprising, since Oates claimed this gap had a great deal to do with the loss of the battle. Also, Robbins said that his men actually engaged the right companies of the 20th Maine, which is highly unlikely. By any reasonable estimation, there was a huge gap between the two regiments while the 47th was near the summit of Round Top, in order to close that gap the 47th would have had to find the right of the 4th under fire and connect with it while both regiments were heavily engaged. This also seems unlikely.

61. Bulger, interview in *New Orleans Picayune*, September 18, 1898.

62. Ibid.

63. Oates' Official Report (OR); Oates, *The War...*, pp. 218–19.

64. Spear memoirs (AMS); Chamberlain, in *Dedication of the Maine Monuments at Gettysburg* (UMO); Spear to Bachelder, November 15, 1892, (Bachelder Papers, NHS). Spear recalled that his suggestion was to bend back two more companies, but this would have moved the 20th's line up to the crest of the spur rather than just below it, thus losing the advantage of the ground. On several occasions, Chamberlain recalled that his response to Spear's request was the attempt to move his two right companies to the left wing. Combined, the two right companies (E and I) of the 20th suffered only six casualties (see Appendix Three).

65. Chamberlain, in *Dedication of the Maine Monuments at Gettysburg* (UMO); Nichols, letter in *Lincoln County News*, April 1882 (AMS); Spear to Bachelder, November 15, 1892, Bachelder Papers (NHS).

66. Howard Prince, in *Dedication of the Twentieth Maine Monuments* (UMO, AMS); Chamberlain's Official Report (OR); Chamberlain, in *Dedication of the Maine Monuments at Gettysburg* (UMO). The gap between the right of the 20th and the left of the 83rd apparently grew to well over one hundred feet, but the angle of the two in relation to the enemy prevented an assailable gap from presenting itself to the Alabamians. The flank markers, placed where they stand today by veterans of the fight, show the left of the 83rd Pennsylvania and the right of the 20th Maine more than two hundred feet apart. Since they left no record of whether each of these markers represent the opening, middle, or end of the fight, it is hard to determine how they relate to one another. These

are, however, consistent with the maps of John Bachelder, the official historian of the battlefield who visited the field personally with Ellis Spear, Joshua Chamberlain, and other veterans and used their advice in making his maps.

67. Chamberlain, "Through Blood and Fire at Gettysburg"; Chamberlain, "The Maine 20th..." in *The Maine Farmer*, December 28, 1865.

68. Chamberlain to Lieut., July 6 (20th Maine Corr., MSA); Chamberlain, "Through Blood and Fire at Gettysburg." William Livermore later remembered that the Springfields were not necessarily better weapons in a fight, they were just easier to clean, and cleaning a rifle was a daily chore for which an easier method was always preferred (Livermore to Charles, July 6, AMS).

69. Chamberlain, "Through Blood and Fire at Gettysburg."

70. Ibid.

71. Oates, *The War...*, p. 755.

72. Oates, *The War...*, pp. 612–13.

73. Gerrish, *Army Life*, p. 109; Howard Prince, in *Dedication of the Twentieth Maine Monuments* (UMO, AMS).

74. Howard Prince, in *Dedication of the Twentieth Maine Monuments* (UMO).

75. *Maine at Gettysburg*, pp. 261–62; John Morin Pension Records (NA).

76. Chamberlain, in *Dedication of the Twentieth Maine Monuments* (UMO). None of the veteran's recollections explain how a private, not usually eligible for the color guard, was serving in that role, but Coan was definitely there, and was definitely still a private.

77. Livermore to Chamberlain, May 22, 1899 (AMS).

78. Chamberlain, "The Maine 20th..." in *The Maine Farmer*, December 28, 1865; Chamberlain, "Through Blood and Fire at Gettysburg."

79. Ibid.; Spear memoirs (AMS).

80. Ibid.

81. Herbert Heath to Chamberlain, February 7, 1903, (Collection 10, Box 1, F. 8, MHS); Chamberlain, "Through Blood and Fire at Gettysburg." After the war the Alabamian who was struck by a "queer notion" (he was in the 15th Alabama) wrote to Chamberlain to relate this story. He said that he was glad he had not fired, and hoped that Chamberlain was also.

82. *Maine at Gettysburg*, p. 261. Chamberlain received a "tearing cut in the right instep by a piece of shell or a splinter of rock, and a contusion on the left thigh by the steel scabbard being doubled against it, struck by a minnie ball."

83. Oates, *The War...*, pp. 218–19.

84. Oates, *The War...*, p. 221; F.A. Dearborn, to J.L. Chamberlain, March 13, 1903, Maine Historical Society, Portland, Maine (Collection 10, Box 1, F. 8).

85. Oates, *The War...*, p. 218.

86. Ibid.; Edwards to W.R. Painter, November 11, 1915 (15th Alabama Regimental History File, ADAH).

87. Chamberlain, in *Dedication of the Twentieth Maine Monuments* (UMO); Chamberlain, "Through Blood and Fire at Gettysburg"; Keene to

Sarah (wife), July 3–5, 1863 (AMS). Thomas was sergeant of pioneers on the march but Chamberlain detailed him to act as orderly during the battle.

88. Spear memoirs (AMS); Howard Prince, in *Dedication of the Twentieth Maine Monuments* (UMO, AMS).

89. Oates, *The War...*, pp. 218–19, 226. Reports vary that either six or eight bullets hit John Oates.

90. Spear, "A Visit to Gettysburg," *Lincoln County News*, July 1882.

91. Oates, *The War...*, p. 219; Spear, Ellis, "A Visit to Gettysburg," *Lincoln County News*, July 1882. Park thought he had seen two battle flags across the field behind Company B's stone wall, but the only troops in that vicinity were Fisher's Pennsylvania Reserves who were not close enough at that time to threaten Oates.

92. Oates to Stoughton, November 22, 1888 (UOA); Oates, *The War...*, p. 219; Spear, Ellis, "A Visit to Gettysburg," *Lincoln County News*, July 1882.

93. Chamberlain's Official Report (OR). About a third of the 20th was then wounded and several other men were carrying messages or helping wounded to the rear.

94. Chamberlain's Official Report (OR). Ellis Spear maintained that the men on the left of the regiment never ran out of ammunition. This is not surprising since the left became engaged later than the right and faced the enemy in waves rather than with regular constant fire as the right did.

95. Chamberlain, "Through Blood and Fire at Gettysburg."

96. Oates, *The War...*, p. 220.

97. Chamberlain, in *Dedication of the Twentieth Maine Monuments* (UMO); Elisha Coan, unpublished manuscript (Coan papers, BCL); Chamberlain, "Through Blood and Fire at Gettysburg." In "Reply to Rear Rank" (*LCN*, May 1883), Coan recalled that James R. Martin, shot below the right eye, was among the wounded in the forward position at the ledge.

98. Chamberlain, in *Dedication of the Twentieth Maine Monuments* (UMO); Elisha Coan, unpublished manuscript (Coan papers, BCL); Chamberlain, "Through Blood and Fire at Gettysburg"; Melcher, "The Twentieth Maine at Gettysburg" (*LCN*), March 13, 1885. Melcher claimed that his men moved "almost before" the order arrived, but in fact, Chamberlain admitted on two occasions that he never got the words "charge" or "advance" out before the movement began, though it was clear what the next step would be. In "Through Blood and Fire," he wrote: "It was vain to order 'Forward.' No mortal could have heard it in the mighty hosanna that was winging the sky."

99. Spear memoirs(AMS); Spear, unpublished essay on military surprise (AMS); Howard Prince, in *Dedication of the Twentieth Maine Monuments* (UMO, AMS); Spear to Bachelder, November 15, 1892 (Bachelder Papers, NHS).

100. Spear memoirs(AMS); Spear, unpublished essay on military surprise (AMS); Howard Prince, in *Dedication of the Twentieth Maine Monuments*,

(UMO, AMS); Spear to Bachelder, November 15, 1892, (Bachelder Papers, NHS).

101. Oates, *The War...*, p. 220; Livermore diary (AMS), July 2. According to Livermore's diary, the three men captured were all from Company B: privates George Leach, George Stone, and Henry Sanders. Stone and Sanders apparently freed themselves, though Sanders was wounded. Leach did not, and he died five months later in a Richmond, Virginia, prison.

102. Morrill to Chamberlain, July 8 (Bachelder Papers, NHS).

103. F. A. Dearborn to J.L. Chamberlain, March 13, 1903 (partial letter in Chamberlain Papers, MHS).

104. Spear to Mildred, March 14, 1910, TMs copy in possession of Abbott Spear, Warren, Maine; Spear, unpublished essay on military surprise (AMS). The farm lane led to the Jacob Weikert farm. A worm fence was constructed in a zig-zag pattern by piling rails on top of one another.

105. John O'Connell memoirs (MHI).

106. Chamberlain, in *Dedication of the Twentieth Maine Monuments* (UMO); Livermore to Chamberlain, May 22, 1899 (AMS); Elisha Coan, unpublished manuscript (Coan papers, BCL).

107. Chamberlain, "Through Blood and Fire at Gettysburg"; Oates, *The War...*, pp. 771–72; Chamberlain, in *Dedication of the Twentieth Maine Monuments* (UMO).

108. Oates, *The War...*, p. 220. Keels died later that night.

109. Chamberlain, "Through Blood and Fire"; Jordan, *Events and Incidents...*, pp. 43–44.

110. Jordan, *Events and Incidents...*, pp. 43–44.

111. Morrill to Chamberlain, July 8 (Bachelder Papers, NHS); Oates, *The War...*, p. 221; F.A. Dearborn to J.L. Chamberlain, March 13, 1903 (MHS). Captain Shaaf was 30 years old at Gettysburg and a veteran of the 1st Kentucky Volunteers, C.S.A., a twelve-month regiment. He had been in command of the company for eleven months and was generally a reliable officer. He was present for twenty-eight of the regiment's thirty-two engagements and was absent sick at the other four (15th Alabama Regimental Histories Files, ADH).

112. Livermore diary (UMO, AMS), July 2.

113. Chamberlain, "Through Blood and Fire at Gettysburg"; Livermore diary (UMO, AMS), July 2.

114. Chamberlain's Official Report (OR); Elisha Coan, unpublished manuscript (Coan papers, BCL).

115. Spear memoirs (AMS). The material of the Confederate's uniform struck Spear enough that he remembered it more than forty years later. It was a heavy cotton duck.

116. Oates, *The War...*," p. 217; Chamberlain, "Through Blood and Fire at Gettysburg"; Bulger, interview in *New Orleans Picayune*, September 18,

1898. Bulger stated that he was taken to a barn by Colonel Rice and cared for by a Dr. Clark of New York. Augustus Milton Clark was acting surgeon in chief of the First Division, Fifth Corps. The only way Bulger could possibly have had a 22nd Maine sword is if it had been given to him by another Confederate somehow. The 22nd Maine was not at Gettysburg. Chamberlain later claimed to have captured Bulger, but both Rice and Bulger remembered differently. It is likely that many people passed by Bulger in the confusion after the battle ended, so it is not surprising that many officers felt that they had "captured" him.

117. Livermore diary, July 2; Chamberlain to Lieut., July 6 (20th Maine Corr., MSA); Chamberlain to Coburn, July 21 (20th Maine Corr., MSA).

118. Oates' Official Report (OR); Oates, *The War...*, p. 222.

Chapter 3. THE BIGGER HILL

1. Chamberlain to Bachelder, January 25, 1884 (Bachelder Papers, NHS). Most of this letter is a reprint of a memorandum written by Chamberlain on July 5, 1863, from which he made his official report.

2. S.L. Miller, in *Dedication of the Twentieth Maine Monuments* (UMO).

3. The best and most detailed description of the struggle for the right flank of Vincent's Brigade at Little Round Top is contained in Pfanz, *Gettysburg: The Second Day*.

4. Boothby to "Folks at Home," July 4, 1863 (NOR); Fernald diary (PHS), July 2; Livermore diary (UMO), July 2.

5. Keene diary (AMS), July 2;

6. Chamberlain, "How General Chamberlain...," *Lewiston Journal*, May 25, 1912; 20th Maine Descriptive Rolls (MSA). Land was originally Spear's first lieutenant in Company G.

7. Oates to Stoughton, November 22, 1888 (UOA); Spear, "A Visit To Gettysburg," *Lincoln County News*, July 1882; Oates, *The War...*, p. 225; Jordan, *Incidents During the Civil War*, p. 43; Campbell's Official Report (OR). The figures of Campbell and Oates seem to correspond with the diary entries of Fernald, Spear, and Livermore of the 20th (written that day) which indicate that the Mainers had around 250 prisoners before the occupation of Big Round Top, where they captured more than two dozen more. Also, the existing muster rolls for the 47th seem to confirm the figures as well (ADH).

8. Chamberlain to Governor Coburn, July 21, 1863 (20th Maine Corr., MSA); Keene to Sarah, July 3–5, 1863 (AMS); Chamberlain to Bachelder, January 25, 1884 (Bachelder Papers, NHS); S.L. Miller, in *Dedication of the Twentieth Maine Monuments* (UMO).

9. Chamberlain manuscript (BCL).

10. S.L. Miller, in *Dedication of the Twentieth Maine Monuments* (UMO); Chamberlain to Bachelder, January 25, 1884 (Bachelder Papers, NHS);

Chamberlain manuscript (BCL). Fisher's command was the Third Brigade, Third Division, of the Fifth Corps.

11. Chamberlain to Bachelder, January 25, 1884 (Bachelder Papers, NHS); Livermore diary (UMO), July 2. Most of the letter is a reprint of a memorandum written by Chamberlain on July 5, 1863, from which he made his official report.

12. Morrill to Chamberlain, July 8 (Bachelder Papers, NHS); Chamberlain to Bachelder, January 25, 1884 (Bachelder Papers, NHS); S.L. Miller, in *Dedication of the Twentieth Maine Monuments* (UMO). The regiment ascended the hill just to the left of the current park road and pathway.

13. S.L. Miller, in *Dedication of the Twentieth Maine Monuments* (UMO). In his field notes in *Maine at Gettysburg* (p. 260), Chamberlain mentions capturing a Captain Christian, but Oates later corrected him (Oates to JLC, March 8, 1897, UMi) by saying that it was Lt. Thomas Christian of General Law's staff.

14. Ibid.; Spear memoirs (AMS); Coan, "Round Top," in *National Tribune*, June 4, 1885.

15. Spear memoirs (AMS).

16. Chamberlain to Bachelder, January 25, 1884 (Bachelder Papers, NHS); S.L. Miller, in *Dedication of the Twentieth Maine Monuments* (UMO).

17. Ibid.

18. S.L. Miller, in *Dedication of the Twentieth Maine Monuments* (UMO); Coan, "Round Top," in *National Tribune*, June 4, 1885; Chamberlain to Bachelder, January 25, 1884 (Bachelder Papers, NHS). John Bradford and Eugene Kelleran escorted the prisoners to the provost guard.

19. Ibid.; *Maine at Gettysburg*, p. 260; Lamson to Father in Engert, *Maine to the Wilderness*, p. 73.

20. Spear memoirs (AMS). Spear's servant was John Vinal of Company G.

21. Oates, *The War Between the Union and Confederacy*, pp. 674–75.

22. Bulger, interview in *New Orleans Picayune*, September 18, 1898. Bulger may have been taken to the George Spangler barn, east of the Taneytown Road and south of the Schoolhouse Road (on what is now the Blacksmith Shop Road). A history of the 22nd Massachusetts (Carter, *Four Brothers in Blue*) mentions an Alabama lieutenant colonel that was treated there and this would have to be Bulger or Feagin (of the 15th). Feagin was wounded on the far side of Devil's Den and did not fall into Yankee hands until much later. Also, the Spangler farm is quite near the position of Rice's brigade on July 3, making his visit to see Bulger on that day easily possible. Many believe that this is the same place that Gen. Lewis Armistead was taken on July 3 after Pickett's Charge.

23. Garrison, *John Shaw Billings*.

24. Ibid.; Pierce, *What a Young Girl Saw...*, pp. 56–59; Graham, "On to Gettysburg." Lieutenant Graham found it contemptable in numerous visits to Little Round Top in the years after the war that Weikert's son bragged about

the "wonderful acts of heroism" his family had done to care for the wounded during the battle.

25. Nash, *History of the 44th*, p. 151. Quoted from the diary of Sgt. E. R. Goodrich, Company A, 44th New York.

26. Chamberlain to Bachelder, January 25, 1884 (Bachelder Papers, NHS); Spear diary (PHS), July 3; Livermore diary (UMO, AMS), July 3.

27. Livermore diary (UMO, AMS), July 3.

28. Wescott to Chamberlain, February 1896 (Chamberlain Papers, LC).

29. O'Connell memoirs (MHI).

30. Ibid.

31. Keene to Sarah, July 3–5, 1863 (AMS).

32. O'Connell memoirs (MHI); Livermore diary (UMO, AMS), July 3.

33. Ibid.

34. Livermore diary (UMO, AMS), July 3.

35. Ames to Chamberlain, July 3, 1863 (copy in JLC General Order Book, PHS). It is interesting that for some unknown reason the typescript of this letter in Joshua Chamberlain's personnel file (NA) differs from the manuscript copy in that it excludes the closing sentence and replaces it with the "God bless you..." sentence.

36. Oates, *The War...*, pp. 236–37. Company H of the 15th Alabama guarded 1,100 prisoners taken around Devil's Den and was not engaged here (Houghton *Two Boys...*, p. 232).

37. Ibid. Oates at first said that Farnsworth shot himself in the head, but after being informed that the body had no head wound he changed the story to a shot in the heart. The story among the men, according to Houghton, was that one of the two Alabamians who approached him ordered him to surrender and he did not, so the other man shot him.

38. Oates, *The War...*, pp. 237–38. Oates indicated that the monument erected to Farnsworth is at least 150 yards north of where he fell.

39. Ibid., pp. 598–99.

40. John Chamberlain to Charles Desmond, July 11, 1863 (BCL).

41. Ibid.; John Chamberlain's journal.

42. John Chamberlain's journal.

43. Wescott to Chamberlain, February 1896 (Chamberlain Papers, LC); "Incident After Gettysburg," *The Northern Monthly*, May 1864, pp. 207–8.

44. Oates, *The War...*, p. 237.

45. Ibid., p. 238.

46. Ibid., pp. 238–39.

Chapter 4. SEARED BY THE HORRORS OF WAR

1. Livermore to "Brother Charles," July 6–9 (AMS).

2. Chamberlain, "The Maine 20th..." in *The Maine Farmer*; Chamberlain, "Through Blood and Fire..."

3. Chamberlain to Fannie, July 4 (Chamberlain papers, LC).

4. Fernald diary (PHS), July 4; Spear diary (AMS), July 4; Jordan, *Incidents...*, p. 45.

5. *Bangor Whig and Courier*, July 3 & 4, 1863; Muffly, *The Story...*, p. 245.

6. *Aroostook Times*, July 3, 1863.

7. John Chamberlain's journal (PHS). Brewer and Bangor are opposite one another along the Penobscot River.

8. Oates, *The War...*, p. 239.

9. Keene to Sarah, July 3–5, 1863 (AMS). The *Annual Report of the Adjutant General* for 1863 indicates that Hill was discharged for disability February 6, 1863.

10. John Chamberlain's journal (PHS). Joshua Chamberlain was named Lawrence Joshua Chamberlain at birth but switched the first and middle names while in college. With his family, however, he retained his childhood name, Lawrence.

11. Ibid.; unpublished Chamberlain manuscript on Gettysburg, original manuscript in the Chamberlain papers, Bowdoin College Library Special Collections.

12. Ibid.; O'Connell memoirs (MHI).

13. John Chamberlain's journal (PHS).

14. Livermore diary (AMS, UMO), July 5; unpublished Chamberlain manuscript (BCL). The barn was the Sherfy barn. The Peach Orchard, across the road, is actually the Sherfy Peach Orchard. The barn has since been rebuilt.

15. Ibid. Most of the dead were Union soldiers as the Confederates had apparently removed many of their dead and buried them before retreating.

16. John Chamberlain's journal (PHS).

17. Ibid.; unpublished Chamberlain manuscript (BCL); Livermore to "Brother Charles," July 6–9 (AMS); Livermore diary (AMS, UMO), July 5.

18. Clark diary (MSA), July 5.

19. Keene to wife, July 3–5 (AMS); Clark diary (MSA), July 5.

20. Livermore to "Brother Charles," July 6–9 (AMS); A rod is 16.5 feet. In all likelihood, most of the horses near the Trostle house were from the 9th Massachusetts battery.

21. Spear diary (AMS), July 5; Clark diary (MSA), July 5; Fernald diary (PHS), July 5; John Chamberlain's journal (PHS).

22. Fernald diary (PHS), July 6; Spear diary (AMS), July 6; John Chamberlain's journal (PHS); Keene diary (AMS), July 6; Engert, *Maine to the Wilderness*, p. 73.

23. Clark diary (MSA), July 6; Keene diary (AMS), July 6.

24. Chamberlain to "Lieut.," July 6 (20th Corr., MSA); Chamberlain, "Official Report," July 6 (OR).

25. Fernald diary (PHS), July 7; *Annual Report of the Adjutant General of Maine for 1863*, p. 576.

26. John Chamberlain's journal (PHS); Keene diary (AMS), July 7–8; Spear diary (AMS), July 7; Livermore to Charles, July 6–9, 1863 (AMS).

27. Carter, *Four Brothers*...p. 314; Norton to Nicholson, September 28, 1888 (GNP). Rice's order was dated July 12.

28. Livermore to Charles, July 6–9, 1863 (AMS).

29. John Chamberlain's journal (PHS).

30. Ibid.; Fernald diary (PHS), July 8.

31. Livermore to Charles, July 6–9, 1863 (AMS).

32. Spear diary (AMS), July 9; John Chamberlain's journal (PHS); Keene diary (AMS), July 8. According to Keene, Strobel's friend was named Leaser.

33. Livermore to Charles, July 6–9, 1863 (AMS); Engert, *Maine to the Wilderness*, p. 75; Clark diary (MSA), July 9.

34. Prince in *Dedication of the Twentieth Maine Monuments at Gettysburg.*

35. Clark diary (MSA), July 10; Spear diary (AMS), July 10.

36. Spear diary (AMS), July 10. The skirmish took place just south of the town of Fair Play, Maryland.

37. Chamberlain to Clark (report to Third Brigade adjutant) July 30, 1863 (JLC Personnel File, NA); Records of the Adjutant General of Maine (MSA). The 2nd Maine men wounded at Gettysburg were: Erskine (G), Grindle (A), Hall (F), Knapp (C), Leach (B), Lester (I), O'Connell (C), Pinkham (D), Surry (A), Wyer (F). The men of Company E captured on Sharpsburg Pike were Lowell Brock, Charles Brown, Alvin Cutler, William Davis, Lewis Flanders, and John Lenfest—all privates.

38. John Chamberlain's journal (PHS).

39. Isabella Fogg Pension File (NA); Moore, *Women of the War*, pp. 122–23; Brocket, *Women's Work...*, p. 508; Records of the Adjutant General of Maine, Civil War Relief Files (MSA)

40. Wescott to Chamberlain, February 1896 (Chamberlain Papers, LC).

41. Records of the Adjutant General of Maine, Civil War Relief Files (MSA); *Annual Reports of the Adjutant General of Maine*, 1863–65.

42. "Incident after Gettysburg," *Northern Monthly*, pp. 207–8.

43. Ibid.

44. Kennedy to Gov. Coburn, July 25, 1863, (20th Maine Corr., MSA); C.C. Hayes to Gov. Coburn, July 21, 1863 (Civil War Correspondence, Relief Agencies, MSA). During the Battle of Fredericksburg, Bulger was in Alabama recuperating from the Cedar Mountain wound.

45. Oates, *The War...*, pp. 674–75. John Oates was taken to a tent hospital (Second Division, Fifth Corps) on one of the farms on the White Church Road. He was initially buried near the Fifth Corps hospital on the Fiscel farm.

46. Edmond C. Burnett, "Letters of Barnett Cody and Others, 1861–64." *Georgia History Quarterly* 23, pp. 372–4. The tribute was published in the *Spirit of the South* in Eufala, Alabama, and in the *Christian Index*, September 18, 1863.

47. Oates, *The War...*, pp. 674–75.

48. McGuire, *Recollections of Prison Life in Fort Delaware* (ADH). Confederate casualties were treated at David's Island (in New York Harbor), Chester, Pennsylvania, and at the West buildings in Baltimore.

49. McGuire, *Recollections...* (ADH).

50. Ibid.

51. Ibid. A good example of a trial and hanging of Union prisoners by Union prisoners at Andersonville can be found in Michael Dougherty, *Diary of a Civil War Hero* (New York, 1960).

52. Oates, *The War...*, pp. 604–5, 710.

53. McGuire, *Recollections...* (ADH).

54. Hopkins, *From Bull Run to Appomattox*, pp. 171–72. That area of Maryland was heavily secessionist.

55. List of Union dead buried at Andersonville (Andersonville National Cemetery). Andersonville data: Alvin Cutler died March 20, 1864, buried in grave 80; William Davis died March 29, 1864, buried in grave 227; Lewis Flanders died March 19, 1864, buried in grave 69.

56. Lenfest family letters (PHS); Lavinnia Lenfest, Widows Pension file (NA).

57. Ibid.; Records of the Adjutant General (MSA). Leach died December 1, 1863.

Chapter 5. IN GREAT DEEDS SOMETHING ABIDES

1. Chamberlain, *Passing of the Armies*, pp. 385–86.

2. Records of the Adjutant General of Maine (MSA). Oates, *The War...*, p. 571. The regiment's total loss was 308, or 19 percent, who died in service. The surrendering Confederates included 172 of the 15th and about one hundred of the 47th (Oates, *The War...*).

3. Chamberlain Service Record (NA).

4. Chamberlain Service Record (NA); *Official Records*; Chamberlain Papers (BCL).

5. The salute he ordered was a secondary honor in army etiquette, not the one of highest honor used in military matters. Still, it vexed many in the North. Southerners took it more positively, and Chamberlain was unusually welcomed in the South after the war.

6. For more on Chamberlain's post war life, see Wallace, *Soul of the Lion* (New York, 1960), and Trulock, *In the Hands of Providence* (Chapel Hill, 1992). In Maine politics at that time it was customary for a governor to be reelected to at least three consecutive terms.

7. Oates, *The War...*, p. 543. Oates estimated that no more than two hundred men of the 15th were captured during the war. Twenty-seven of those captured at Gettysburg later died in prison. Even by rough estimates, upwards of 30 percent of the men in the regiment died while in service.

8. Oates, *The War...*, pp. 276–79, 384.

9. Oates, *The War...*, pp. 791–92.

10. *Memorial Record of Alabama*, p. 998.

11. For a detailed description of the postwar lives of the men of the 15th Alabama, see Appendix A of Oates, *The War...*, pp. 569–772.

12. Oates, *The War...*, p. 543; Oates to Chamberlain, March 8, 1897 (UMi).

13. *Memorial Record of Alabama*, p. 998; *Reminiscences of Public Men in Alabama*, p. 659.

14. Oates, *The War...*, pp. 698–99.

15. Oates, *The War...*, pp. 698–99.

16. Ibid.

17. Ibid., p. 710.

18. Ames to Chamberlain, August 18, 1863 (Chamberlain Personnel File, NA). For insight on the plot to have Ames relieved of command of the regiment, see 20th Maine correspondence, MSA, particularly a letter from "Undersigned Officers," "To whom it may concern," February 5, 1863. Much of the animosity toward Ames seemed to stem from his weeding out of ineffective officers while in winter camp.

19. Miller, *Reunions of the Twentieth...*, p. 20; Spear, "The Left at Gettysburg," *National Tribune*, June 12, 1913. The *National Tribune* was the official paper of the Grand Army of the Republic, the Civil War equivalent of the American Legion. For more on Ames' life, see Ames, Blanche A., *Adelbert Ames: General, Senator, Governor, 1835–1933*, (New York, 1964).

20. "An Interesting Case," *Lincoln County News*, August 2, 1888.

21. Ibid.; U.S. Census Population Schedules of 1870 for Union, Maine. The 1870 Census valued George Sidelinger's real estate at $600 and personal estate at $300.

22. U.S. Census, Population Schedules for Union, Maine, 1860–1870; Adjutant General Records, Civil War Towns Correspondence for Union, Maine (MSA).

23. Lenfest family letters (PHS); Lavinia Lenfest, Widows pension file (NA); Collins to Governor, May 29, 1866 (Town corr., Union, MSA).

24. Ibid.

25. Details of John's later life from the Chamberlain–Adams family correspondence at Radcliffe College's Schlesinger Library, and from records in the Chamberlain Family Bible at the Brewer (Maine) Public Library. John likely died of something akin to, if not exactly, tuberculosis.

26. Details about Tom are evident in Chamberlain correspondence in the Frost Family Papers at Yale University Library and in the Chamberlain–Adams family correspondence at Schlesinger Library, Radcliffe College.

27. Ibid.; Tom Chamberlain Pension Record (NA).

28. Ezra Tozier Pension File (NA); Andrew Tozier Pension File, (U.S. Department of Veterans Affairs); Andrew Tozier Service Record (NA); 20th Maine Order Book (NA); Chamberlain to Secretary of War, March 28, 1898 (Tozier Medal File, NA).

29. The U.S. Census Population Schedules for 1870 show Andy, Lizzie, and Andy, Jr. living with the Chamberlains on Maine Street in Brunswick as servants. Tozier's Medal of Honor probably burned in a fire that destroyed his son's home.

30. Coan to Brother, August 5, 1863 (MSA).

31. Composite of Coan's life from Coan papers (BCL).

32. "In Memoriam: Holman Staples Melcher," Pamphlet printed by the Maine Commandery of the MOLLUS (Soldiers Obituaries, MSA).

33. Holman Melcher, "Diary of Holman Melcher" TMs in Maine Historical Society, entry for January 7, 1865.

34. Obituary in *Portland Post*, June 25, 1905; *Portland Board of Trade Journal* 6 (1893): 143; *Portland Board of Trade Journal* 16 (1904): 336. Melcher's building, still standing, is located at the corner of Market and Commercial Streets, exactly one block from Joshua Chamberlain's last workplace, the Portland Customs House.

35. Probate Records, Piscataquis County, Maine, 1912.

36. Fernald to Chamberlain, March 4, 1897 (Chamberlain Papers, BCL); *Maine at Gettysburg*, p. 268. Gerrish's service record shows that he was sick in U.S. General Hospital beginning June 9, and is not listed as having returned until September. The morning rolls taken on June 30 at Union Mills for the monthly returns show him absent sick as well (Regimental Records, Rolls, NA).

37. Gerrish, *Army Life*, p. 108.

38. Ibid., p. 110; Gerrish, *Portland Advertiser*, March 13, 1882; Nichols in *Lincoln County News*, April 1882; Gerrish, "Battle of Gettysburg," *National Tribune*, November 23, 1882.

39. Nichols in *Lincoln County News*, April 1882; Chamberlain in *Dedication of the Twentieth Maine Monuments at Gettysburg*.

40. "Rear Rank," (*LCN*) April 1883; "C" (Elisha Coan), "Reply to Rear Rank" (*LCN*), May 1883; Melcher, "Still Another" (*LCN*), May 7, 1883; Prince, "A Probable Theory" (*LCN*), May 22, 1883. Miller is listed as "acting sergeant major" in *Maine at Gettysburg* but, in a letter to Chamberlain in 1895, he corrected the misnomer, which Chamberlain apparently overlooked anyway (Miller to Chamberlain May 15, 1895, Chamberlain Papers, LC). The 20th Maine Regimental (reunion) Association dubbed the *News* the official newspaper of the group.

41. Coan, "Reply to Rear Rank" *Lincoln County News*, May 1883; Melcher, "Still Another" (*LCN*), May 1883. Prince, "A Probable Theory,"

(LCN), June 1883; Livermore, "A Veternan's Diary" *(LCN)*, June 1883. In his *National Tribune* (June 4, 1885) article "Round Top," Coan claimed to have been a corporal when all other evidence, including his service record, indicated that he was a private. This was one of many errors in Coan's representation of details about the battle.

42. "Twentieth Maine at Gettysburg: List of Officers and Men Actually Engaged in the Battle." *Lincoln County News*, 1897 (copy in the Henry Burrage Collection, MHS); Hamlin to Chamberlain, July 7, 1896 (Chamberlain Papers, LC).

43. Spear diary, May 16, 1863 (AMS); Spear memoirs (AMS).

44. Gilmore Pension file (NA). Gilmore sustained his Lee's Mill injury on April 16, 1862.

45. Gilmore Pension file (NA); Gilmore Service Record (NA); 20th Maine corr. (MSA).

46. Ibid.; Spear diary (AMS); Spear memoirs (AMS); Gilmore Service Record (NA). The lawsuits apparently stemmed from his prior service as sheriff of Penobscot County.When Gilmore resigned, Holman Melcher became major and Walter Morrill moved up to lieutenant colonel. Morrill offered to resign and let Spear return to the lieutenant colonel's spot, but Spear refused.

47. Adjutant General to Meade, April 24, 1865, in Gilmore Service Record (NA).

48. Gerrish, *Army Life*, pp. 69–71.

49. Ibid., p. 69.

50. Fogg to G.W. Dyer, February 26, 1863 (Civil War Relief Records, MSA).

51. State v. Alden Litchfield, Docket #223, Supreme Judicial Court Records (1871), Knox County, Vol. 7, pp. 223–226 (MSA); *Rockland Courier Gazette*, May 1870. Litchfield's collaborators were Langdon Moore of New Hampshire, Jack Rand, and two others known as Daniels and Haight, all from Boston.

52. "Reports of the Warden and Inspectors of the Maine State Prison," *Maine Public Documents*, 1874, Vol. 2"; Gerrish, *Army Life*, p. 71. There is no stone for Buck in the National Cemetery at Gettysburg, though he may be in one of the "unknown" graves.

53. Oates, "Gettysburg—The Battle On the Right," *Southern Historical Society Papers*, VI (1878) 172–82.

54. Oates, "Gettysburg—The Battle On the Right"; Oates, *The War...*, pp. 339–41.

55. Ibid.; Gerrish, *Army Life*, pp. 107–108; Coan, "Round Top," *National Tribune*, June 4, 1865. In his *National Tribune* article, Elisha Coan estimated the numbers at 1,000 Alabamians versus 308 Mainers.

56. See Appendix One.

57. Miller, *Reunions of the Twentieth Maine Regiment Association*.

Waldoboro, Maine: 1881. Thirty-one years after the inaugural meeting, the association held its 38th reunion at Gettysburg's 50th anniversary.

58. Gerrish, *Army Life* (Portland, 1882); Spear, Ellis, "A Visit To Gettysburg" (*LCN*), June 9, 1882; *National Tribune*, November 23, 1882, and June 4, 1885; *Lincoln County News*, March 13, 1885; Johnson, et al., *Battles and Leaders of the Civil War* (New York, 1884–1889). For a complete list, see Appendix Two.

59. Fisher, *OR* 27(1):658, Crawford, *OR* 27(1):654. Sykes to Crawford, December 17, 1863 (Chamberlain papers, LC).

60. Coan in *National Tribune*, June 4, 1885. Coan made numerous errors in this account, including the statement that his rank in the battle was corporal when he was actually a private.

61. Doubleday, *Chancellorsville and Gettysburg*, p. 174.

62. Nash, *History of the 44th...*," p. 148.

63. Miller, *Reunions of the Twentieth...*, pp. 3–7. The veterans formed the association on Little Chebeague Island off Portland, August 10, 1876.

64. Ibid.

65. Miller, *Reunions of the Twentieth...*, pp. 3–7.

66. *Portland Press*, August 11, 1881.

67. Spear, "A Visit To Gettysburg," *Lincoln County News*, June 9, 1882. The gathering at Gettysburg was organized by Col. John Bachelder, the official historian of the battle. Among the more prominent attendees were Generals Sickles and Crawford.

68. *Maine at Gettysburg*, pp. 249–50; Miller, *Dedication of the Twentieth...*; Monument files (GNMP).

69. The left flank marker is no longer in its original position and its disappearance is a mystery. Maps clearly show it in position prior to 1900 but it apparently disappeared after 1904 when William Oates visited the site. A sketch he drew contains the left marker and the monument.

70. Chamberlain in Miller, *Dedication of the Twentieth...* Each of several news accounts of the ceremony as well as the official pamphlet published by Samuel Miller list the veterans in attendance. None of these, nor the photo of the event, includes Spear.

71. Oates to Robbins, February 14, 1903 (Oates corr., GNP). In 1893, Congress appropriated $50,000 to the War Department for the battlefield.

72. Oates, *The War...*, p. 779; Oates to Robbins, February 14, 1903 (Oates corr., GNP); Oates to Elihu Root, June 2, 1903 (Oates corr., GNP).

73. Oates to Nicholson, February 11, 1903 (Oates corr., GNP). A monument to all Alabama soldiers, erected in 1933, now stands in this area.

74. Robbins to Nicholson, February 19, 1903 (Oates corr., GNP).

75. Oates to Elihu Root, June 2, 1903 (Oates corr., GNP).

76. Chamberlain to Nicholson, August 14, 1903 (Oates corr., GNP).

77. Chamberlain, *Passing of the Armies*, pp. 385–6.

78. Ibid.

79. Chamberlain unfinished autobiographical sketch, original in Special Collections, Bowdoin College Library.

80. Ibid.; Hatch, *History of Bowdoin College*, pp. 253–55. Pierce was elected U.S. President just two months after that commencement.

81. George Adams' diary (First Parish Church, Brunswick, Maine).

82. Chamberlain to Fannie, July 17, 1863 (LC); Sarah to Tom Chamberlain, May 26, 1863 (Chamberlain–Adams family correspondence, Radcliffe College). The last portion of the July 17 letter was destroyed, reportedly by a family member, to prevent some unseemly words on his part from being discovered.

83. Chamberlain to Fannie, November 20, 1868 (Frost Papers, Yale University). In some of their later years, Fannie and Joshua traveled extensively but separately and even occasionally communicated through their children.

84. Composite look at later life from Chamberlain papers (BCL); Chamberlain Pension file (NA).

85. U.S. Congress, *Medal of Honor Recipients*, p. 401.

86. Evidence of the motivations for the recruiting work of these educated men is made evident in correspondence between Ellis Spear and Lysander Hill (AMS) and in Spear's *Memorial Day Address, 1888* (AMS).

87. Spear, "The Story of the Raising…," p. 443.

88. Spear, *Memorial Day Address, 1888* (AMS). The soldier Spear referred to was probably Andrew Herscomb of Wiscasset, a private in Company G who died of disease October 11, 1862 (*Adjutant General's Report for 1863*).

89. Spear diary, June 22, 1863 (AMS); Spear memoirs (AMS); Spear, "The Hoecake of Appomattox," and "The Story of Raising…," *War Papers*, Washington, D.C., MOLLUS.

90. Spear "Memorial Day Address" (AMS). Spear later married Keene's widow.

91. Spear to Bachelder, November 15, 1892 (Bachelder Papers, NHS).

92. *National Tribune*, June 23, 1913.

93. The style of these magazines was bombastic and sensational, and editors often embellished on original writings. "Through Blood and Fire" was originally intended as a series of articles but was cut back to one, and more than once Chamberlain expressed great disappointment at the manner in which the editors changed it.

94. Chamberlain to Elliot Dill, June 12, 1913 (Gettysburg 50th Reunion Files, MSA).

95. *National Tribune*, March 20, 1913.

96. Douglas S. Freeman, *R. E. Lee: A Biography*, 4 vols. (New York, 1934–35), II, p. 462.

Chapter 6. American Legend, American Shrine

1. Chamberlain, "Address at the Dedication...," in Miller, *Dedication of the Twentieth Maine Monuments...* (UMO).

2. Law, "The Struggle for 'Round Top,' " in Johnson, *Battles and Leaders...*, Vol. 3, p. 322; Oates, *The War...*; "The Twentieth" in *Lincoln County News*, August 24, 1881.

3. Oliver W. Norton to J.L. Chamberlain, May 8, 1901. In this letter, Norton, who acted as Vincent's bugler in the battle, wrote, "I went in my search for ambulances a mile beyond the house where Vincent was carried, and when I returned found Welch [colonel of the 16th Michigan] with the colors and the right wing of his regiment in the [Taneytown] road near the house where Vincent was. I was much surprised to see him there and asked him where Col. Rice and the rest of the brigade were. He told me that he did not know where they were; that the brigade had been driven off the hill and he had been separated from the other troops."

4. U.S. Congress, *Medal of Honor Recipients*, p. 401.

5. Oates, *The War...*, p. 245–7.

6. Oates, *The War...*, p. 586. After describing Shaaff, a prewar veteran of the regular army, as one of his best officers, Oates then criticized him. "When he could not capture the Union ordnance train he should have speedily rejoined the regiment in its assault on Little Round Top, where it was hotly engaged. Instead, he remained with his company concealed in the woods but three hundred yards distant."

7. The only position on the hill from which artillery could have fired against Meade's July 3 line is the ground that today surrounds the 155th Pennsylvania monument and on small flat spaces south of it toward the crest. The rest of the ground is either too slanted downward, does not offer open ground, or is occupied by boulders which would hinder the guns' recoil.

8. Oates, *The War...*, p. 244.

9. Oates, *The War...*, pp. 219, 227.

10. Figures include all three regiments which fought at the spur. The 20th Maine suffered approximately 32 percent casualties, the 15th Alabama roughly 37 percent, while the seven companies of the 47th lost around 40 percent; this last figure not exclusively inflicted by the 20th. The three regiments sent from Maine shortly after Gettysburg were nine months regiments.

11. 20th Maine Regimental Records and Rolls (MSA).

12. Powell, *The Fifth Army Corps*, pp. 530–531.

13. Tucker, *High Tide at Gettysburg*, p. 266.

14. Roberts, *Trending Into Maine*, pp. 42–51; Catton, *Glory Road*, pp. 292–93.

15. Roberts, *Trending Into Maine*, pp. 42–51.

16. Chamberlain to Fannie July 4 and 14, 1863 (LC); Prince in *Dedication of the Twentieth...*

17. Chamberlain's Official Report; Chamberlain, "Through Blood and Fire at Gettysburg."

18. Annual Report of the Battlefield Commission, 1902 (GNP). The process by which the road beds were constructed was called "Telferdizing." The altered nature of the monument boulders is clearly made evident by the photograph, taken in 1882, of the veterans choosing the site.

19. Chamberlain to Nicholson August 14, 1903. Photographs taken throughout the 1880s show no walls other than the one that Chamberlain protested and another running from the monument toward the left flank. The latter is now gone.

20. The opening chapter of U.S. Army Field Manual 22-100 depicts parade-ground style maneuvering and assumes that Chamberlain had a consciousness of details which was simply impossible in Civil War battles. In a sense, Chamberlain was in direct violation of Vincent's orders to "Hold the ground at all hazards," when he charged from the very ground he was ordered to hold. This does not seem the best leadership trait to develop in young officers while Chamberlain's other actions most certainly do.

Appendix One. NUMBERS OF COMBATANTS

1. Chamberlain to General Elliott, April 25, 1913 (Gettysburg 50th Reunion Records, MSA).

2. "Twentieth Maine at Gettysburg: List of Officers and Men Actually engaged in the Battle." Published in *Lincoln County News*. Copy in the Henry Burrage Collection, Maine Historical Society.

3. Many collections of letters, including those of Chamberlain, Spear, and others, contain letters to or from veterans regarding their place in what they often referred to as the report of the "Monument Commission." Neither Prince nor Gerrish are counted in this list, but Sgt. Daniel Donovan of Company E was added by Chamberlain after *Maine at Gettysburg* was published and he is counted here (see Gettysburg Reunion Records, 20th Maine folder, MSA).

4. *Consolidated Morning Report of the Twentieth Maine, 1862–65* (MSA); Regimental Records (NA).

5. Chamberlain to Hodsdon, July 11, 1863 (MSA).

6. Oates, *The War...*, p. 225; Oates inscription in Oates Correspondence (GNMP). Oates pointed out that men later straggled out of the woods and rejoined the regiment after the roll was taken, but an estimate of more than two hundred late returnees seems highly unreasonable.

7. J.Q. Burton, "Forty-Seventh Regiment Alabama Volunteers," Regimental Histories File (ADH); T.F. Botsford, "Sketch of the Forty-Seventh..." Paragon, 1909 (ADH); *Muster Rolls* (ADH). At Cedar Run the regiment lost 98 men killed and wounded, and this was nearly a third of the unit at that time. At Antietam only 115 men went into battle.

8. Oates, *War Between the Union and Confederacy*, p. 222. The lower numbers take into account all of the data for the late stages of the fight including estimates of early casualties. Adjutant Waddell of the 15th Alabama recalled that most of his regiment's casualties were the result of the first "galling" fire of the 20th which evened the odds considerably.

BIBLIOGRAPHY

Articles and Books

Ames, Blanche A. *Adelbert Ames: General, Senator, Governor, 1835–1933.* New York, 1964.

Brewer, Willis. *Alabama: Her History, Resources, War Record, and Public Men, from 1540 to 1872.* 1872.

Brockett, Linus P. and Mary Vaughn. *Woman's Work in the Civil War: A Record of Heroism, Patriotism and Patience.* Philadelphia: Zeigler, Mc-Curdy, & Co., 1867.

Botsford, Theophilus F. and Joseph Q. Burton. *A Sketch of the Forty-Seventh Alabama Infantry Regiment, Volunteers, C.S.A.* Montgomery: Paragon Press, 1909.

Bowdoin College. *Bowdoin in the War.* Brunswick, 1870.

Burnett Edmond C. "Letters of Barnett Cody and Others, 1861–64." *Georgia History Quarterly* 23:265–99. 362–80.

Carter, Robert G. *Four Brothers in Blue.* Austin: University of Texas Press, 1979.

_____. "Reminiscences of the Campaign and Battle of Gettysburg" in Maine Commandery, *War Papers* 2:150–83.

Casey, Silas. *Infantry Tactics.* Dayton: Morningside Press, 1985.

Chamberlain, Joshua L. "Through Blood and Fire at Gettysburg." *Hearsts Magazine.* June 1913. Reprinted by Stan Clark Military Books, Gettysburg, 1994.

_____. *Passing of the Armies: An Account of the Final Campaign of the Army of the Potomac Based Upon Personal Reminiscences of the Fifth Army Corps.* New York: G. B. Putnam's Sons, 1915.

Doubleday, Abner. *Chancellorsville and Gettysburg.* New York: Scribner, 1887.

Ellison, Joseph M. "War Letters." Edited by Calvin J. Billman. *Georgia History Quarterly* 48:229–38.

Engert, Roderick, ed. *Maine to the Wilderness: The Civil War Letters of Pvt. William Lamson, 20th Maine Infantry.* Orange, Va.: Publishers Press, 1993.

Garrett, William. *Reminiscences of Public Men in Alabama for Thirty Years.* Atlanta: Plantation Publishing Co. Press, 1872.

Garrison, F. H. *John Shaw Billings: A Memoir.* New York: W. L. Borland, 1889.

Gerrish, Theodore. *Army Life: A Private's Reminiscences of the War*. Portland: Hoyt, Fogg, and Donham, 1882.

Graham, Ziba B. *On to Gettysburg*. Detroit, Winn and Hammond, 1893.

_____, "On to Gettysburg." Military Order of the Loyal Legion of the United States, *War Papers*, I (1983): 1–16.

Hatch, Louis C. *History of Bowdoin College*. Portland, 1927.

Hays, Gilbert Adams, *Under the Red Patch*. Pittsburg: Sixty-third Pennsylvania Volunteers Regimental Association, 1908.

Hopkins, Luther W. *From Bull Run to Appomattox*. Baltimore: Fleet McGinley, 1908.

Houghton, Mitchell B. *From the Beginning Until Now*. Montgomery: Paragon Press, 1914.

_____, and William R. Houghton. *Two Boys in the Civil War and After*. Montgomery: Paragon Press, 1912.

Ingram, William P. *History of Tallapoosa County*. Birmingham, 1951.

Johnson, Charles F. "The Short Heroic Life of Strong Vincent." *Journal of Erie Studies* 17: (Spring 1988).

Johnson, Robert U. and Clarence Buel, eds., *Battles and Leaders of the Civil War*. 4 vols. New York: The Century Co., 1884–1889.

Jordan, William C., *Events and Incidents During the Civil War*. Montgomery: Paragon Press, 1909.

Judson, A.M. *History of the 83rd Regiment, Pennsylvania Volunteers*. Erie, Pa., n.d.

Lafantasie, Glenn, "The Other Man," *Quarterly Journal of Military History* 5:69–75.

Lary, Samuel D. "Sam Lary's 'Scraps From My Knapsack." Edited by W.W. Wright. *Alabama History Quarterly* 18:499–525.

Linderman, Gerald, *Embattled Courage: The Experience of Combat in the American Civil War*, New York: The Free Press, 1987.

Longstreet, James. *From Manassas to Appamottox*. Philadelphia: J. B. Lippincott 1896.

_____, "Lee in Pennsylvania." *Annals of the War*. pp. 414–416. Philadelphia: Times Publishing Company, 1879.

Maine Adjutant General. *Annual Reports of the Adjutant General of the State of Maine, 1861–67*. Augusta: 1862–68.

Maine at Gettysburg Commission. *Maine at Gettysburg: Report of the Commissioners*. Portland, Lakeside Press, 1898.

Maine Commandery, Military Order of the Loyal Legion of the United States. *War Papers*. 4 vols. Portland, 1897–1915.

McClendon, William A. *Recollections of War Times, by an Old Veteran While Under Stonewall Jackson and Lieutenant General James Longstreet*. Montgomery: Paragon Press, 1909.

Memorial Record of Alabama: A Concise Account of the State's Political, Military, Professional and Industrial Progress. Madison, WI: Brant & Fuller, 1893.

Miller, Samuel, ed. *Dedication of the Twentieth Maine Monuments at Gettysburg. Oct. 3, 1889*, Waldoboro, ME: 1891.

_____. *Reunions of the Twentieth Maine Regiment Association.* Waldoboro, ME: 1881.

Moore, Frank. *Women of the War: Their Heroism and Self-Sacrifice.* Hartford, Conn.: S.S. Scranton Co., 1866.

Muffly, Joseph W. ed. *The Story of One Regiment: A History of the 148th Pennsylvania Vols.* Des Moines: Kenyon Printing & Manufacturing Company, 1904.

Nash, Eugene. *A History of the Forty-Fourth Regiment, New York Volunteer Infantry.* Chicago, 1911.

Newcomb, Jonathan. "A Soldier's Story of Personal Experience at the Battle of Gettysburg." *Maine Bugle*, III (January 1896): 100–102.

Northern Monthly: A Magazine of Original Literature and Military Affairs. Portland: Bailey and Noyes, 1864. Volume I.

Norton, Oliver, W. *The Attack and Defense of Little Round Top.* New York: Neale Publishing Company, 1913.

_____. *Strong Vincent and his Brigade at Gettysburg, July 2, 1863.* Chicago: 1909.

Oates, William C. *The War Between the Union and the Confederacy and its Lost Opportunities.* New York: Neale Publishing Co., 1905 (Reprinted by Morningside Bookshop, Dayton, Ohio, 1985).

_____. "Gettysburg—The Battle On the Right," *Southern Historical Society Papes* 6:172–82.

Pfanz, Harry W. *Gettysburg: The Second Day.* Chapel Hill: The University of North Carolina Press, 1987.

Pierce, Matilda J. *At Gettysburg: What a Young Girl Saw and Heard of the Battle.* New York: 1889.

Pullen, John J. *The Twentieth Maine: A Volunteer Regiment in the Civil War.* Philadelphia: J. B. Lippincot Co., 1957.

Reunions of the Twentieth Maine Regimental Association at Portland. Waldoboro: Samuel L. Miller, 1881.

"Reports of the Warden and Inspectors of the Maine State Prison." *Maine Public Documents, 1874,* vol. 2. Augusta: Sprague, Owen and Nash, 1874 (MSA).

Revised Report of the Select Committee Relative to the Soldiers National Cemetery. Harrisburg: Singerley & Meyers, 1865.

Rice, Larry H., "The Role of Colonel Strong Vincent in Determining the Outcome of the Battle of Little Round Top." *Journal of Erie Studies* 1 (Fall 1972).

237

Smart, James G., ed. *A Radical View: The Agate Dispatches of Whitelaw Reed*. 2 vols. Memphis: Memphis State University Press, 1976.

Spear, Abbott, ed. *The Civil War Recollections of General Ellis Spear*. Orono: University of Maine Press, 1995.

Spear, Ellis. "The Story of the Raising and Organization of a Regiment of Volunteers in 1862." Military Order of the Loyal Legion of the United States, Commandery of the District of Columbia, *War Papers*, (1903): 441–53.

_____. "The Hoe Cake of Appomattox." Military Order of the Loyal Legion of the United States, Commandery of the District of Columbia, *War Papers*, (1913): 387–96.

_____. "Memorial Day Address, Warren, Maine 1888." Unpublished Essay in the hands of Abbott and Marjorie Spear.

Trulock, Alice R. *In The Hands of Providence: Joshua Chamberlain and the American Civil War*. Chapel Hill: University of North Carolina Press, 1992.

Wallace, Willard. *Soul of the Lion: A Biography of General Joshua L. Chamberlain*. New York: Thomas Nelson and Sons, 1960.

U. S. Congress Senate. Committee on Labor and Public Welfare. Subcommittee on Veterans' Affairs. *Medal of Honor Recipients, 1863–1963*. Washington, D.C., 1964.

_____. *Report of the Joint Committee on the Conduct of the War at the Second Session, Thirty-eighth Congress, Army of the Potomac...* Washington D. C.: U. S. Government Printing Office, 1948.

U.S. War Department. *War of the Rebellion: The Official Records of the Union and Confederate Armies*. Washington: U.S. Government Printing Office, 1880–1901.

Youngblood, William. "Unwritten History of the Gettysburg Campaign." *Southern Historical Society Papers* 38:312–18.

Manuscripts and Other Collections

Alabama Department of Archives and History, Montgomery, Alabama (ADH)
    Civil War Period Flags Photograph Collection
    Confederate Muster Rolls Collection
    Deceased Soldiers Accounts
    15th Alabama Correspondence and Regimental Histories Files
    47th Alabama Correspondence and Regimental Histories Files
    Photographic Collection
Bangor Public Library, Bangor, Maine (BPL)
    Reunions of the Twentieth Maine Regiment Association (pamphlet)
Fogler Library Special Collections, University of Maine, Orono, Maine (UMO)
    William Livermore Diary
    Chamberlain Family Papers
    Joshua Chamberlain Scrapbook
    Dedication of the Maine Monuments at Gettysburg (pamphlet)

Gettysburg National Military Park, Gettysburg, Pennsylvania (GNP)
    Bachelder Maps
    15th Alabama File
    47th Alabama File
    Monument Commission Files
    Oates Correspondence File
    20th Maine File
Hawthorne-Longfellow Library Special Collections, Bowdoin College, Brunswick, Maine (BCL)
    Joshua Chamberlain Papers
    Elisha Coan Papers
Library of Congress, Washington, D.C. (LC)
    Joshua Chamberlain Papers
Maine Historical Society, Portland, Maine (MHS)
    Henry Burrage Collection
    Joshua Chamberlain Collection
    Holman Melcher Diary, 1865
    Holman Melcher Papers
    Holman Melcher Scrapbook
Maine State Archives, Augusta, Maine (MSA)
    Civil War Diary of Nathan Clark
    Records of the Adjutant General of Maine
        Civil War Correspondence, 1861-1866
        Civil War Photographs
        Gettysburg Reunion Records
        Regimental Rolls
        Relief Organizations Records
        Soldiers Obituary Files
    Supreme Judicial Court Records, Knox County
    U.S. Census Population Schedules for Maine
National Archives, Washington, D.C. (NA)
    Civil War Soldiers Service and Pension Records
    20th Maine Regimental Books
    20th Maine Muster Rolls
New Hampshire Historical Society, Concord, New Hampshire (NHS)
    John Bachelder Papers
New York Historical Society (NYH)
    Joshua Chamberlain Papers
Norlands Living History Center, Livermore, Maine (NOR)
    Civil War Collection
Pejepscot Historical Society, Brunswick, Maine (PHS)
    Albert Fernald Diary
    Alice Trulock Collection

Joshua Chamberlain Files
Joshua Chamberlain General Orders Book
Journal of John Chamberlain
John Lenfest Letters
Photographic Collection
Shore Village Museum, Rockland, Maine (SVM)
    Hezekiah Long Civil War Letters
Spear Collection, Abbott and Marjorie Spear, Warren, Maine (AMS)
    Diary of Ellis Spear, 1863–1865
    Diary of Samuel Keene, 1862–1864
    Papers, Photographs, and Correspondence of Ellis Spear
      and Samuel T. Keene
    "Memorial Day Address, Warren, Maine" (typescript) given by Ellis Spear,
    1888.
    "Two Stories of Fredericksburg," unpublished essay by Ellis and Abbott
    Spear
    "Turning of the Tide," unpublished essay by Abbott Spear
Sterne Library, Special Collections, University of Alabama, Tuscaloosa, Alabama
    (UOA)
    William C. Oates Papers
U.S. Army Military History Institute, Carlisle, Pennsylvania (MHI)
    Brake Collection (Joshua Chamberlain Papers)
    Civil War Miscellaneous Collection (John O'Connell Memoirs)

INDEX